THE
UNKNOWN GRANVILLE BARKER:

Letters to Helen and Other Texts 1915-18

THE
UNKNOWN GRANVILLE BARKER:

Letters to Helen and Other Texts 1915-18

Edited by Simon Shepherd

Society for Theatre Research
London
2021

First published in 2021
by the Society for Theatre Research
PO Box 78086, London, W4 9LP

ISBN 978 0 85430 085 3

Typeset in Garamond Classic 12pt / 14.3pt
Blot Publishing
www.blot.co.uk

Printed and bound by
Henry Ling Ltd., The Dorset Press, Dorchester DT1 1HD
http://www.henryling.co.uk

TABLE OF CONTENTS

ACKNOWLEDGEMENTS

Thanks are due to the following:

For permission to reprint material from the archives of Barker and Huntington, The Society of Authors as the Literary Representative of the Estates of Harley Granville Barker and Helen Granville Barker.

For grants towards research and publication expenses, the Central School of Speech and Drama and the Society for Theatre Research.

For archival, biographical and military help and information, Joan Dean, David Porter, Mick Wallis; archivists Siân Mogridge, Royal Artillery Museum; Marianne Hansen, Bryn Mawr College Libraries; Eleanor Hoare, Eton College; staff at British Library Boston Spa.

For commentary on drafts, Maureen Bell, Iain Bruce, Colin Chambers, Janette Dillon, Helen Henry, Annie Lloyd, and Mick Wallis. I have learnt so much from you all.

LIST OF ILLUSTRATIONS

I

PREFACE

Harley Granville Barker's plays are still performed and studied. His *Prefaces to Shakespeare* are still read. Some of his writings on theatre have recently been reprinted. So two questions arise: what is this 'unknown' Barker? And what is the point in making it known?

The unknown Barker writings included here date from the period 1915-1918. The published texts consist of articles and essays together with reports of lectures. The unpublished texts, the largest proportion of the book, consist of selections from the letters he wrote over a four-year period to the woman who became his second wife, Helen Huntington (1867-1950).

The published pieces have not so far been listed in any scholarly bibliography of Barker's work. Most of them came to my attention because Huntington comments on them in her letters. Together these pieces articulate a specific development in Barker's thinking about the efficacy of theatre.

But the most revealing insight into his life and thought comes from his letters. Here we must pause to note that Barker disliked exposing his private life to public scrutiny. He banned reference to it in at least two other people's autobiographies and told Hesketh Pearson (1951: 85): 'd'you know I fear I don't *like* personal reminiscences.' Unsurprisingly he requested his letters be destroyed after his death. So all of this might make publication now of these very private letters an apparent treachery to the memory of the man. But actually that treachery has already been done in a sequence of malign misrepresentations started by Pearson himself. It is, therefore, only by publication of these letters that the historic misrepresentation can finally be exposed for what it is.

For years it had been assumed that Barker's wishes had been honoured and that most of the letters to Huntington had been destroyed. They were clearly not available to his first biographer C.B. Purdom (1955), though, curiously, he seems to have had sight of her diary, but, just as curiously, makes next to no use of it. Nearly thirty years later Eric Salmon (1986) read and reprinted a small selection of letters to her written in the months immediately before their marriage (these are held at the Harry Ransom Center at the University of Texas). But he didn't know there were any others. Most of the letters printed here only became available to scholars after the British Library acquired them in the late 1990s. They seem to have arrived there in a disordered pile, and were dutifully foliated as such. So it remains a difficult archive to use, which is perhaps why no extract from it has so far been reproduced in the public domain.

There is another small cache of letters from this period, which, again, is largely unknown. These are archived with the William Wiseman papers at Yale University Library. Wiseman served as head of station for British Intelligence in New York and thus oversaw Barker's intelligence gathering during his lecture tour of the United States in the first three months of 1917. These letters help us to complete the picture of his war-time military service, which is closely, and sometimes hilariously, detailed in letters to Huntington.

Now to establish whether it is worth making any of this material better known we need first to face the fact that it all comes from a very limited period of years. True it is that we don't know enough about it from the full-length biographies, basically because neither Purdom nor Salmon had accurate information. Since then, Colin Chambers and Richard Nelson (Barker, 2017) sought to fill in the picture and made a convincing case for Barker's war-time productivity up to 1922. But although they refer to the British Library letters they quote nothing from them and crucial details of the picture are still missing. Recently, Maggie Gale (2020) gave a brief account of Barker's war-time service in America based on the relatively few Wiseman letters supported by muddled secondary sources. It's consequently another distorted picture, sensationalising his supposed 'spying', ignoring the full extent of his service, and leaving him, yet again, unknown.

Only by exploring and engaging with the rich detail of the unfamiliar texts printed here can we begin to see how, at a specific juncture, the artistic work connects into Barker's wider thinking. From here we can then begin to see how this brief period links and, in turn, gives new significance, to the work of the years either side.

These links can initially be mapped as creative phases: the acting career modulated after 1905 into a directing and management career, with the management activity ending in 1915. Plays were written throughout, but they were of two main sorts: some modelling a re-worked, modernised, 'New' realist drama, from *The Marrying of Ann Leete* (1902) to *The Secret Life* (1923); others exploring episodic – 'non-realist' or 'epic' – dramaturgy, starting with *Prunella* (1904), then *The Bowarra* (?1909), *The Pied Piper* (1909–10), and *Harlequinade* (1913) through to *The Three Musketeers* (?1919), with the final play, *His Majesty* (1927), blending both modes. Non-dramatic fiction continued from 1909 with 'Georgiana' through to the early 1920s with 'Out of These Convertites'. Of this at least five stories were written between September 1915 and September 1916, with two, including 'The God of Good Bricks', being started in mid-late 1917. Dramatic and non-dramatic works are linked thematically, especially the interest in relationships mutating in time: 'Georgiana' (1909), 'Trivialities 1' (1916), *Farewell to the Theatre* (1917), *The Secret Life* (1923). The campaign for a national theatre from 1904 continued (as in his British Drama League speech opening the theatre design exhibition of 1922), but to it were added arguments about theatre in the life of a nation (the American theatre essays, the role of theatre in national reconstruction, the work around the British Drama League). There is, then, no creative break-point, simply overlaps and mutations.

These phases are in turn crossed and pressured by external circumstances. First the 1914-18 war. Barker did three sorts of war work: propaganda writing and lecturing (the Red Cross book [1916] and some 1915 New York speeches); military training in artillery; Secret Intelligence Service work, office-based with three months on the road in America. The Red Cross work sharpened awareness of the contrast between upperclasses safe in London and soldiers at the front. The months of military training focussed questions around war, nation and democracy. The intelligence gathering intensified his already strong interest and reading in international affairs. But he found it largely boring and he seems later in 1917 to have engaged with peace initiatives and the Labour Party, though some of this may have overlapped with Intelligence work. The second set of circumstances was his change of partners. His own sense was that the first marriage (in 1906) was already desiccated well before 1914 and that by 1915 he was becoming a 'hack' as a writer. Meeting Huntington was, he said, a new dawn, the beginning of a new period of creative productivity. And it produced in him, for the first time since boyhood, an emotional flowering. What began in 1906 was obviously broken by 1915; what began in 1915 continued until his death in 1946.

Barker's view of the full significance of meeting Huntington has hitherto been hidden from us, and instead we've had manufactured Barkers. From the 1920s onwards theatre gossip had accused him of deserting the theatre. This notion found its way, largely via George Bernard Shaw, into Pearson's *The Last Actor-Managers* (1950). Here he says that, having married Huntington, Barker 'practically abandoned the theatre', failed to become a country squire and went to Paris to become 'a sort of professor'. Clearly, for Pearson, being a professor is much less reputable than being a squire. Barker, he concludes, 'had become donnish and respectable' (1950: 78), an outcome to the dangers of which Pearson must have been alert, being himself a failed actor turned light-weight biographer. But whereas Pearson's attack is directed at Barker's own apostasy, that of Shaw had a very different target. In the same year, immediately after Huntington's death, Shaw used the second volume of Pearson's biography of him (1951) to publish a statement about Barker's supposed rejection of both theatre and socialism. The blame for this was now focussed solely and intensively onto the person and indeed body of Huntington. The level of venom here tells us more about Shaw than Huntington perhaps, but nonetheless, as we shall see later, coming from a theatre 'celeb', it did its damage.

When four years later Purdom published his biography of Barker, Shaw's slander, now more decorously phrased, reappeared: 'his second wife', says Purdom, 'was against his stage connections'

(1955: 192). Accompanying this was a suggestion that Barker was an emotionally cold man who conveniently married a rich woman. That woman was, in fact, against only two of his 'stage connections'. One was his first wife, the actress Lillah McCarthy (1875-1960), whose influence on Purdom's book, with its prejudices and unsubstantiated suggestions, was noted by both the second biographer, Salmon (1983), and the author of perhaps the most perceptive book on Barker's artistic work, Dennis Kennedy (1985). The other connection was of course Shaw, whose behaviour during the divorce was seen as treacherous by Huntington. Embarrassed at the time, Shaw's affronted egotism simmered for three decades until her death usefully provided him with the opportunity to take revenge by publishing his venomous fantasy about her. Although seventy years later the story of the morally dubious theatre man and his rich wife is clearly – what shall we say? – conspicuous trumpery, it dies hard. For it once again twitches into life in Gale's account (2020), which though brief might be said to be confidently Shaw-footed.

Although scholars such as Chambers and Nelson (Barker, 2017) have usefully critiqued the ancient slander, the main people involved seem still to be substantially unknown and misunderstood. It is only when we can read their own words that we begin to understand – and more compellingly feel – the richness, the importance, of the relationship. Further than this, we gain, in a much more expansive way, new insight to the mind – the feelings and ideas – of perhaps the greatest British theatre-maker of the twentieth century.

The letters here may have been produced over a limited period but there is a great deal of writing in them. Running to about 500 folios, many double-sided, and taken as a whole, interconnected, unit, the British Library archive comprises one of the most extended pieces of Barker's writing that we have. Indeed, for Huntington, merely receiving a fortnight's letters and diary from him was 'like an entire book', which she titled 'Letters to my Dear by H. Granville Barker' (71914/117). Produced on a daily basis for months at a time, this 'book' reveals the detail of Barker's activities, feelings and thoughts. For this particular moment in his life we can read his opinions, speculations, frustration and devotion. He reflects on his past and plans for his future. And while of course this is only how he sees things at this point in time, it is nevertheless a very significant point.

It comes, quite neatly, halfway through his working life. This is the moment he turns his back on theatre management and explicitly engages his attention on drama as community expression. It's also the moment he breaks from one partner to live with another. And it is to her, I think, that we owe the particular richness and significance of these letters. In Helen Huntington, Barker found a kindred spirit. She was a writer and a reader. She was a thoroughly well-informed intellectual with an interest in art, ideas, politics. A sense of this emerges from her letters, also archived in the British Library, which are quoted here in the contextual essays and the notes. While she and Barker did not always agree, they were comfortable with discussion and argument. Above all he loved her. In loving her he entered emotional territory that he said he had not known as an adult. It was for him a new and vibrantly intense way of relating to another human being. So he wanted to tell her all the details of his life and, in doing so, felt he had the space, the understanding and support to enable him to articulate ideas not only about society, politics and writing but also about his own emotional life, his desires, his sense of who he was. Alongside the cool brief letters to his first wife, the ones sent to Helen Huntington are full of ideas, description and, above all, passion. If Huntington had not been exactly the woman she was it is very probable we would not have these letters. And Barker would not have embarked, half-way through his career, on what he saw as his new beginning.

II

TIME LINE

1914
15 December: Barker and Huntington meet

1915
January-March: Wallack's Theatre (New York) season (*Androcles and the Lion* and *The Man Who Married* opened 27 January; *A Midsummer Night's Dream* opened 16 February; *The Doctor's Dilemma* opened 25 February)

15 May – 12 June: Greek plays tour of eastern university stadia

18 June: Barker and McCarthy return to England

August/early Sept: Red Cross book research in France

Late summer-autumn: writing 'Trivialities 1: Acids in Solution' and 'Trivialities 2: The Man to whom life owed nothing' (unpublished)

19/20 September: Barker arrives in USA

Late October-late November: lecture tour ('Art and Democracy' and 'New Ideas in the Theatre')

1916
8 January: sails to France (research for Red Cross book), arriving 18 January

29 January: travels to London

February: probably revises 'Bigamist'

c.5 February: returns to France

c.17 February: travels to London

23/24 February: finishes Red Cross book (in London)

24 February: Huntington's father dies

11 March: Barker leaves Bordeaux for New York

Late March – June: Barker in Williamstown, MA, working on *The Morris Dance*; the 'Williamstown' story; starts *Farewell to the Theatre*

April 'Souls on Fifth' published both in *The Century* 91 and as a book by Little, Brown and Company

15 April: article on Leo Hogan's work published in *The Evening Post* [New York]

8 July: returns to England to enlist, arriving 17 July

6 August: first day in St John's Wood barracks, London

August: writes short story 'Picket: July 1916' (published in *The Sun* [New York] Sunday, 22 February 1919). Salmon, in Barker 2004, says this was never published

10 September: finishes 'Promise of an American Theatre'

11 September: arrives at Trowbridge barracks

2 October: arrives for Coast Defence training in Weymouth

11 October: commissioned as Second Lieutenant

12 October: begins work in Secret Service Bureau, Whitehall, London

Mid-October – November: writes new lecture 'Why worry with art?' (working title) and new act of *Prunella*

15 December: served with papers for the first divorce suit

23 December: leaves Liverpool for New York, arriving 1 January

1917

13 February: *The Morris Dance* opens (dir. Winthrop Ames, Little Theatre, New York)

February to mid-March: six-week lecture tour (two 1915 topics plus 'What is Wrong with Art?' and 'The Staging of Shakespeare'); simultaneously working for British Intelligence and finishing *Farewell to the Theatre*

31 March: returns to England, arriving 10 April

19 April: hearing for restitution of conjugal rights

May: Huntington finishes her novel *Eastern Red*

9 July: the Huntingtons sail to France

11 July: Barker's 'The Eden Theatre' in *Manchester Guardian*

Summer-autumn: planning *Peer Gynt*

Late autumn-winter: working on/planning two stories, one of which became 'The God of Good Bricks'; the other ('Mrs M—') aborted

October: Huntington begins her novel *Ada*

10 November: decree nisi granted

December: planning *The Betrothal*

16 December: *Vote by Ballot* performed by Stage Society at Court Theatre, London

27 December: the Huntingtons separate

28 December: Barker at Labour Party conference

1918

'Introduction' to reprint of Leonard Merrick's 1897 novel *One Man's View* (London: Hodder and Stoughton)

January: planning *Deburau*

8 January: lecture to Dalcroze Society

23 January: Labour Party conference

27/28 March: Huntington leaves Paris for England

31 July: Barker and Huntington marry

1919

20 February: article 'Reconstruction in the Theatre' in *The Times*

July: Barker becomes Chair of Council of the British Drama League

December: planning *The Romantic Young Lady*

1920

16 September: *The Romantic Young Lady* opens (Royalty Theatre, London)

23 December: *Deburau* opens in New York (Belasco Theatre)

1921

8 January: *The Betrothal* opens (Gaiety Theatre, London)

March: 'The Fire that Burned in the Corner' *Fortnightly Review* (109: 518–527). Salmon, in Barker 2004, says this was never published

2 November: *Deburau* opens in London (Ambasssadors Theatre)

III

LECTURES AND JOURNALISM 1915-1918

INTRODUCTION

After meeting and marrying Helen Huntington, Granville Barker continued to direct, write plays and campaign for theatre, with her full encouragement. The key change in 1915 was that he stopped working as a theatre manager. His decision to do this was made independently of Huntington.

Barker arrived as a celebrity on the New York theatre scene in December 1914. He had been invited to direct a season by the Stage Society on the strength of his innovative productions in London. His stature was seen as equal to that of Craig and Reinhardt. He was also in New York because he had been asked to manage a new theatre, based on the fame of his management expertise as seen principally at the Court Theatre, London. After his Stage Society-sponsored season at Wallack's finished in mid-spring 1915, he formed a company with Lillah McCarthy to tour two Greek plays. By the time they both sailed back to England in June he had turned down the 'New Theatre' initiative and taken a decision no longer to do projects such as the Wallack's season and the Greek plays. In the following summer, when his friend Winthrop Ames invited him to head up a new Shakespeare Theatre in New York, Barker refused, saying he had 'given that up' (71897/75).

Although the press the previous year reported he had given up directing, by at least summer 1917 he was thinking about a production of *Peer Gynt*, followed by a series of other projects. And he continued to write plays, beginning *Farewell to the Theatre* in spring 1916 along with his adaptation of Stevenson, *The Morris Dance*.

1

Through summer and autumn of 1916 he was researching a series of history plays, now done, not as a theatre or company manager, but as a solo artist. This work was accompanied by a conscious repositioning of himself in relation to theatre as an institution. He had always disliked theatre conceived simply as a 'business', which is why he was interested in experiments such as the Court Theatre. In America he was exposed not only to a more extreme version of theatre as business but also to the huge wealth and privilege of those who sponsored 'art' theatre. Barker was alienated by both.

This alienation may have been felt the more strongly because at the same time he was developing his idea that dramatic creation did not need money or theatres or even a profession. We first see the articulation of these ideas in the lectures he gave in America in the spring and autumn of 1915. Here he explored the nature of acting. While, on one hand, he introduced American audiences, perhaps for the first time, to the careful rehearsal techniques of Stanislavski, on the other hand he suggested acting is an activity that is part of everyday behaviour. These ideas would be refined until they appeared in his publications from the early 1920s onwards.

Running alongside the exploration of acting there was an interest in the places where dramatic creativity takes place. In the spring of 1916 he encountered the work of Leo M. Hogan, who was using drama and music in classes for children with learning difficulties. The concept of drama as a means of facilitating non-theatrical expression, as it were, expanded considerably once Barker began military service. His experience in the army prompted much thought about class and democracy. Like his friend John Masefield, he saw the army as potentially a democratising force. The enemies of democracy, for Barker, were the 'exploiters' and the newspapers which they used as their tool. Newspapers sought to manage how people thought. Democracy would only come when communities learnt how to express themselves.

An early statement of this idea came in a lecture in March 1915 and then was more fully developed in an essay commissioned for the *Manchester Guardian's* 'American Number' issued on 3 October 1916. The publication was propaganda intended to persuade America of her closeness to Britain and so to join the war on

Britain's side. Barker used the opportunity not so much to write propaganda as to explore drama's efficacy as a means by which American minority communities could learn to express themselves. This exploration emerged from, but extended the implications of, one of his regular themes. He had argued for a number of years that the distinctive feature of drama was that it was a 'communal' art. It had to be made by bringing together different elements in a way which was cooperative. By autumn 1916 he was arguing that this communal art could undertake the specific job of enabling expression by a local community. Thus communal methods meet community purpose.

His own role in relation to such community work, as a middle-class intellectual, is hinted at in the conclusion to the *Guardian* piece. Here he describes the two forces working towards a new future for American theatre. On the one hand there are the local community makers and, on the other, university-trained intellectuals. In America of course, unlike Britain, it was at this date possible to study drama at university. Barker, though not university-trained, was clearly one of those intellectuals capable of arguing for a new vision. And it's in that role that, in 1919, he took on the chairmanship of the newly formed British Drama League. A major purpose of the League was to promote drama-making among a range of different communities. For this initiative Barker modelled a prospectus and infrastructure (letter to Geoffrey Whitworth, 18 July 1919 in Salmon 1986: 556). The ex-theatre manager now put his management skills to the service of a communal art being made in communities. This, though, viewed with the eyes of a traditional theatre man, might well be evidence of how Barker the producer 'degenerated into a professor' (Pearson 1951: 85). That opinion, and the coagulated theatre snobbery it articulates, neatly indicate something of the radicalism of Barker's project.

Its articulation is mapped in the extracts and pieces which follow. Each shows the developing interest in what theatre-making is, who does it and what for. Barker's later published work in this area has its roots in the ideas first formulated here.

1. American Press Interviews and Reports of Lectures: extracts

The lecture topics were 'Art and Democracy' and `New Ideas in the Theatre' (1915), to which were added `What is Wrong with Art?' and `The Staging of Shakespeare' in 1917.

i. Granville Barker, 'Bad Drama Bad as Typhoid', *New York Times*, 31 January 1915

'A play', according to Granville Barker, 'is anything that can be made effective upon the stage of a theatre by human agency. [...] 'Then, as a social force, the theatre has the immense value of bringing different arts together in its service. The thing that I myself want to do is to get together all the arts that have to do with the theatre – music, painting, decorating, speaking. Every one joins in. The work is essentially communal. [...]'

ii. Stanley Olmsted, 'The Asceticism of Granville Barker', *Morning Telegraph* [New York], 21 February 1915

'In my ideal school of acting', proceeded Mr. Barker, 'they would all be taught for at least four years to fence, to ride, to wrestle, to run across country, to raise, lower, inflect and modulate the voice. The feeling for colors, tones, rhythms, melodies, harmonies, all that sort of thing would be developed in each student to the limit of his individual capacity for sensitiveness along those lines. Thus as his appercetiveness grew the unimpeded bodily expression would have to follow along. For on the development of plastic power in his body would a large proportion of his energies be expended. That no aspirant would be admitted to my school of acting who lacked at least a rudimentary physical perfection goes without saying. Physical perfection is, of course, absolutely essential in an actor.'

[Each of the above extracts shows how misguided is the assumption that theatre-making of this period was uniformly subservient to the idea of written text as primary.]

iii(a). Report of a speech to the American Academy of Dramatic Arts, *New York Telegraph*, 20 March 1915

'I learned the particular method that Stanislofsky uses in rehearsing the parts. He says to study a play, and to study a part, and not to merely learn it mechanically, you should do this: You should first study the character; then when you come to the actual staging of the thing and you want to learn to work with the other people, you should set up in your mind certain milestones in that character and that part. ¶ And those are the points to which you have to travel in your conception of the part, in your acting of it, when you know it. You have to say in such and such a scene there are two milestones; there is one at the start and then in a certain scene you have to reach the other, and so on. ¶ He said if you will do that and you will get that fixed, then you need never become a mechanic, you will find that your performance is really spontaneous; and if the performance that I saw there is a test, it is certainly very wonderful.'

iii(b). The same speech as reported by the *New York Herald*, 20 March 1915

That the profession of acting really extends outside of the theatre and plays an important part in a number of callings was one of Mr. Barker's statements.

Think of the number of callings that depend upon the person attached to that calling being really a good actor, not in the sense of being an impersonator of some one else, but in really being a good interpreter.

[The speech was also reported in the *Tribune.* My assumption is that 'Stanislofsky' was a journalist's rendering of Barker's pronunciation of 'Stanislavski'. The concept of acting as interpretation rather than impersonation runs through Barker's writings.]

iv. 'Granville Barker Talks on Drama', *New York Columbia Spectator*, 27 March 1915

'I feel that the theatre can be something more than an entertainment, although I never want it to be less. I feel that it can be more than a collection of expert people, that it can be the mouthpiece of a community expressing itself. ¶ It is vitally important that a community should learn to express itself. I think the theatre, to a great extent, can furnish the highest type of the expression of a community's feelings. The theatre should come from the community, and not from the experts of the communinty [*sic*]. The Greek drama began that way. It began by a concourse of people coming together and singing and dancing and giving expression to their natural feelings. In time, as individual poets arose, they began to formulate and elaborate and to reduce to words and more artistic forms the feeling of the people, and ultimately you have the things which we now know as Greek tragedy. ¶ The theatre, it seems to me, is a thing in which all people should be a little more trained. To know a little bit about the art of acting is the best way to appreciate the art of the theatre. After all the art of acting is only the art of good and graceful behavior. We want a race of people who will walk beautifully, speak beautifully and be sensitive to beautiful things. This is not idealism, but common sense. This is the world in which you would choose first to live. ¶ And finally, we need, as a nation, to learn how to express ourselves and our national feelings.'

v. Report of a lecture at Vassar entitled 'New Ideas in the Theatre', *Poughkeepsie Miscellany News*, 19 November 1915

Mr. Barker first gave a short history of the English drama which showed throughout the dependence of the drama for its success upon its relation to the people and the part it plays in interpreting the life of the people. This significance of the drama lies in the fact that it is the one art which operates most directly with human material and is most dependent for its success upon the cooperation of the audience. The Mystery Plays with which the English drama originated were given by the people and for the people and touched their lives in that serious religious interest which was so vital to them. The Elizabethan drama was great because it was an expression of the customs and habits and life of the times. Then came the period of the Commonwealth, a time when the popular interest turned from the broad social culture to political affairs and the stage suffered accordingly. Nor did the Restoration under Charles II bring back the real theatre. Instead, it was a foreign thing that was introduced for the amusement of the court. [...] There lies with the people the answer which will determine for the future the cultivation of that living art of community imagination and expression.

vi. Report of a lecture at Harvard [entitled 'Art and Democracy'?], *Kansas City Times,* 11 December 1915

'The theater has always been at its best when it has been regarded as a perfectly natural means for the expression of the emotions of the people themselves handed over to experts to look after, not as a foreign thing, but a thing which the audience who do not earn their living by it are quite as capable of doing in their time as the actors on the stage who do earn their living by it. Acting is as common a thing to all of you in your everyday lives as it is to me in my professional life. We all of us act. We acted in our cradles. Go into any nursery and you will see the children acting, playing at soldiers or policemen. It is a sort of instinct. As we grow up we dramatize our lives. We are the principal characters and the rest of the world's business is to play up to us. If you doubt that you have got that dramatic point of view about your lives, ask yourself whether, when you are going to have an important interview, with your father for example, in the morning, you do not as you take your bath catch yourself saying, I shall say so and so, he will reply thus and thus, and then I shall say so and so. You dramatize the whole scene as you go down to that unpleasant interview. Sometimes it doesn't come off as you thought it would. He didn't take up your cues. He plays the scene in a different way; he plays you off the stage. You see he has dramatized the thing himself, he has done it in his own way, and perhaps he is rather more expert in his way than you are in yours. ¶ It is the man who is the best actor who will manage to get the best of it in the interview. Why? Because acting does not mean pretending to be somebody else. That is the lowest form. What it means, as I take it, is the interpretation of what you are through the medium of your own personality. There is not very great difference in principle between an actor interpreting Hamlet on the stage and a judge interpreting justice on the bench or a doctor interpreting medicine in a hospital. People talk about acting as if it were a sort of falsifying of human nature. In reality, it is the only way you can express yourself. I think it is true that the man who can act best on the whole will be the most successful man. I do not mean he will be the man who will make the most money. I mean he is the man who will stand most successfully for the things he wants to stand for. The healthful and natural drama has always been that expression of the people. I imagine the beginning of all drama was simply as that.' [...]

[The argument here precedes by several decades Erving Goffman's hugely influential *Presentation of Self in Everyday Life* (1956). Another version of drama's origins, in similar vein, is offered in 'The Eden Theatre' (*Manchester Guardian*, 11 July 1917). See below pp.22–24.]

vii. *Boston Sunday Globe*, 25 February 1917

Granville Barker, in the course of a lecture recently delivered in New York, said that the 'nearest to a National expression of art he had observed in this country was the dancing of patrons in cafes and restaurants'.

viii. Report of a lecture at Stanford entitled 'The Staging of Shakespeare', *The Stanford Daily*, 7 March 1917

'If I were running this University, I would put the study of Shakespeare into a Department of Physical Expression, make it a part of every normal course of study, and couple it not with literature, but with athletics.'

2. 'Backward Children Developed by Rhythm', *The Evening Post* [New York], 15 April 1916

They Sing Nursery Rhymes and Act Fairy-Tales
Those with Criminal Instincts Find their Better Selves in
the Ungraded Classrooms of Public School 19
Self-Effort an Aid to Progress
Folk Dances, Recitations, Songs, and Plays Given Once a Month
They do Constructive Work

Salvatore put the little horn to his lips. He blew a sweet blast upon it, and then went on with the little verse which has been classed as a Nursery Rhyme, which begins and ends, 'Little Boy Blue, come blow your horn'. But, someway, as Salvatore spoke it, his grimy hands fingering his little, old, red sweater, his big, dark eyes seeming to see the sheep on sunny uplands, the cows knee-deep in corn, Little Boy Blue left forever the pigeonhole of Nursery Rhymes, and became one of the most beautiful of the poems which tell of shepherds and their sheep. It took on a thrilling, magical tone – with its unconscious Italian caesura, after the 'Little Boy Blue' and its musical entreaty that the shepherd boy come at once – which made one think of Pan and the strange, white sheep of fancy which run so swiftly to his piping.

Salvatore is one of the deficient children in the ungraded classes of Public School 19, on East 14th Street – the exceptionally interesting and effectual ungraded classes taught by Leo M. Hogan and Miss Farley, and the way he made the jingle into poetry seemed symbolic of the work which Mr. Hogan and Miss Farley are doing in turning poor, puzzled, half-frantic children, "high-grade defectives with criminal instincts", into sensitive, understanding, skilled, interested human beings, with the power to see and hear and tell again what they know. The deficiencies never can be altogether made up, but every possibility that the children have can be developed. They are learning how to learn, how to be interested and industrious and ingenious, how to take the initiative, and to work together. And the new rhythm and balance of their bodies, which comes from gymnastics and music, makes new rhythm and balance in their brains.

Rhythm as a Teacher

This rhythm is the fundamental idea upon which Mr. Hogan builds, and it has been proved a good one, for boys have gone out from his classes to earn their own living, and are doing it. His class is of older boys, up to sixteen, who have graduated from all the other ungraded classes in the East Side. They are not all of the immediate vicinity of East 14th Street, as are those in Miss Farley's class of younger boys, in which is Salvatore. And many of them come to him in hopeless condition, not knowing how to do things for themselves, destructive, dangerous, "ready for a rough-house", as he says. Some are lazy, some melancholic, some seem to have no ability to think. Some of them come from reformatories, juvenile courts, other places. One boy in the class came a week ago from the Catholic Protectory, where he had been for a year because he stabbed another boy. One boy who had just come into the class is now being held for murder, for stabbing a man who tried to inter-fere with him one day. There is need of help, evidently, for the high-grade defective, and the kind of help which is being given them is apparent after a half-hour spent in Mr. Hogan's class room.

The room itself says a great deal. Mr. Hogan says: "Just now we're working on Spring". Their efforts seem to have been successful. On the green burlap which the boys have stretched over the rather dilapidated wall of the room where those of criminal instincts study, are the improvised yellow chickens and the blue-birds of the season. The green burlap is held up at the top by a stained wood moulding made and put into place by the boys, for "shop work" or carpentering takes up all the afternoons. The cabinet where the tools are kept was made by them, and one of the tables, and they do much of the repairing of the furniture in this and other rooms. They made the window-boxes where the flowers are. And this is where the initiative, the co-operation which Mr.

Hogan says they so much need when they first come, may be seen. They work out all the problems of measurement and construction themselves. The measurements are put on the blackboard, and they set to work, three or four boys working together in a way which saves labor and makes for efficiency.

They No Longer Fight

"It takes a while to get them to working together instead of fighting each other", Mr. Hogan says. "And I do not help them in the work. If they were working for a boss they could not run to him every minute to find out what to do next". It is very remarkable, almost miraculous, to see the puzzled looks which the boys' faces often wear, lightening up as they work, to see the eagerness of their eyes and hands, and the quickness and exactitude and immeasurable pride with which they turn out a picture-frame or an umbrella-stand, or a knife-box. The younger children are taught chair-caning, basketry, brush-making, and clay-modelling by Miss Farley, and the baskets thus made come in handy to represent the porridge bowls when the children dramatize their favorite tale of 'The Three Bears'.

About once a month there is an assembly of all the ungraded classes. The next one will be on the 14th of April. Then there are folk dances – Salvatore is now learning to lead off in the Virginia reel – recitations, songs, gymnastic drills, and dramatizations.

The rhythm is given by the marching, the beating of time, the gymnastic exercises with the windows wide open – as they are anyway all the time in this room, so that the boys wear caps and coats all day long in winter – the music and singing. This singing is a regular thing: recess is as well-ordered for these children as any other part of the day, filled largely with gymnastics, and in the middle of it the boys step up close to the piano in a double row and sing as if they wished to get rid forever of all the voice they have. It would be a pity for them to do this – especially for two Italian boys who sing, one embryonic bass and one embryonic tenor, in a very wonderful and extremely foreful [*sic*] way. This is no light matter – the singing of 'We are at home, we are at home, we are at home', and 'Heave, Ho, my Lads'. How they do sing! –

and that little one, with golden-red hair and the look of a cherub, lifts up his face in the way choir-boys in pictures do on Christmas morning. He wears no robes, but probably no pictured seraph could have discovered as quickly as he did, immediately after recess, that if a man has $48 for car-fare for a year, he has $4 of it for one month. He did not have to trace the division signs madly in the air with his first finger, either, as did the highly excitable youth on the end of the row.

A Self-Government System

On the blackboard of the big boys' room is the explanation of the Self-Government System. The room is run entirely by them. There is a Mayor and Assemblyman and a Fire Department and a Health Department to keep things clean and a Police Department and all other kinds of departments. On the window-sills of the room are the evidences that this is indeed a democratic and artistic municipality in which the man in the street knows what he likes – great scrap-books for the time when the boys are waiting for school to open, in which they can all paste the pictures they like best and bring with them. "And there is everything here from Charlie Chaplin to Pope Pius the Tenth", says Mr. Hogan.

Everything that is done is for a purpose. When the children join hands and make a circle and one boy chases another and they dodge in and out, in and out of the circle, it is developing their judgment and their quickness, but they don't know it. And probably nothing is more significant than the dramatizations which the little children give of the stories they love. Petie was the baby bear, and Goldilocks was a little boy who never spoke at all before Christmas, but who finds it impossible to keep silence any longer in such a world as this has proved to be.

"Somebody has eaten my porridge all up", says Petie, aggrieved. But first Salvatore himself tells the whole story. Says he in his musical, magical voice – who was it that said Salvatore had criminal instincts? – "What lovely house! I guess I sit on this chairs". Poignant drama is this, when the Father Bear says, "Let us go eat the porridge", and they go and find it eaten.

But just here the bell for fire drill rang, and Goldilocks and the bears ran together, their differences forgotten, to get their coats and "go quietly, single file".

[**Leo Michael Hogan** (1893-1943), born in Massachusetts to Irish parents, graduated from New York University, obtained his doctorate at Fordham and lived in Brooklyn. After Public School 19 and war service he taught American History and Literature at Brooklyn Academy for 25 years. **Italian cæsura**: A cæsura is a slight pause produced by meter and syntax within a line of poetry; an Italian cæsura, strictly speaking, falls after the fourth and most important but not word-final syllable in a syllable unit, thus potentially making a clash between linguistic and metrical sense. Here it falls neatly on the comma after Blue (Little Boy Blue, /Come blow), so Barker has got his learned insight slightly wrong. **'new rhythm and balance of their bodies'** making the same in the brains: His piece on eurhythmics speaks of 'that perfect physical or emotional poise which eurhythmics seems to give - that sense of rhythm in everything they do' (see below pp.25-26). Such personal discipline and expressivity are then related to democracy.]

3. 'THE PROMISE OF AN AMERICAN THEATRE', AMERICAN NUMBER, *MANCHESTER GUARDIAN*, 3 OCTOBER 1916

How soon the American genius will be found fully expressing itself in an American drama one cannot, of course, say. But the omens are good. The curses of the theatre there are the curses here – a cut-throat commercial policy and a debauched public. The way of salvation there is in some respects easier, because that public, though debauched, is at heart not apathetic; it will still react quickly, if uncertainly, to a new sensation. But there again is the mischief; a sensation must be provided, and the sensation must be sudden and strong. As an adventure, artistic or financial, the theatre has as fair a chance in America as anywhere. As an institution, there, as in England, it simply does not exist. For a theatre, properly considered, must not be a place merely for the production of new plays. Does a library fulfil its purpose by throwing to the public as many thousand copies of the latest novel as can be absorbed? A theatre is a place for keeping plays and the co-operative art of acting alive, and it must be organised with that end in view.

In America there is business organisation to be found. It is, on the whole, expert and efficient. An entire continent could not be supplied (and mostly from one centre, New York) with elaborate and constantly shifting entertainments if it were not. The booking staffs of those big New York exploiters of drama that call themselves managements are at their desks day by day year in and out. The treasurers and accountants of separate theatres work in touch with them; so that problems of travelling, printing, and advertisement can be regulated to a nicety. You may even find a permanent producer or two who will drill a company in double-quick time and halve the cost of carpentering your scenery.

A Vital Self-Criticism
Valuable and valued people these; for the worth of their activities spread over a hundred productions a year may in itself spell profit

instead of loss on a final balance-sheet. But for artistic organisation – for a permanent company, or a studio of designers and painters, for a finished idea of staging, or a school of playwrights making new methods from old – for anything of that sort you would search America, as you may search England, almost if not quite in vain. Not quite in vain, though, if you will search with the eye of faith and if the cold, critical eye winks on occasion. For there is no country better at boxing its own ears and calling itself names than America – except perhaps England. But while England owns to her special stupidities with a helpless smile that amounts almost to boasting, America, resentful at least that anyone else should level a charge against her, does attempt vaguely and wildly anything and everything to remove the reproach, never fearing (inestimable virtue!) to make a fool of herself in the attempt, confident that from the many wrong efforts snuffed out some right one will survive.

And so it is there at this moment with the theatre. A feverish and not too well-informed criticism of these exploiters who operate from New York, and deal out drama to the hungry public as a trader deals out glass beads to savages; a fever of attempts to 'do something different' breaking out all over the continent, both in get-at-able centres and noticeably in un-get-at-able corners, where the Movie (in whose bright lexicon there's no such limiting word) has dished the unwieldier play of whatever quality, has left even the lighter-travelling comedian and his kind a luxury forbidden by his railroad fare.

The Great Problem

For America means to have a drama. That much is clear. It is obvious, too, that she needs one, and needs it more than any other form of popular art. She that a hundred years ago was a nation – that was a nation fifty years ago, asserting and proving it in blood – has now through the haphazard immigration of the last thirty years run back very dangerously to being but a congeries of peoples, living, it is true, under much the same law, struggling, many of them, with Nature for their livelihood, struggling, more of them, only with each other by the light of no practical law save the

survival of the sharpest and (these new-comers of one or two generations) with no guiding national consciousness or purpose at all –
nothing at least, that the New Englander, the Virginian, the
Quaker, those truer souls and voices of American tradition, would
care to dignify with that name. That theory of the Melting-pot is an
easy-going hope and nothing more. You do not make a man a
citizen of your country by giving him freedom to live in it if he can,
and die in its gutters if he can't. He may have whole-heartedly
ceased to be Ruthenian or Slovac or Russian Jew while America
may still be nothing to him but a name. If he is Greek or Italian, it
is ten to one that, taking his vote and using it either to serve his
fancy or earn its price, he yet thinks of the land he has left as his
native land and plans to return, even though also it is a hundred to
one that he never will. If he is a German he plans, apparently, not
to return at all, but to plant his essential Germany in this soil as the
English planted England here. This is the hyphen trouble which is
so rudely dissipating the Melting-pot fiction. It has taken the
European War to bring the conscious American to a full sense of
what the conscious hyphenate may stand for. But, further, he is
seeing now what the unconscious hyphenate, the uncalculated
millions of him, may quite fail to stand for – those ideas and ideals
on which all he proudly means by America is founded, – and may
fail in the not far future at some fatal moment to the nation (so he
thought it) which he and his fathers gave faith and love and
suffering to create.

The Community Drama
The lookers to the future, then, in that land whose future may well
mean the future of the world, are searching for any and every
means by which in these new-come millions an American
consciousness may be gendered. Quite naturally – and, thank
goodness, quite simply – they turn to the theatre as one – though
one of the least – of these. We may rule out a few superior efforts
to improve the mind of the people through the influence of Art.
Such things are never vital. Nor need we spend sympathy with a
well-known authority in New York who laments that the limited
vocabulary of the playgoer (his English still a foreign tongue to

him) rules out the worthy play. There is no law that connects a play with complex literature. It is not lack of words that will leave the Movie at its most emotional no more than a frigid debauch, but rather lack of that peculiar gift of drama – the directly human touch and its response. And not in the recognised theatres of New York, in spite of much good work which with pocket-denial good workers try to do there, are (I think) the true foundations of the new American drama being laid: the art that shall first do its small share in creating the new America, which shall then find its less humble reward in expressing that new America to herself. But look to the so-called Neighbourhood and Community Playhouses (again to the simplest of them, where art, if it is mentioned at all, has no capital A), unpretentious little places to which gather, their day's work done, the butcher and baker and candlestick-maker and amuse themselves by singing and dancing, by staging and acting little plays. Look fifteen hundred miles or so west. There in the State Agricultural College of North Dakota is a department giving a good part of its time to the encouragement and help of village plays and playing. Through the hard winter not much work can be done on the farms, and the little communities scattered over the great State are very isolated. So to keep their minds busy at least they stage and act plays. This, however embryonically simple, is truly the theatre as an institution. In North Dakota they write the plays sometimes. And a group of Icelanders, one winter there, contrapted a little scene of the old Icelandic winter to show to their new countrymen. And so on and so forth.

The Well-Spring of Art

One must not, I know, over-measure the importance of such things or trust yet to their permanency. Notions strike root quickly in America; they may not therefore strike deep. And it is far enough, no doubt, from the amateur acting of popular farces in village halls (even though an occasional semi-folk play is thrown in) to a national art form. But we have here quite genuinely the people trying to express themselves; and that, surely, is the foundation of all true art. Moreover, in that little Icelandic play may we not see a contribution brought in the right spirit by those strangers to their new home? It is in the blending of many and diverse races that the spiritual strength of America will lie, but if – and only if – they really can be blended. And certainly from such a blending the richest art may spring, but if – and only if – each people brings its genius generously, humble-mindedly, content to lose its soul with faith to find it, content to make no particularist and hyphenated claim. Certainly in that blending, in the clash of emotion and idea which must precede and go along with it is all the stuff of drama. And in that fact lies chiefly my hope for a great American theatre, my even dearer hope for a theatre that shall serve and vivify a great America.

There is the other road to be travelled. In New York, leavening the lump of the mere exploiters of drama, one finds men to whom the theatre stands for both a calling and an art. They took to it at their universities, and (marvellous this to an English ear) their professors encouraged them. So that while one would find in our dead past the stage-struck young man from Oxford merely ambitious to be Romeo, his cousin from Harvard or Yale, Williams or Dartmouth, come with a more disciplined mind on the subject, demanding opportunities to manage a theatre and make something of it; and this, after some years of apprenticeship in the school of the exploiter (the only school available), he is about now coming to do. One could list the names, telling off with much pride and praise the theatrical children, older and younger, of Baker of Harvard and Phelps of Yale and the others – Ames, Williams, Sheldon, Hopkins, – but the progeny is such a growing one. They must work in New York and mainly on the conditions they find there; must be creative, that is to say, upon terms laid down by the exploiter for his own profit. Does that sound a small difficulty to surmount? Try it and see. Therefore I say that most criticism of their shortcomings is but ill-informed. But by sheer persistence and good judgement, by the patient enthusiasm which thrives on abuse and survives even misunderstanding, they are winning their way. They are winning and – more hardly – holding a public to whom drama is food rather than strong drink. In their hands is the future. In any others (as far, at least, as the New York commercial drama is concerned) it seems that it will be but an inane repetition of the past.

Democracy and Self-Expression

The goal, then, is at the meeting of these two roads; the one, travelled spontaneously by the people, who shall find in dramatic expression an outlet and a means of cultivating that sense of themselves which is after all a step, and not the smallest, in the climbing from amoeba to angel; the other, along which the consciously creative artists are leading the but half-willing public by the nose. Between the two, other forces make for good. The vogue of the Pageant Play is remarkable. It burgeons out in one big city after another – conceived and carried through on an enormous scale – too unwieldy for true health, I incline to think. But certainly it brings again a sense of unity and self-expression to the crowd. No man or woman having had a share in it need ever feel again that drama is a wild beast show. One learns, as actor, to demand that the audience too must take its active part of sympathy and understanding. As audience one is less likely ever again to begrudge that share.

For first and last, and in general and particular, it is by this co-operation that the drama lives. Pipe we never so wisely, the souls of our hearers will not dance unless the sense of drama is living in them too. And the need for self-expression – personal, communal, national – is a need that must be filled if democracy is not to be a byword for the fooling of the people, if the voice of the people is to be anything more than a parrot-cry. Now in the theatre, that common meeting-house of sex and class and creed, where an epitome of our world gathers for an hour or two to recognise some epitome of our life – in that social solvent that the theatre at its best can be, there is to be found, if we will, some fulfilment of that need.

Nowhere than in America is this need greater – of self-realisation, of self-expression, of the creation of a national sense. Nowhere are the dangers threatened by the lack of it, though distant, more threatening. There are wise souls who mean that the self-centred, the spendthrift, the petted and despised theatre shall be brought to do its part in the fulfilment.

[Commissioned in September 1916, while Barker was in barracks, this essay appeared alongside articles by: James, Lord Bryce, ex-British Ambassador to the United States, author of *Neutral Nations and the*

War (1914); Charles Eliot, President Emeritus of Harvard, a supporter of the British war aims; Gilbert Murray (1866-1957), Barker's friend, translator of Euripides and war propagandist; the celebrated associate editor of *The New Republic*, Walter Lippman, a convert to the cause of American intervention in the war; and James Walker, a leading New York Democrat, who wrote on 'The Meaning of Preparedness'. That title, together with the range of authors, indicates the purpose of the *Guardian's* 'American Number'. It was a contribution to the propaganda campaign to persuade the USA to enter the war as an ally of Britain. While much of the rhetoric was expected to engage Americans as friends who shared the same civilised values as the British, Barker's essay annoyed a number of people associated with New York theatre. Helen Huntington heard gossip that the critical hostility towards his play *The Morris Dance* in February 1917 was motivated by anger at the views he had expressed.

nation/congeries of peoples: Here as in the letters to Huntington, Barker gives particular importance to a concept of nation as organic wholeness. **the hyphen trouble**: Many Americans of German extraction had a hyphenated surname. As the war progressed there developed a feeling among those who were pro-British that members of the German community in America were more loyal to their Kaiser than to the country of their adoption and that they were resisting and disrupting the process of the racial blending implied by the 'Melting Pot' metaphor. By the time of the presidential contest between Woodrow Wilson and Charles Evans Hughes in the autumn of 1916, political rhetoric was full of racist slurs against those with 'hyphenated' names. Barker told Huntington he was writing 'an article about the American stage – in which I'm saying some things – not about the stage at all – that you want said' (71898/62). These 'things' may derive from Huntington's forcefully stated opinions about the 'hyphenated' and their loyalty to Germany. **The Agricultural College**, founded in 1890, is now North Dakota State University. George Pierce **Baker** (1866-1935) founded the Harvard Dramatic Club in 1908, following this with Workshop 47 in 1912, set up to perform plays written by students under Baker's tutelage. Failing to get a drama degree established at Harvard, he moved to Yale in 1925. William Lyon **Phelps** (1865-1943) taught English literature at Yale. Winthrop **Ames** (1870-

1937), theatre director and friend of Barker, founded the Little Theatre in 1912 in order to do experimental work, and the Booth Theatre in 1913. Percy G. **Williams** (1857-1923), theatre owner and manager, especially of vaudeville, was famous for bucking the management trend and giving performers generous pay and good conditions. Edward Brewster **Sheldon** (1886-1946), playwright, wrote such works as *The Nigger, Romance* and *The Song of Songs*. Arthur **Hopkins** (1878-1950), Broadway producer and director, was to take an interest in Expressionist drama, staging Sophie Treadwell's *Machinal*. Barker considered sending him the scenario for *The Three Musketeers*. **Pageant Play**: Widespread American interest in this form from around 1905 led to the founding of the American Pageant Association in 1913. Huntington commented on the essay: 'A good thought that the really successful theatre will come into being at the meeting point between those working <u>down</u> (like Winthrop Ames, etc -) and those working up - (like the Dakota farmers and their Icelandic play) - In other words between those who <u>know</u> - and those who <u>do</u>. If only these two forces could always work toward each other instead of in opposite directions it would mean a great deal for general civilization - wouldn't it? ¶ And I liked, particularly in your article, the idea that the theatre may have a big share in the "making" of this country' (71901/121). To which Barker responded: 'always - always you see clearly the thing that I had dimly seen - the thing that unknowing I had been struggling to say. When you speak of "the junction between those that know" and those that do - in everything yes that is a truth - and fruitful - that is <u>live</u> thought' (71898/219).]

4. 'THE EDEN THEATRE',
MANCHESTER GUARDIAN, 11 JULY 1917

This is a story of the time when Cain and Abel were young. Adam was busy from dawn till dark digging and planting and picking in the little field in the little field he had made, and Eve was busy too in their little hut of branches and leaves, keeping it tidy and getting ready the meals, and they had no time at all for the children. Cain was eight years old and Abel seven, and they were very bored. They could stand and watch father digging, or they could walk about or they could run, but they mustn't run far because of the wild animals that might eat them up. So they had walked and run and crawled and hopped, from the biggest tree of all to the biggest second tree and back again till they were very bored indeed, and there was really nothing else to do. But one day as they stood looking towards the edge of the forest and wondering what was inside it, and if there was another side, they saw on the short grass a squirrel eating a nut. He was enjoying every bit of that nut, and he had come away from the trees and his home and his friends that he might enjoy it all by himself. Behind him out of the wood came stalking a young wild cat, and Cain and Abel watched.

The squirrel felt danger. He dropped the nut and gave a bound forward, and round he turned, and when he saw the cat his tail quivered. Perhaps the cat could have had him then with one big spring, but, again, perhaps it couldn't, and a missed spring is a missed squirrel. So it lay down, there where it stood, and seemed to go straight off to sleep. And now the squirrel could have got away. But no: back he would go for that nut. And just as he reached it the cat sprang; then very soon there was no more squirrel.

It made Cain and Abel feel rather solemn as they began their walk again backwards and forwards between the two big trees. Presently Abel said –

"The squirrel was holding the nut like this, and when he felt the cat was there he turned his head twice – like this he turned it, – and then he jumped!"

Abel jumped; and it wasn't at all unlike the squirrel.

"I don't believe the cat was really asleep," said Cain.

"No," said Abel, "but it wanted the squirrel to think so. And then it jumped, like this." And he jumped again.

"Not a bit like that," said Cain. Then Abel jumped five or six times more, and jumped a little differently every time. But still Cain said that it wasn't like it a bit.

Abel was a slim child with straight hair and large dark eyes, while Cain, as everyone remembers, was a hefty youngster, red and curly-headed, and had a turn-up nose.

"If you'd sit down there like the squirrel," said Abel, "I believe then I could jump just like the cat."

"I won't," said Cain, "and you don't look like the cat. You be the squirrel, and I'll show you how the cat jumped. I know how. I feel like it."

So Abel took a little pebble for the nut and squatted with his back to Cain and lifted his head and turned it and jumped and swerved around, and there was Cain with his head down and his eyes shut, just as the cat had been. Then Abel crept back for the pebble and Cain sprang – oh, very like the cat indeed, for his eyes went quite red. He sprang so hard and fell so heavily that Abel went clean over backwards and hit his head against a stone and hurt himself and howled and howled.

Eve, who was getting the sweet potatoes ready for dinner, wiped her hands hastily on her fig-leaf apron and ran to see what the noise was.

"He's a cat and I'm a squirrel," sobbed Abel, "and he's killed me for his dinner, and my head's hurt awful – oo!"

"Dear me, what a tragedy!" said Eve.

Cain called Abel a cry-baby, but Eve kissed him and dried his eyes and smoothed his hair. Then she took them both by the hand and walked them up to the top of the hill mound from which the lake could be seen.

It was spring-time, and among the stones and the scant grass down by the lake edge two water-birds were building their nest. One of them ("That's the wife", said Eve) was standing on one leg by the spot they had chosen, preening her feathers and looking very proud, while the other was running around and making a lot of fuss, picking up bits of grass and leaf and stick and scuttering in to add them to the growing nest.

"Just like father," said Cain.

"But they must have a nice house, you see," Eve told the two, "or what would happen to the little Cains and Abels when they arrive?"

Abel sniffed; his head felt bad.

"You might play at being birds till dinner's ready," said Eve. "But you can't stand on one leg, Abel, can you?"

"'Course I can," said Abel.

So he did, there on the top of the mound, sniffing a little from time to time. Cain ran about and fetched bits of leaves and stick, and soon there was a nest. They put round stones in it for eggs, and Abel sat on them, and then they talked about things in general, and in particular about how nice it would be when the little feathered Cains and Abels came. It seemed only a short time till the sweet potatoes were done and Eve was calling them to dinner.

This probably happened on a Tuesday, though we can't be sure of the day of the month or even quite sure of the year. If we could the anniversary would always be celebrated in the theatre. For on that day the two first plays were acted – a tragedy and a domestic drama.

[In the 1915 lectures Barker suggested that drama emerged as a mode of community expression. By contrast this piece seems in line with the general proposition that drama is a mode of everyday behaviour. The most influential contemporary research into the origins of theatre was that of the so-called Cambridge Ritualists. This group included Gilbert Murray, Jane Harrison (*Ancient Art and Ritual* [1913]), Francis Cornford (*The Origin of Attic Comedy* [1914]) and A.B. Cook. Their thesis was that Greek tragedy originated in the ritual practice of seasonally killing the god. 'Eden Theatre' lays the emphasis instead on the ordinary activities of observation and imitation. In doing so it secularises the model of origins. In this its tone as a jokey – and indeed sometimes quite arch – 'children's fable' is crucial. Presenting an almost poemical contrast to scholarly accounts of ritual practices, it proposes that acting arises out of everyday play.]

5. EXTRACT FROM *EURHYTHMICS PAPER NO. 3: ADDRESSES DELIVERED AT THE ANNUAL MEETING, JANUARY 1918.* PUBLISHED BY THE DALCROZE SOCIETY OF GREAT BRITAIN AND IRELAND

[...] It seems to me that the essentials of the art of acting are things which practically every single man or woman should study. They should be part of general education. There is a very great misconception (especially among English people) that the art of acting consists in pretending to be something that you are not. But what acting really consists in is expressing through the medium of your own personality something which you have spiritually and emotionally absorbed. And there is really no very great difference in principle between an actor interpreting the soul of Hamlet on the stage, or a judge on the bench interpreting the principles of justice, or even, if I may say so, a priest interpreting the word of God in the pulpit; the power of expression is necessary to them all. [...] For this is the great choice which the rival ideas of civilisation offer us. What is to be the view and the treatment of the individual? Are we to think of the State as the great power of which we ourselves are mere soulless, irresponsible units, or are we think of [*sic*] the State as the highest common factor of the expression of all the individuals in it, however diverse those individual expressions may be, however much we may disagree with many instances of them? If the choice is between these two things, have we not made ours once and for all? We have chosen the expression of the individual as being the basis on which we will build our future lives and the future lives of our race. On that encouragement of the individual to develop himself to the highest pitch of self-expression, on that and on that only can we hopefully build a great democracy. When we face the problems of our education, we can test our solution of them by our faith in the fact that we shall never greatly err as long as our discipline comes from *within* and we encourage the individual to express himself. That appears to me to be the great claim that eurhythmics has upon our attention as educators and as learners ourselves. Its relation to the arts is in one sense incidental – but in a sense that the arts are but the expression of the spiritual vitality of the people – the only sense, I think, in which it is profitable to consider them at all – the relation is fundamental. [...]

[The **Dalcroze Society** of Great Britain and Ireland was founded by Marie Eckhard in 1915. Emil Jacques-Dalcroze at this time ran his own institute in Geneva. The meeting was held on Tuesday 8 January 1918. Barker shared the platform with Edward Lyttelton and Arthur Clutton-Brock. In 1918 Lyttelton was rector of Sidestrand in Norfolk, but up to 1916 had been a reforming headmaster of Eton, committed to freeing the child's creative imagination. Clutton-Brock wrote on art and literature. His *Socialism and the Arts of Use* was published by the Fabian Society in 1915. The comments on the **expression of the individual** seem to show the influence of J. A. Hobson (see p.156) and are in line with the New Ideals in Education conferences (from 1914 onwards), which were committed to the freedom of the child in the classroom and experimental praxis (Howlett 2017). That context gives extra significance to the 'Eden Theatre' essay. Barker in Spring 1918 wrote: 'Did I ever show you this in any form – this Eurhythmics thing – Oh but the verbatim report – Whatever on earth I actually said!' (Texas 'At the Club. Monday 7-5PM.')]

IV

LETTERS

Barker to Huntington calendar entry: 'You are my inspiration'
(Harley Granville Barker papers, British Library 71898/188)

INTRODUCTION

Your dear – dear letters – they never leave me Helen (except for bath-times!) night or day. Oh my darling I am made a new man by your love – they promise me – give me proof of that dear the letters – I read them and life is a different thing – they add something to me – I've always told you – a spiritual strength – an inspiration (5 February 1916: Boulogne) (71897/28)

Barker and Huntington were forced to be separate from one another for much of the time between falling in love early in 1915 and marrying in July 1918. From the summer of 1916 onwards he had to do military service in England, but even when he was residing in the United States it was difficult for the two to meet. Her husband Archer, once alerted to the relationship, kept a jealous eye on both her movements and her communications. In order to bridge the gap between them the couple wrote to and for each other on a very regular basis. Sometimes they wrote several times a day.

In addition to letters they wrote what they called 'diary' and 'calendar'. The calendar was kept separate from the letters and diary. Barker characterised it as the place where he put the more 'abstract' thoughts, though it might also describe the same events as the diary. The diary was usually written into a letter. Often separately titled, it recounted how he had been filling his days, what he had been working at, who he had been visiting. By contrast the letter itself was much more directly expressive of emotion, usually his love and admiration for Huntington and his frustration and impatience at his own circumstances. When they met in their necessarily secret meetings – in the public spaces of department stores, galleries, tea-rooms – they were constrained in what they could say to each other. It was in the letters that they exchanged on these occasions that they expressed all the passion that they could not speak aloud.

For both of them it was emotionally important, and comforting, to write down their feelings as a way of trying to make real contact across the enforced separation. For those outside the relationship the writing is not invested in the same way and can simply appear repetitive in its sentiments and phraseology. So most of my editorial cuts fall here. They are all marked, even if it's merely a sign-off line that's gone. It is, of course, ironic that what I am choosing to cut is precisely what was for Barker and Huntington the central function of the letters, the communication of the constant presence of love.

Deeply attached as they were, the non-arrival of expected letters caused considerable distress, and they worried for each other. These absences were frequent however. It was war-time. Mail across the Atlantic was even more disrupted than usual (though things improved when Barker could use War Office channels). But on top of war-time difficulties, their own circumstances had particular problems. Because of Archer Huntington's controlling vigilance, letters had to be smuggled through by friends, or whole sequences of friends. In one case a letter passed through four sets of hands in its journey from Barker to Huntington. The complexity and fragility of these arrangements, at all levels, had two main consequences. First, because they could not post a letter regularly, the two lovers would write part of a letter each day over a sequence of days or indeed weeks. Second, letters posted in one particular order might, in transit, get disordered and overlap one another. If this became confusing for them, as it did, then it is even more so for those of us trying to read the letters a century later. That confusion is at its most intense when we try to date the letters.

In very many cases Barker, in particular, puts the day of the month, without the year, on a letter, though not always. The letters written early in 1918 simply have the day of the week. Problems are made worse in the case of the British Library letters by the chaos of the archive. The foliation, the order in which the papers are numbered, bears only a casual and intermittent relationship with actual dates of writing. Letters from different years are bundled together and, even worse, pages of different letters are shuffled together. Sometimes the foliation is also back-to-front. Such disorder clearly compromises the accessibility of the archive.

Fortunately we can arrive at some dates by other means. Barker and Huntington frequently discuss events in the world around them, for example the US election, which can be easily dated. They also have their own key dates, such as their first meeting, of which they note anniversaries. After he left the United States in July 1916 Barker adopted a convention of putting a double time-scheme at the top of his letters. Huntington had given him a travelling clock which he kept set to New York time, as a way of keeping close to her. If a letter written in England doesn't have this double time-scheme then it dates from before July 1916, or after July 1917 when she travelled to France, though this feature does not apply to 'calendar' entries. As already noted, a letter may be written over several days or indeed weeks, and thus they assumed that by the time the letters arrived the events they described would be long over. On 28 September 1916 he responded to a letter she wrote twenty days earlier. Having written in a rush to catch the post, he said it all again at more length the following Sunday. This sort of repetition regularly affects the relationship between calendar, letter and diary. Writing so often, Barker sometimes could not remember what he had said when. If they needed to communicate urgently they didn't write letters; they cabled. But you can't do much love in a cable.

There is a particular problem in dating the 'calendar'. These are usually single sheets of paper headed only with the day of the week. They were sent off to Huntington in small batches to accompany letters. Several of these sheets might be written in one sitting, thus pieces headed Tuesday or Thursday could have been written on a Sunday. Rather than reflections on actual events they may be abstract thoughts. Thus 'calendar' entries don't necessarily correlate with actual datable days, so it would be artificial to tie them together. Where a calendar piece seems to grow out of or refer to a specific day, I have tried to date accordingly. Otherwise I indicate a general period of composition. My dates are in square brackets; my guesses are prefaced with a question mark. The same applies to conjectures about place of writing.

The need for reliable precise dates is perhaps less pressing given that these texts are all from a fairly tightly circumscribed group of years. It seems to me not much to matter whether Barker was setting down his beliefs in 1915 or 1917, given that his career extended several decades either side. Where precise dating matters much more is in sequences that have been hitherto confused in writings about Barker. First, there is the marital breakdown. Very obviously we now find out that Barker met McCarthy face-to-face on three occasions in 1916; he also tells us that he never settled down to regular life with her after leaving America in June 1915. Less obviously the more precise dating can enlighten us to the behaviour of the other parties in this story: George Bernard Shaw and of course McCarthy herself. What Barker called McCarthy's 'tricks' fall into place as part of a sequence (as detailed in 'Archer Huntington's Wife', below). From Huntington's letters we learn she went directly to France from the US in July 1917. Salmon's ignorance of this led to mistaken ordering of and commentary on the letters he reprinted. Second, there is the military service. Gale (2000: 121) says Barker 'returned to America in early 1917, reportedly to lecture', and from there did intelligence gathering about the activities of supporters of Germany. The phrasing suggests the lectures were merely cover, grounding its assertion rather perilously in that slippery word 'reportedly'. In reality the letters show that he planned the lecture tour, in order to raise money, before he was even enlisted as an officer-cadet in the artillery. He was only formally recruited to the Secret Service Bureau, also known as the Secret Intelligence Service, two months later, although he had met with them prior to that. Once recruited to them they made use of the tour, which was standard practice. Correct dates here again allow us to see the fantasies that have been woven around Barker.

My decision to organise the extracts from the letters into themed sections is an attempt to foreground different sorts of thinking and description without losing these in an undifferentiated plod through a chronological sequence. Being written across several days, letters and diary covered a range of topics, and could run to fifty or more pages in length. But the moves from one topic to another, especially in the diary, are quite sharp. Given there is a clean break either side of a passage on a particular topic, it becomes possible, without doing damage, to do extractions. I believe that seeing thematically linked passages together enables insights that may be lost if one were reading one whole letter after another. It may be arguable that lifting out extracts destroys the flow of a letter, but where it is written in stages across several days or weeks, changing topic and mood, one has to decide what constitutes a complete unit ... and then what more is gained in being able to bathe in the flow of that unit. Calendar entries are usually complete in themselves, fitted often onto one sheet and with a coherent thought.

Some longer extracts here run across several thematic topics. In such cases I have placed the letter according to its dominant concern. Where a letter or extract is relevant to more than one topic, it can be found by searching names or key terms in the Index. For example parts of 'the military mind' describe features of England; Shaw turns up in at least two sections: England and Shaw can be found via the Index. Explanatory notes on individuals or events are given at the first mention of the name, but all such occurrences are listed in the Index. Subsequent mentions of a name can be referred to the Index and thence to the note. In the explanatory notes, birth and death dates are given only for those people with whom Barker closely engaged, intellectually or emotionally. The dates of such people as American presidents are thus not relevant to the story.

While his unhappiness with the situation is clear enough, and while his views on the topics he discusses give us new insights, we don't have here the full picture of Barker the correspondent. We know from Huntington that when she was in Paris he bought her a dog and was threatening to send it from England (which worried her because her husband had also bought her a dog). During the discussion of this she suddenly got a letter from the English dog, introducing himself as Peter Imperator Noodles, becoming eventually called Imp for short (a name Salmon [1986: 309] misreads as Mop). When she was in England and planning to take a drive to meet Barker in the country she got a letter from him warning her about lions, tigers and highwaymen en route. Their letters were so much more than a communication of feeling. They were places for thinking, describing, analysing and - just as importantly - joking.

In many ways the letter was also a gift, part of the regular flow of gifts between them. Habitually these were shared quotations or cuttings or whole books. Barker said he much enjoyed sending her books, and asked whether he overburdened her with them – bear in mind that these were subject to the same pressures of secrecy as the letter and they arrived on a regular basis. But alongside the books there were other often whimsical gifts: dried flowers, pussy willow, vast quantities of cologne, a gardening apron, three mechanical ducks.

It is easy enough when reading the letters to get drawn into the sense of longing and desperation, a world where letters have to stand in for someone who is physically absent, where they seek to conjure into being an impossible closeness. And that's why it's worth always remembering that the writer and recipient were also capable of wit, fantasy and shere (as he spells it) silliness.

Editing of the letters

The punctuation is transcribed exactly as Barker wrote it, including his wildly inconsistent use of inverted commas. He was a great user of the dash, in lieu of most other marks. But the dashes are highly various, some being as small as a full stop, others much longer. Some marks look like a dropped pen. The distinction between full stops, commas and short dashes is blurred. In these cases I have been guided by such things as capitalisation of following words and relationships with other neighbouring marks. Sometimes there is no punctuation where it would be syntactically useful, so I have placed a gap between syntactic units. Overall I have tried to avoid providing Barker with the punctuation he didn't use, because it changes the character of the voice in the letters. My main intervention is to provide marks thus [...] to indicate that an extract has been taken from a more extended text that precedes it or follows it or both. Most of the letters are referenced by their BL folder/folio numbers. See Sources for abbreviations and listings of all letters. Of the Texas letters here, none is in Salmon (1986).

1. THE ATMOSPHERE OF WAR

[Monday 17 July 1916] Hotel Russell London 1-10am – <u>7-10PM.</u>
[...] The atmosphere of war is heavier in London than ever – crushing to the spirit of the finer people – coarsening the spirit of the less fine – I can't deny that. And the strain seems greater – and the sense that we are battling in the dark for we know not what – because some blind fate has led us into it – Is stronger than ever it seems. And that is the finally tragic sense. Oh it is too early to be summing it up but that – I record as an impression for you now. [...] **71897/100**

> [Written on the day Barker arrived in London from America, in order to enlist. The use of the double time scheme began when he left America (see p.30).]

Tuesday July 18 [1916] 10 am – <u>4 am</u> [Hotel Russell, London]
[...] The strain of this war! I'm not re-adjusted yet to the half organised welter of work – and the quite unorganised welter of opinion that England now is   It falls queerly on me but it is right it should. Once in it and if you are not careful your brain gets dulled to the meaning of it all – and that is bad.   This blind fighting! [...] **71897/100**

Friday July 21. [1916] 12-15 – <u>6-15</u>. [The Garrick Club, London]
[...] Some things – which are little things beside winning the war – sex one nevertheless – hurt rather. London is full of these "Revues" – and the soldiers on leave crowd to them. Silly and vulgar at the best (what should that matter at all one would say!) they are now becoming more and more frankly indecent – and drink and prostitution and drug taking among the soldiers are becoming very bad indeed. Poor wretches – cut off from all natural life and sent into

that hell (it is such a <u>boring</u> hell too) – let out for a week or so – what can one look for. <u>Still</u> it makes me unhappy – and one turns to think of Gallipoli – and the things they did – unbelievably heroic things – I must send you a first copy of Masefield's   I wish you could have heard his uncensored talk about it though. [...]
71897/109-10

[The attempt to seize control of the Turkish straits at **Gallipoli** was a major Allied defeat, with many dead. John **Masefield:** (1878-1967), poet and playwright. The **first copy** was probably his book *Gallipoli,* published by Macmillan in 1916.]

Wednesday July 26th [1916] 6PM – <u>Noon</u> with you.   [?Hotel Russell, London]

[...] In some things I'm so proud of England – in some things so ashamed. At my club they have ceased to take all the Radical papers. Think of it – the pettiness and folly. And you can't talk to people about the war or politics – they are nearly all just sick in mind. One must try and understand – the strain has been and is – bad. Ah – but there's more than that to trouble me in it [...]
71897/117

[His **club** was the Garrick Club, not simply an institution for those who are or fancy themselves 'theatrical' but also for the legal professions and indeed, at that date, senior military officers.]

Wednesday. [?25 October 1916 Bloomsbury, London]

London is a queer place these nights. When I come out of the office about seven it is pitch dark – I have to cross Trafalgar Square and there are crowds of people hurrying to get home – they tumble into each other – and cabs toot and work their way – none too slowly   and if it's raining and there are umbrellas up!! – The stretch from Piccadilly Circus past Leicester Square – usually disreputable – now more disreputable than ever. But usually of course in a blaze of light – all the Music-halls – now disreputable in the dark. But that seems to make it not more furtive but more bold. There's one thing though   On a clear night stars shine quite brightly One has never seen the stars bright above a big city and – what is the feeling it gives one? I couldn't get it into thought, much less into words – You must – for me. There's a certain stillness added at times. The place is full but people move more quietly. Perhaps it is that terrible dignity of starlight shining down on – a lot of bricks – and people crawling very slowly (it must seem from the stars) in and out of holes. No – it's more than that – and different. [...] **71898/180**

[Barker's **office** was in Whitehall Court. **dark**: A restricted lighting order was introduced in London with the end of Summer Time on 1 October, and extended to vehicles on 22 October.]

Friday. [?late October 1916 London]

Today at Charing X Station – I was having my boots cleaned – standing there – and the Hospital train was arriving and the ambulances driving the wounded men away. A little crowd – not very many – some men taking off their hats as the wounded passed. And a flower woman selling little roses and calling out "Flowers for the soldiers" And then – since no-one seemed to have bought any – I saw her run after one of the ambulances and throw some flowers in herself – a little excited she was but very ugly and ungainly. And a great lump came into my throat – it does now. I felt at once that I must buy some flowers – and then at once I felt I shouldn't let even that slight shadow of money spoil it. But I think that tomorrow I must go and buy some from her and tell her to throw them in – from me I shall say – but it will really be from you [...] **78198/139**

Friday Nov 3. [1916] 11-30am – 6-30am [Whitehall Court, London]

[...] once a week one has the feeling – oh better get out to the front and run the risk of being killed – for that's what war wants of people really – not cleverness and brains – even at war-work (you see the war is passing beyond all that) but just killing – kill enough people and when the fury is exhausted somehow it will stop.

However time will show what the demands are. The only <u>real</u> soldiers in this department are men who have been wounded and are sent back to this sort of work. Of course they are picked men – the average soldier might not do it very well. But in a years time there'll be no lack of picked men who'll be half smashed in that way. And then – if the fury still goes on – it'll be our turn. So I keep the gunnery books and my slide-rule and things – I can take that up again where I dropped it at least. People do seem to see a decision and a finish next year though. This winter there hardly can be – I take it no one really expected one. There may of course be no military decision at all – it may come simply through exhaustion – empoverishment of life – the nation's life – not the army's That's the tragic thing – but I suppose a wholesomely tragic thing – War ceasing to be military in its decisions altogether – passing out of the "chivalry" stage which it entered in late feudal times – which it had in Roman times – back into the ways of Attila and the dark ages – when it really did mean whole nations preying on each other We may the sooner stop it that way The empoverishment of life is bad of course – not the <u>material</u> empoverishment one could bear – one gains on the balance in the attack it makes on luxury – (and yet do you know luxury seems <u>more</u> rampant than ever in London now!). But the moral empoverishment One gains in the balance in that too – you may say – for the war has brought out all sorts of heroic qualities in the people. Well – yes – at the front I think that is so – though of course not universally so – one mustn't expect it or mind the other side of things the side that remains unpublished. But here in England! Every day lands me in deeper depression – yes – really. The good men stick gamely to their jobs but the rest – our public life rushing downhill people losing sense of decency – of honour – of chivalry – and openly unashamed of it There was a debate in the House of Commons last night about an old German soldier who since 1872 (he's 75) has lived here and for pure love of the work catalogued the Persian M.S.S. in the India Office Library (about as relevant to the war and our quarrel with Germany as the teachings of Confucius – or Christ!!) And a set of men hounding at the government to turn him out (probably to intern him) – playing up to the very lowest mob passions in their speeches. I had meant to cut out the debate to send you – and I was too ashamed. But the best of England is <u>not</u> like that you know – oh but too much of it is. [...] **71898/218**

[The **department** is the Secret Service Bureau, founded in 1909 and formally overseen by the War Office. For more on the **gunnery** see pp.90-98, below. The **old German soldier** is Hermann Ethé, a distinguished philologist who taught at what became University College Aberystwyth. In the middle of October 1915, when he and his wife returned from holiday, he was hounded out of town as an 'enemy' by a mob of 2-3000, earnestly demonstrating the patriotism of Aberystwyth citizens. In the **Commons debate**, one MP said 'Every German in this country was a professional spy'. Ethé died two years later, never having been able to return to his home.]

2. FRIENDS AND ASSOCIATES

[Tuesday 18 July 1916] 10-45PM. – <u>4-45PM.</u> [with the Masefields in Cholsey]

[...] As I write this I am at Masefield's for the night – at Cholsey in Berks – under the downs in the Thames valley (the place he writes of in his later poems and in "August 1914") A little moated farmhouse – and oh such divine country – the peace of long civilisation in it . We walked after supper half a mile up the down to the site of a battle that Alfred fought with the Danes. Miles you can see – and the landscape all grey-green and blue – green corn in the fields and bright scarlet poppies crowded in among it and blue cornflowers. Constance Masefield talking learnedly to me as we went – and my heart saying all the time only Helen – Helen – that you were here and could see all this beauty   oh you'd have cried with the joy of it – I wanted to feel its beauty through the beauty of my dear love instead of only through my own duller senses. To have been alone with you on that hill top in the twilight and the dead stillness – the country all damp and cool.   Oh beloved – how soon. [...] **71897/101-2**

> [John **Masefield** in 1903 married **Constance** de la Cherrois Crommelin (1867-1960), a friend of Laurence Binyon and a teacher with a university education in both mathematics and literature. They lived at Lollingdon Farm, Cholsey, just south of Wallingford, which at this time was in Berkshire. **Alfred** fought his battle in 871 at a site called 'Ashdown', probably to the west of Cholsey.]

Wednesday night [19 July 1916] 11-15PM – <u>5-15PM.</u> [with the Shaws in Ayot St. Lawrence]

[...] After some delay GBS met me at the station and we walked along   After a minute or two he referred to you. And then I went for him. Not a traitor – no. Or I shouldn't be here. And I did

always know that. Not in any malignant sense. But insensitive –
unapprehensive. Some lump left out of of his spiritual composition. Apparently in pure wanton stupidity he had done it – not
knowing what he had done – not knowing at least how one must
feel about it. Can you believe that – and yet not believe him either
stupid or monstrous through and through? Without knowing him
– no one can't. I spoke to Barrie about it – just the fact of his
having done the thing – and Barrie's eyes went "dangerous". Then
he said – mainly what I've just been saying. If you know him – you
know him capable of these amazingly "impossible" things. Pretty
damnable – and when you're fond of him – as both Barrie and I are
(in the teeth of much abuse of him – open abuse) more damnable
still. I'm not making excuses for him – my dear – I'm as angry as
ever   What more he'll have said to explain I don't know for just
then Charlotte drove up in the car and that ended it. But I'd said.
In future I must hold my tongue   He'll refer to it again – for I can
see he's hurt at having hurt me. Amazing creature   So big – and
yet with these flaws that would damn a lesser man completely, a
mystery. But no deceit in him – one may be sure of that – or the
shadow of a lie or a prevarication. The worst always on the surface
And not over this a traitor in intention or thought – no double-
dealing. Believe that for that at least (after years of knowledge) I
know. Angry as I am I know that. **71897/104-5**

[**GBS**: the playwright and radical polemicist George Bernard Shaw (1856-
1950); **Charlotte** Payne-Townshend (1857-1943) was a socialist and translator
– and like Huntington a millionaire – who married Shaw in 1898. **Ayot St
Lawrence** is a village between Harpenden and Welwyn in Hertfordshire.
Barker had spoken to J.M.**Barrie** (1860-1937), the playwright, on the day he
arrived back in London. What Shaw **had done** was to tell Lillah McCarthy
something about Huntington and Barker's arrangements, and for this
Huntington felt he had behaved like a **traitor** to Barker (see 'Archer
Huntington's Wife' p.220). Shaw had been much abused in public for his
stance on the war.]

Thursday July 20 [1916]. 5 PM. <u>11am</u> [with the Shaws in Ayot]

[...] Letters this morning – a walk   much talking about the inside things of English politics – the Casement trial (a lot of information that will never be public). I fight G.B.S. and that is stimulating to the mind as a rule – but I'm weary of it now – his occasional but very persistent perversities do weary me. Last night he read me the beginning of a new play – most of the usual charm and dash but he begins to repeat himself – that is inevitable – And we both fought poor Charlotte (I say "poor" because she hadn't much chance – I said I should go round to her side!) who has become a sort of religious anarchist – anti-war – anti-conscription   And I'm reading – an English life of Lincoln – one of my heroes – and my heart is not here. [...] **71897/107**

[For **Casement** see p.110. The **play** was probably *Augustus Does his Bit*.]

Thursday [20 July 1916] 11 PM. <u>5 PM.</u> [Ayot]

A day of devilish depression ending   What since I wrote? More reading – talking – walking. A swarm of bees found on a plum tree – great interest in seeing them shepherded into a hive – aeroplanes passing over. G.B.S. and Charlotte carrying on a conversation after dinner through the medium of the little white Highland Terrier that has their hearts – Charlotte addresses the dog – GBS answers for the dog. I read steadily on at this "Life of Lincoln". It is by a Lord Charnwood – a first-rate book too. And what a great man. Great in great things – and therefore essentially great   Isn't it true that in ordinary times – ordinary men seem to answer all the purposes of the world (They don't – but with our lazy souls we let them). But when the crisis comes – then the 'essential' qualities count – and only those [...] **71897/108**

[Godfrey Rathbone Benson (Baron **Charnwood**), *Abraham Lincoln* (London: Constable, 1916).]

[Tuesday 25 July 1916] 11-45PM – 5-45PM – [?Hotel Russell, London]

... Today – dear – oh – to the City and letters to the War Office and to the Red Cross – I begin to <u>loathe</u> the Red Cross people here in London – almost to wish I hadn't done the book – they are the vilest most parasitical crew in England – these "smart" people that run it. More business – and then to supper with Laurence Housman and his sister She is a charming grey-haired woman with a serene face and a beautiful voice – and they live in a quiet little house in the quietest corner of Kensington – all very simple – they do nearly all their own housework – she does the cooking (and does it very well) Very few things in the house – except books (lots of those) but each thing quite beautiful of its kind – all serenely simple. But if ever a place had an "atmosphere" and reflected the lives of the people that owned it – that has. I wanted you there so all the time – for it would have pleased you – a really English thing. I don't believe you could find it anywhere else just like that – (in Scandinavia you might) – a real feeling for beauty and knowledge of art without any fussing after it – I'd be proud for my dear one to see it. I want her to think well of England – and love me the more because I'm English in <u>that</u> sense – she does. After supper Housman read me the draft of the new act of Prunella and a one act play about St Francis – and their enormous sandy cat sat in my lap and stuck a claw into me occasionally out of pure contentment Then a long walk towards here through dark and silent London (I like it better at least than light and noisy London) – thinking of you – talking to you [...] **71897/115-16**

[The **book** is *The Red Cross in France*, published later that year. **Laurence Housman** (1865-1959) was an illustrator and playwright; his **sister,** Clemence (1861-1955), an illustrator and author (their other brother was the poet A.E. Housman); both Housmans were active in support of socialism and female suffrage. *Prunella*, a joint work by Barker and Housman, was first performed in 1904; thereafter it went through several revivals, mainly negotiated by Housman, with revised texts, including a film by Maurice Tourneur (1918). The **one act play** presumably became one of Laurence Housman's *Little Plays of St Francis* published in 1922.]

Friday [28 July 1916] 11-30 PM. – <u>5-30PM.</u> [with the Galsworthys in Manaton, Devon]

[...] Today I went up to the barracks and first they kept me hanging about for half an hour – and then the doctor spent three minutes examining me – and then they kept me hanging about an hour – and then I was told that I was passed fit for army service and that I could join on Wednesday next   I am in the "ranks" for a little – then I'm to be recommended for a "cadetship"   then I am to be trained in artillery work for four months and a week and then I may get a commission.   And then I shall get my furlough – all being well to come back to America for three months.   After that – service I suppose in England or France if the war is still on.   I write this at Manaton – Devon – at the Galsworthys   I have come down for the week end – I haven't seen them for two years – oh what a world of change in that time – but they are as friendly and fond of me as ever – and I like him better – the war has left him less "pontifical"   he had begun to get <u>slightly</u> ridiculous laying down the humanitarian law.   A crowded hot journey down – one of the minor "horrors of war" in England is that there are half the number of trains and twice the number of people travelling – they don't pretend to provide seats for them all   But this place is high up on the edge of Dartmoor – that means nothing to you.   It shall my darling someday for Dartmoor is a beautiful place and the Devonshire people are real unspoilt English – gentle – and homely – not the vulgar blatant sort. [...] **71897/118-19**

[**Galsworthys:** John Galsworthy (1867-1933), novelist and playwright; and Ada Galsworthy (née Cooper) (1864-1956). She had been married to John's cousin Arthur Galsworthy. John was a campaigner for reform of the divorce laws, which he discussed with Barker (see 71897/121-23). **Manaton** is in south Devon, on the eastern side of Dartmoor. The love for the **Devon** countryside, and the life there, may have been recalled when he and Huntington bought a house in east Devon, near Honiton. While their residence at Netherton Hall, bought in mid-January 1920, has been seen as an attempt to live the life of gentry, the sentiments of the letters from Manaton suggest a different motivation.]

[Monday 31 July 1916] 12-45am. – 6-45PM.   [Manaton, Devon]
My darling – diary?! – We took sandwiches out for lunch and sat in
a thick wood by a tumbling stream to eat them (I somehow think
you wake and call to me at 8 o'clock now – for it is at two that I
always feel you so near)   Then we climbed a hill and lay in the hot
sun – and walked – discussing politics quite furiously – so back to
tea. And then I read and J.G. and Ada back to their work on proofs
– and oh my dear one my heart did ache for this quiet life here in
the still country of work and thought and walking – Oh if I could
have shown you those woods today – is our life – and I want it. Well
– well my sweet. And after dinner more talking some music – more
talking till late as you see – rather despondently – on our uselessness
to a world like this – anger at the war and some of the vile things the
war is letting breed in England (vulgar low newspapers angering us).
And now – sleep. Are you near me my dear love? [...] **71897/125**

[The **proofs**: Galsworthy's diary for 26 July reports 'Readying A Strong
Character and The Mother Stone for Marie José book and the Nation'
(Marrott 1935: 421).]

Wednesday [2 August 1916] 11-15PM – <u>5-15PM</u> Ayot.
... I am here alone with G.B.S. – glad of the country quiet and the
cool of it. And he – amazing creature – and inexplicable if you
don't know him. Such big qualities such faults   But in fundamental things – true. I know you can't believe that – but try to
believe it because I know it – and be sure that now I don't give again
his vanity and incontinence a chance of not being true in things
which he (amazing) doesn't think fundamental   Such things he
does as would shake faith in him in all things – if you didn't know
him. Trust me dear [...] **71897/128**

Sunday Aug 6. [1916] (Ayot) 2-45PM – 8-45am.
[...] A longish walk this morning – the pace forced to 5 miles an
hour I should think by Beatrice Webb – thin and determined
Webb – placid self-sufficient – stamping behind her   I like them –

they have always been good to me and interested. I can't love them. Brilliant they are - more full of shere knowledge than any other two people in England (you can find them mercilessly caricatured in 3 or 4 of Wells s books. They had a great row with him)   But they are so dogmatic and dictatorial and satisfied with their ideas and positive in their views. If they weren't very good in themselves they'd be intolerable in every way - as it is they keep my mind on the strain and spiritually rather repel me. I now know so well just what I want in life   just what makes me fruitful of good in myself and what makes me barren. This is <u>arid</u> - it keeps me barren. What I want - what is fruitful - we know beloved. [...] **71897/133**

[**Beatrice** (née Potter) **Webb** (1858-1943) was a social scientist who married Sidney Webb (1859-1947) in 1892. His degree was in law. Both contributed to the founding of the London School of Economics, founded the *New Statesman* magazine and were active members of the Labour Party as well as, with Shaw, being active Fabians. Sidney Webb wrote the Labour Party's Clause IV, which called for common ownership of industry. The Webbs appear as Altiora and Oscar Bailey in H.G. Wells, *The New Machiavelli* (London: John Lane, at Bodley Head, 1911).]

Sunday [6 August 1916] 11PM - <u>5PM</u>. [Ayot]

... Diary - for me - Well - reading and a little more walking - and talking. Literature - aspects of the war - England after the war - National service - the position of women   Webb more full of information and original thought on things that ordinary mortals like myself can conceive! - and yet I stand up to him if need be Shaw and Webb fighting each other - close comrades of 35 years they've been. I suppose - though one says it as shouldn't - as brilliant talk as you'd find in England. And yet - to me my dear arid - arid - you understand. ¶ Oh my dear this is our bad time apart. And my mind so empty - that is the imaginative side of my mind - it needs you. [...] **71897/133-34**

Saturday Sept 2. [1916] 11pm – <u>5 PM</u> by our little clock – in front of me. [with the Wheelers in Kent]

I am down at the Wheeler's – an old farmhouse in Kent – very old and solid – low ceilings – oak beams – great open fireplaces but charming – good furniture good books and two good people in it – happy in their lives though no big prizes have come to them or ever will I daresay. We have sat in the dark over the wood fire this evening – and talked – much at our ease about books and people and politics – and always England <u>after</u> the war. What is it to be? And oh – always your darling face coming between me and the fire as I looked into it. [...] **71898/1**

[**Wheelers**: Charles Edwin Wheeler (1868-1947), known as Christopher, doctor, homeopath, author and translator; and Penelope Wheeler (née Ethel Mary Drew Arundel) (1868-1950), actress. They married in 1895. Christopher did the literal translation of Barker's *Anatol* and Penelope worked with him on several stagings of *Euripides:* see p.179. Salmon, on the basis of a misreading, somewhat bizarrely suggests that Barker and Huntington called Wheeler 'Hopher'. In fact they abbreviate his first name by replacing 'Chris' with a cross, thus +topher; the cross and t are read by Salmon as H, though Barker crosses the second stroke in an H not the first, and doesn't often cross a t.]

Saturday [23 September 1916] midnight – <u>6PM.</u> [Ayot]

[...] I am at the Shaws for part of my week-end just tonight and tomorrow morning. Charlotte back from her Irish holiday full of the beauties of her beloved country – GBS from wandering round England – both very quiet and friendly. I – tired and my head all dull. For I was up in the dark this morning – the old moon and a bright star still shining – up to town – to see Barrie and his "boy" back from the front – the boy "Peter" (Peter Pan) with a poisoned face caught in the trenches – 19 he is and looks thirty after a months dose of the Somme battle. Good God – what a world! [...] **71898/77**

["**Peter**" (1897-1960) was the third of the five Llewellyn-Davies boys whom Barrie had befriended, along with their mother; he entertained them with stories, one of which was that Peter, as a baby, could fly, because babies began as birds, which led eventually to Peter Pan; the eldest brother was killed in the war in 1915.]

Sunday morning [24 September 1916] 11-30am – 5-30 am. (You are sleeping   I lean and kiss you) [Ayot]

[...] Are you troubled at all by the way - at my being at the Shaw's - do you think of him still as a traitor? I mean. Trust me over that my dear It isn't easy to explain him. That particular subject he has never reverted to - he knows he was wrong - and - his curious pettiness - hates to own it. And indeed on the whole subject we're apt not to talk now   He asks for news - and we may sometimes speak of L.M. - <u>never</u> further - never of you I mean of course - never in any "discussive" way certainly. But traitor in spirit or intention - well - whatever the ties were or had been - if I knew that it would be an end of them and of everything   Trust me that this is so [...] **71898/79**

[See letter above 'Wednesday night' (19 July) for more on Shaw's mistake in relation to **L.M.** (McCarthy). The **ties** may pre-date Barker's marriage to her.]

Monday 25 Sept. [1916] 8-30am – <u>2-30am</u> [Trowbridge barracks]

[...] Yesterday I walked with GBS round the meadow. He and I and the little white Highland Terrier - grossly disobedient and G.B.S. mildly and endlessly requesting it not to be - scolding it and then taking the dog's side - He's comic with all animals. Then lunch - then to town and tea and a long talk with Barrie. How we hate the war and hate the military with their needless stupidities - all the things that happen that you seldom hear of - and then we shut our mouths and our teeth and say - well it's their job they've got to carry it through - truly by means of <u>us</u> - but we must just "carry on". Then by train to Westbury - struggling to interest myself in fuses and explosions on the way. And then I walked the five miles here - under wonderful stars - through misty fields - the cattle the only living things I saw And now - another week begun. An examination at the end of it – I must do my best but it'll be a poor best – my brain won't <u>want</u> to do it. [...] **71898/80**

[The **fuses and explosions** were part of the theory for artillery training: see pp.87–88. The **examination** was towards his commission.]

Saturday Sep 30. [1916] Midnight – <u>6PM.</u> [with Barrie, Adelphi Terrace, London]

[...] here I am at Barrie's – we have been alone to dinner and since having one of our old long talks. Well as I know him – it takes him an hour or two to blossom out with me – I think you'll love Barrie – I know well how he'll fall down before you – my <u>dear</u>. **71898/86**

Sunday [?1 October 1916] [Adelphi Terrace, London]

A London Sunday it is with me – true English autumn – grey in the morning – later a little cold sun – but a certain sweetness lighting up everything – rather than warmth – the year beginning to be tired. I'm at Barrie's – a little flat that you must someday see (I got it him) perched in a corner of the Adelphi looking over the river – a back-water in the busiest part of London. We've been alone and talking intimately – of people and of work he telling me a plot for a new play – great sign of intimacy – I responding with the same. The life contemplative and creative – that's a good life my dear. An oasis this day in the midst of "barracks" – and now I'll be alone till 6 – and that means (oh but if it did) with you – with you in the sense that I can put thoughts on paper for you. [...] **71898/96**

[**Adelphi** Terrace was built by the Adam Brothers in the eighteenth century, between the Strand and the River Thames. Other residents included the Galsworthys, Thomas Hardy, McCarthy and the Shaws.]

Thursday [?5 October 1916 Weymouth]

Snobbery is a subtle sort of thing. Hardy lives quite close here – and I mean to go up and see him. Now I don't go quite simply because I like him – though I do but I know him so slightly – but because he is Hardy – and I shall like – more to have been – than to go. A sort of snobbery isn't it – and not fair to him. Oh yes – this is "considering very curiously"   Nothing wrong – something extremely right in a way in making a little pilgrimage to an old and quite distinguished personage. But we do need so to do things for their own sake – don't we ¶ Snobbery only begins as a form of cowardice – and that again as a form of modesty – we think we ought to admire and ought to reverence – and (often with relations) ought to love. I believe I'd teach a child first of all never to be ashamed of its tastes and feelings ¶   Beloved of my heart – all this one sided talking – I want to <u>hear</u> you talk. [...] **71898/107**

[Thomas **Hardy** (1840-1928), poet and novelist, lived at Max Gate south-west of Dorchester. The **quotation** is recalling an exchange between Hamlet and Horatio in Act 5 scene 1 of *Hamlet*. Hamlet asks: 'Why may not imagination trace the noble dust of Alexander till he find it stopping a bung hole?', to which Horatio replies, ''Twere to consider too curiously to consider so'.]

Tuesday [10 October 1916] 10PM – <u>5PM</u>. [Weymouth]

[...] I've been up to the Hardys in Dorchester to dinner – and please Helen – I am a nicer human being than I was two years ago when I last saw him – for now I can discover through him the fineness of his work – and all his fussiness and petty ways seem little unimportant things – rather loveable – because the other is there – while before I remember they obscured him to me And we all talked and made harmless jokes – and his dog bullied us all – and a fidus Achates of his who drives him and his guests to and from the station and about the country and writes bibliographies of his books – and looks like an Elizabethan mariner – I wished you had been there – **71898/150-51**

[**Two years ago** Barker was preparing his staging of Hardy's epic poem, *The Dynasts,* which opened in late November 1914. I suspect the **fidus Achates** – faithful friend – was A.P. Webb, whose *Bibliography of the Works of Thomas Hardy 1865-1915* was published in 1916.]

Thursday. [19 October 1916 London]

[He encloses an obituary cut from the *Times*]

A very dear friend of mine has just died. I may have mentioned her to you. She was 84 – nearing 70 when I first met her – she had been failing lately and I had not seen much of her – but the friendship remained fresh – and her daughter wrote to me that the other day when she had given her a message I sent to say she had been in my thoughts after a long time she said (she was very weak) "That does me good" Good to think that quite simple things like that can be simply true. The cutting is frigid as such things always are and it doesn't tell you <u>the</u> thing because it can't. I never saw her in any company in which she was not easily the most distinguished person there – Never an effort If you'd been asked what most struck you about her you'd have said her gentleness – then you'd have had to add that she wasn't "soft" a bit – no effort to be gentle. Charmingly witty and yet she never seemed to say obviously witty things very critical and firm in her opinions – but she always managed to seem more interested in yours than in her own Her husband (he was the old Queen's Secretary) used when they were apart to write every-thing to her and when they were together I'm pretty sure to discuss everything she had a hand in ruling England for 20 years or so I think! But never "portentous" with knowledge – and it was hard to get her to talk because it took so long to make her realise (this was quite genuine) that you wanted her to talk about herself. Always and to the very last keen on what was happening around her I remember she was once too ill to be able to talk at all but one of her sons (he's in Parliament) went to see her and she had him tell her all about the debate the night before and nodded her comments – ¶ My darling - you know why I tell you all this –She was the only being I've ever known who was in the least like <u>you</u>. (No one in the world of course can be very like you – that is high treason) But – stranger still do you know my feeling for her was a faint foreshad-owing – the sort of delighted reverence I had towards her – a faint foreshadowing of that side of my thoughts for you – in the early days dear when our love was growing towards our recognition of it (It was always there in a way full grown and before we ever met – we had but to recognise it) just in those earliest days before it passed "beyond all compare" A sort of hint was it – that there was someone in the world if I could find her and know her that would make life perfectly gracious and beautiful – life – my life and all the world for me Oh my dear my dear it was wonderful to find you [...] **71898/175-77**

[The **friend** was Lady Mary Ponsonby (neé Bulteel) (1832-1916), a supporter of women's rights with the court roles of Maid of Honour, then extra Woman of the Bedchamber. Her husband, Sir Henry Ponsonby, had been Queen Victoria's Private Secretary. Her daughter Magdalen Ponsonby was a close friend of Lillah McCarthy and her son in **Parliament** was the radical politician and activist Arthur Ponsonby. Barker met Lady Ponsonby in 1902, before his first marriage. Huntington enjoyed this comparison of herself to Lady P.]

Sunday morning (Oct 22) [1916]10-30am – <u>5-30am</u> [Ayot]
[...] I've been chased into 3 rooms over this letter already – and now I'm going to be cleared out for a 'walk' – Well perhaps as I'm still fidgeted to that extent (witness my scratchy handwriting) I'd better go and look for peace this afternoon – to be alone with my dear. But you see – I experience a little what you have contended with for years – oh beloved and I'll snatch you away from it – and we'll be ourselves and order our life to the measure of our purpose in it. I'm ungrateful a little over this actual present grumbling. People are good to me – these two especially – but ——! You know
3-30PM – 10-30am.
A long walk – lunch – a furious war argument with Charlotte – and now – beloved heart – oh if I could just open a door and walk in and find – really <u>you</u> What you say about my friends – the little bit you write across after you've finished the letter I just wonder a little what prompted it – something you thought of – or read in my letters after you'd finished yours some re-action in your own mind?   Dear one they are very good to me – and I ought to be grateful and am But – I get deadly impatient with them sometimes – want only to get away – for it is all "outside" really a thing of the mind – of "affection" in a general cheerful sort of way You know. I can't find words – but – well it is simply darling I'm hungry for your love [...] **71898/196-97**

Wednesday Nov 8 [1916] 11PM. – <u>6PM.</u> [Bloomsbury, London]
[...] Diary for the rest of today – <u>Office</u> – then I lunched with Barrie who was gloomy but glad to see me – I think he is really fond of me but a man so grudging of all exhibition of feeling I never met – and I am shy because of that. Office again – and I'm at the stupid side of my job looking through files and files and giving notes on them to my secretary who sits there patient and chilly – and then retires to type them out – which is at least exercise. At seven the Chief sent for me and talked to me till 8. He seems fond of me too (and I'm sure I don't know why). But he'd amuse and fascinate you   he is such a child – a perfect baby – Very good at his job – naively proud of that – awfully humble about himself – sweet and sharp tempered by turns – Nowhere but in England I think could such a man hold such a position Yet I doubt if you could find a better man. I want you to know him   Then to dinner at the club – and reading Bleak House while I dined [...] **71898/229**

[The **Chief**, who could not be named, was Mansfield Cumming (1859-1923), head of the Secret Intelligence Service.]

Sunday [19 November 1916] Midnight – <u>7PM.</u> [Bloomsbury, London]
[...] Diary then? Well, I made that speech – They said well – but I know <u>not</u> well – for it was not clear, finished, thought. And the people – that "smart" crew   "How wonderful to be able to make speeches!!" There they were after two years of the war – the same as ever – learnt nothing and forgotten nothing. Oh – and I've lunched with people – one interesting man J.L. Hammond first in the army – now on the Reconstruction Committee – to plan a new England after the war – a good man – a writer of good books   that was interesting Besides that my usual round – yesterday afternoon down to the Masefields. Such weather – snow and sleet – John and I walking across fields in the dark by the light of a little torch – I really went to meet Murray – whom I've not seen for a long time but he only arrived five minutes before I had to leave – I had to come back this afternoon for a few hours work. We had some quite good talk

though – except that I didn't want to talk or be with anybody – about our work in the future. He read me one or two new poems – quite good – though he reads them badly and he loaded me with several books of his just out – and suddenly brought in another "Gallipoli" and said – Would I take it for him to "America"? And up to town – more talking [...] **71898/255**

[The **speech** was for an event organised by Concerts at the Front (see p.179). John Lawrence **Hammond** (1872-1949), in collaboration with his wife Barbara (née Bradby), wrote numerous works on social history and was a leading figure in the New Liberalism movement. The **Reconstruction Committee** was a committee of Cabinet, but government would not release the names of its members in July 1916. **Murray**: see p.20.]

Thursday-Friday [23-24 November 1916] 12-45 am – <u>7-45PM</u>. [Bloomsbury, London]

Beloved my own – So late. I have been out to dinner and the people – only 4 others <u>would</u> stay – and I hadn't the bad manners or moral courage (when are the two synonymous?!) to leave first A duty dinner – I was trying to "work" something for a friend (Wheeler) I met my man and he was interesting enough – Sir Robert Morant type of distinguished Civil Servant – Education authority (do you know?) I'm never sure whether it is one of the good products here or one of our bad. And he talked and was pleasant but I fear I "worked" nothing – I am no good at intrigue – even of the mildest – Oh – and his wife was called Helen – and when anybody called her Helen my heart jumped. And now to bed. **71898/258**

[**Robert Morant** had been Permanent Secretary to the Board of Education until 1911, and after that was Chairman of the National Health Insurance Commission. In that latter capacity he would have been relevant to **Wheeler**, a doctor.]

3. WOMEN

We begin with two short extracts from newspaper reports of a speech to a suffrage meeting (Hotel Astor, New York, 8 May 1915):

....

'Granville Barker dwelt on the curse of uncreative labor which makes men machines and on the idleness which makes women soft and sensuous as the obstacles in the way of advance. Many women, he said, cling to the privileges of the harem system and men to its rights. He urged companionship in creative work as the true democracy.' [*Charleston Mail*, 13 May 1915]

'"I hope you will not think there will be a new heaven and a new earth when women get the vote," said Granville Barker. "There will not be much change for a time. When the women voters get into the stride I think they will surprise you. I do not think they will show much sentimentality. I think they will be rather ruthless."' [*New York Times*, 9 May 1915]

Monday. [10 July 1916] 9-45 – 8-45 [on board the 'New York', sailing to England]
[...] Three or four priests on board – 1st class – 3 or 4 nuns 2nd class. I'm amused at the church's naïve distinction between the sexes [...] **71897/69-70**

[Wednesday] July 12 [1916] Five minutes to ten – <u>twenty to eight</u> [on board the 'New York']
[...] I believe I saw today what you mean when you think Englishwomen are 'bold' (was that the word?) There are the usual

professional beauties on the ship and they do seem to exhibit themselves – to be showing off. But the popular woman I am glad to say – at least among my corner of men (I haven't spoken to her yet) is a sharp featured – sharp eyed spinster – very direct and downright looking who has been nursing in Serbia – stands for something – means something. That's not boldness is it – in the wrong sense. But I know what you mean – women making themselves "cheap" – Oh Lord! [...] **71897/79**

Saturday July 15 [1916] 10-30am – <u>6-30am</u> [on board the 'New York']

[...] Oh Helen – you are a dear – and oh – such a <u>woman</u> – and I love you – I do reverence and respect and love you   Little thing in my arms – and not thinking how big you are – that makes me smile and love you – something in you must know. I'm at your feet and I'm not a fool. And I'm as nothing before you – I'm content and proud to be. You'll make me do things big things perhaps. And you like to look 'up' to me and feel small in my arms. I like it too – and to protect and comfort you. And in a way – yes I <u>am</u> the stronger and cleverer – and can "carry more weight" as they say. But I know well enough what it all comes to – and something in you must know – and quietly – happily smile – and be glad – and a little proud dear too (be a little proud) For I turn back to the little fragile one in my arms and – <u>yours</u> is the wisdom – I know. So much for my work and my share of the world. But that by itself was often the old way of things (not less true because it was). And now there's the newer way – the thing we're adding for the world's good – your work your share of the world. The woman inspiring the man – we've had much of it – But why not the man inspiring the woman – if he has enough of 'womanhood' in him to give that unselfish love. Please God I have – I try to have – well I don't have to try – with you it <u>is</u> so. And besides – it is my creed – you know. The world needs the woman's spirit made into a message to it – it wants to hear the thing you have to say. <u>I</u> want to hear it for myself – therefore I know it does. An end to this horrible man's habit of patronage. Big men have always had it least. As Scott said of Jane

Austen "Yes – I can do the big bow-wow – but I can't do that" And – by God my dear! I know that if I want your spirit to help me in my work – am greedy for that and depend on it – oh more that you'll own now – yet apart from that I want your work too – and the things in it and the thing it is that I can never do. And – oh – men have <u>stolen</u> women's strength so. I do want to pay you back a little of that great theft. I do want to give you some and have you spend it for yourself – yes selfishly – for your own satisfaction and honour and glory. Oh Helen dear – <u>take</u> from me – do take   I am proud of you and what you are and can do I'm ambitious for you. I want to see you recognised – quite vulgarly famous – though not for the vulgar 'literary' things. I love good work for its own sake – no matter who does it. I love your work for its own sake as well as for yours – and I mean it shall be the best you can do – and better far better than you've ever done – because – darling (though this sounds an awful "phrase" – still it has real meaning) because you shall write your books in my blood as well as in your own. I give you that – first and last it is what my love has to give. My darling – my little love – yet such a woman – so big – such a <u>human being</u>. [...] **71897/92-3**

> [**Little**: Huntington was short in stature; he often called her 'baby' but liked to think of them both as being childlike – in large part as a rejection of dominant forms of adult sexuality, which I discuss in *The English Theatrical Avant-Garde* (Routledge: forthcoming). In his Journal for 14 March 1826 Walter **Scott** said: 'The Big Bow-wow strain I can do myself like any now going; but the exquisite touch ... is denied to me'.]

Wednesday. [?27 September 1916 Trowbridge barracks]

[...] It would interest you to see the new women workers here in England – the tram conductors and ticket collectors in the stations – telegraph girls and motor drivers. They all seem immensely happy – (1) for that they're earning their own living quite independently (2) that they are doing a real thing. Of course in time the monotony of the work would tell on them as it has told on generations of men. And that's a problem to tackle – how to prevent that wearing monotony. But the 'home' is no longer a real place to women except for the short time when her children are young – as it was in the days when she had to 'create' it every day – baking and brewing and knitting and weaving. That is all organised and created for her – she has but to administer it (that still a great enough task but being more organised every generation) and so – seeking realities as all healthy beings do – a true soil to root themselves in – they search for new spheres   Hence the 'suffrage' and the laying of a new basis of Society. And all to the good – I think – don't you? [...] **71898/55**

Thursday. [?9 November 1916 Bloomsbury, London]
You wonder what I think about women and the vote   whether they should prove themselves worth it first or get it first as a means to proving themselves worth it. Well – I rather approve of our way here of giving it them in instalments, a vote for local government first – which they have – though on a very bad basis. And my quarrel with the English Suffrage party was they would not take trouble to show what they could do with that. But generally speaking I think the vote is a duty rather than a privilege and should be forced on people – who have the privileges of citizens – that and jury service and minor government service generally – and in fact national service I would compel them to accept   I suppose I shall hear in America vast claims both as to what the Womans vote did at the Presidential Election – and what it might have done But that will be from the Suffragists – and I think my 'moral' remains true – We shall do nothing for women now till the Suffrage Question is out of the way and with it the Suffragist. The English leaders have now gone frantic on the subject of Grey and Asquith (especially Grey) being "traitors" and they parade the streets accusing him of treason! (Will talk more of this my darling – on Saturday. [...] **71898/248**

[British women got the right to **vote** in county and borough elections in 1894. The US **Presidential** contest was between the Democrat Woodrow Wilson and the Republican Charles Evans Hughes on 7 November 1916.

More than 3 million more votes were cast than in 1912 partly because in a group of states women now had the vote. In the Women's Social and Political Union newspaper, *Britannia*, Christabel Pankhurst attacked Sir Edward **Grey** for not pursuing the war sufficiently aggressively, calling him a '**traitor**'. Grey, a believer in the efficacy of diplomacy, supported the formation of the League of Nations. He was Foreign Secretary and therefore close to **Asquith** as Prime Minister. Barker hated war and believed in the pursuit of peace, hence his criticism of a war-mongering branch of the Suffragette movement.]

Saturday [11 November 1916 Bloomsbury, London]

[...] And you think that women should learn to support themselves – with all that means   the requirements of sound bodies and steady nerves – before we recognise them as citizens. No – not before – I don't believe one thinks that – because one of the aids to a citizens support is his wife (but we talked of that). But that they should be self-dependent – oh yes. Be quite normally in what one used to call the 'Battle of Life' – Yes. But I don't want that battle to be the fierce cut-throat competition which now degrades 75% of men workers – and which is tending even more easily to degrade women workers too – in the lowest ranks only one sees it yet. I do want women – for their own sake and the worlds to see the world of work as a cosmos not as a chaos – and I even think it right if they refuse to go into it except on those terms.   Men are natural fighters – we must make their fighting emulation instead of competition and destruction – the last word – the last vile word in competition   Are women naturally combative and competitive. Do they naturally look for a cosmos? We artists (you and I beloved) do   that is "our nature". Oh much in this to talk of. [...] **71898/249**

[The distinction between **cosmos** and **chaos** is very close to the terminology both of J.A. Hobson (see p.56) and of Gilbert Murray.]

4. THINGS WERE ENDED BETWEEN US

The process of separating from Lillah McCarthy preoccupied Barker from late 1915 to late 1916. Culminating in two legal hearings in mid- and late 1917, the formal steps began in January 1916. Barker was in France with the Red Cross, McCarthy [L or LM below] was in London and Huntington in and around New York. Barker's close friend George Bernard Shaw acted on his behalf in London. Communication between all parties was disrupted by war and censorship. Urgent news had to be cabled.

Barker had met Helen Huntington in mid-December 1914. By April 1915 they were firmly in love. Although McCarthy and Barker left New York on 18 June 1915 as a married couple, they were never to live together again. Barker planned to be in France until the end of August, to research for his Red Cross book, though he returned to their house in Stansted, near Tonbridge, Kent, for a few days around 18 August to nurse McCarthy who was ill. On 10 September he sailed for New York. Eighteen months later he said he had spent this entire period living out of boxes.

Between June and September Huntington and Barker had resolved to test the strength of their feelings by not communicating. So, back in New York, he did not know if she would welcome him. With no means of contacting her privately he walked up and down the street where she lived, hoping to bump into her. When they met it was clear she was still in love but terrified of both her husband and scandal. Her husband monitored her activity and the relationship had to be secret. On 19 November these pressures forced her to suggest ending the relationship. He responded, once he had quietened down, by telling her that things now had to become public in the sense that he had to tell his wife that he wanted to separate.

At this period divorce in England was extremely rare, favoured the husband and had to take place in a High Court hearing. To avoid all this lovers risked scandal by simply running off together. Huntington, used to more liberal American laws, and conscious of her status, would not do this. So Barker had to take a relatively new course of action, which he describes following a conversation with his friend John Galsworthy, a campaigner for divorce law reform: 'he tells me that it is only within seven or eight years that we have used the method over here which I am set on L.M taking - the getting round the law by a sham suit - at least it is not a sham - but a suit brought in a way the law <u>did</u> not originally intend - a suit for restitution followed by a formal "adultery" with some person unknown' (71897/121). Thus Barker would write formally to McCarthy to notify her of his 'desertion' so that she could then initiate proceedings against him. Once that process started Huntington would sail from New York to join him in France.

But things went wrong. When Barker sailed for France at the beginning of January he wrote a lengthy letter to McCarthy which begins: 'I have made up my mind that I cannot return to you and I want you to set me free' (Salmon 1986: 191). This has hitherto been read as brutally peremptory. But of course it came out of a six-month period during which McCarthy not only knew he had fallen in love with Huntington but also started to take steps to unsettle the couple (as detailed in the contextual essay 'Archer Huntington's Wife': see p.220). Barker's letter is the decision, bluntly stated, that ends that uncertain period. It was to be personally given to McCarthy by Shaw, an old friend of hers, once Barker had completed and sent the 'technical' formal letter. But —

....

[Saturday] Jan 22. [1916] 10PM. [Boulogne]

My dear - my dear - I am in your state for a little now - feeling like a table of weights and measures. The letter from Shaw came this morning - at last. His technical point was merely the letter - the formal letter - I had to write which would give L the proper excuse for bringing suit against me. I wrote it today and sent it off. But he had not waited but had told L. and given her my letter. She took it very badly - with a great deal of bitterness and anger he says - a great deal of misery too - went and walked about the streets half the night. It is no use - all that has to be - it is better in a sense for her to take things that way at first – her nature will provide its own remedy – but I do not know how long it will be before the reaction will come. Meanwhile Shaw hints at delay. She has firmly fixed in her mind that this is a "caprice" of yours – either that you do not mean to go through with it – or that it will be a tragedy if you do – I can't tell. Anyhow – I have written to Shaw at great length to tell him there must not be delay and to give him proofs if it comes to an argument with her that whatever else it may be – it is not caprice – that we haven't taken hold of our lives like this without meaning something pretty serious by it. He doesn't think so – he says he wasn't surprised. I have merely told him a few more of the circumstances that he may bring argumentative pressure to bear on her – if need be. I don't think there will be need. The thing has dropped on her rather unluckily on the eve of her playing a new part – and one must remember that that does mean with a vengeance a strain added to a strain – I think as soon as that is over – perhaps before she will simply accept the situation – When she was told – that was Wednesday night – she did nothing at all – but give her opinion of us both. I do not know what has happened since. [...] **71897/8**

[Writing some time after 1930, McCarthy described the effect on her: 'Some of the great moments in our lives come suddenly, swiftly. A letter which I opened coming home alone from the theatre set me for the time being out of my normal senses. I could not endure the pain, and was frightened, too frightened, to remain alone. I went out to seek companionship from a near neighbour. ¶ For months I was incapable of feeling very much; the doctor said I was suffering from shock' ('Why I Began My Recitals': THM/182). The story of being alone when she received the news differs from Shaw's report of a conversation. **a new part**: The lead role in Thomas Sturge Moore's verse drama *Judith*, presented by the Stage Society at the Queen's Theatre, 23 January 1916.]

Sunday Jan 23 [1916] 10-15 PM (getting towards evening with you) [Boulogne]

[...] I've had no further word from England. I could not have had I think. L. simply must have had to make an effort to put the matter from her until this first performance was over – in fairness

I must be patient till then   But whether I ought to go over - Other things being equal I should leave matters as they are - a week or two would mean nothing to me and would bring naturally a calm counsel to her. But I am leaving you without word - that I can't bear - I'd even say a week or two more of separation for us did not count - as against putting the thing through rightly and as kindly as may be - we are - please God - to have our lives. And if I could tell you everything I know you would be patient - But this concealed cabling - everything counts you see - And besides - things <u>may</u> not be easy for you now at Pleasance - though I don't think that - and I won't think delay could make a difference with us - no my dear one - But yet to leave you without knowledge - it's not fair or right - I can't mould things absolutely as I would - to the day and hour - though I will mould them. Anyhow I will wait patiently till Tuesday morning   Then I must cable you all I can - I hope by then for a telegram from Shaw to say that the business is under way. [...] Dear heart - in spite of all delay I go about so lifted up in soul - my head so clear - ideas coming to me - so - as if I were on the threshold of a wonderful life of activity. I have never felt so before - I feel I can conquer - not only push through - but soar over - Oh my darling - it is wonderful the vision that I have for us. [...] **71897/10**

[**Pleasance** was an estate and house at Baychester (on Long Island Sound, New York) bequeathed to Archer and Helen Huntington by his father. I show in 'Archer Huntington's Wife' why Barker was continually worried about 'things' at home not being 'easy' for Huntington, see pp.232-35.]

[Monday] Jan 24. [1916] 10-30 PM (you - as usual - about to dress for dinner - No - Monday - Opera perhaps - Oh my dear - <u>where</u> are you) [Boulogne]

[...] I hope you don't think and never will - that it was anything like cowardice - even of a subtle sort that stopped me going myself to see L. I have faced that as one does and am satisfied it isn't so. I haven't had only one reason for not doing it. There has been the technical "desertion" reason - then I did think it would hurt her more in the end to see me again than not to – and I ought not to hurt her more than I can help. But chiefly I have thought and do that absence and thought-out "impersonal" letters – would make her realise more definitely that things were ended between us. And since she spoke to Shaw about your "caprice" I am satisfied I was right about this – so apparently is he. She I have no doubt calls me a coward for not coming – had I come she would have tried to persuade me of your "caprice" and whether I was kind in response and reasonable or short and hard – equally she would have thought – had she wanted to think so – that she was convincing me – either directly or against against my will – and that would have meant appeals for delay – suggestions – alternatives – days – perhaps weeks of it. Of course <u>if</u> she turns her face against facts and won't believe that things are inevitable then I must go over and try the fight – and fight – with her own weapons until she is convinced. But I think – I do indeed that by the end of this week all will be well. It is devilishly difficult my dear to cable <u>all</u> this to you not to say more or less than the truth – I <u>want</u> you to start on Saturday – I don't <u>think</u> now you will. If you did and if things <u>did</u> go wrong – I wouldn't see you until they were right [...] **71897/12**

[Wednesday] Jan 26. [1916] 11 PM. [Boulogne]
Oh my dear one – I am sick – sick sick – of this delay – of not hearing from you – but there couldn't be a cable yet – or hardly and hardly a letter – and the delay over in England – though that is nothing yet – granting that L. won't rise at once to the decent thing – isn't it the decent thing to say on the minute of asking – yes – you are free if you want to be free. I can't see any other way of it – except I suppose mistrusting bonafides   and what right has she to do that. However granting that she has to look round and see that there is nothing else for her to do (I hate to wrong people – but I'm getting a little bitter about her now) there has been no real delay as yet. In a way I'm not really impatient – but to feel that there in New York you may be thinking – well – after all it'll never be – that – is damnable. But I know you are patient and have more sense in patience than I have [...] **71897/15**

[Barker makes clear here the second major source of anxiety and the cause of his increasing anger at the delays. He dreads that Huntington will, once again, conclude that a relationship between them is not concretely possible. This is why he is at pains to explain the details of the process as it happens, while repeatedly asking for her patience.]

[Friday] Jan 28. [1916] Midnight. London (you are sitting down to dinner!)

[...] For various reasons I could stand it no more and came over today. I have only seen the Shaw's so far - they are helpful and kind and report progress - but that L was savage about the whole thing - having made up her mind - or pretended to - partly I have no doubt she had or had made herself - that I was "coming back" to her - and that my letter was a shock - which he says will take her a while to get over - long or short depends now on the way the matter is handled But something I will do now I am over First I must see my lawyer tomorrow - to find out whether I <u>may</u> write to L or see her without invalidating the "desertion" for no blunders must be made that way. Then I must decide whether it is better to see her - or what - I am relieved to be doing something - but I must be careful what I do. And no news from you! No letter even - and I think one could have reached me by this - Oh Helen ¶ But I am happy dear about you - <u>yes</u> and it is good to find one's friends that know - the Shaws - happy about me - they tell at once without questioning that this is right - and are glad - glad of my freedom from L.   glad about you   they seem to know about you. I suppose they can see in me - the new thing you have put there - I don't wonder - a blind man could I think ¶ But dearest heart - this delay - is it chafing you badly - are you distrusting yourself or me at all because of it. I don't believe so but I wish I could be near you ¶ Well I shall be - if you don't come over - I go back and within a week or two - that is certain sure. [...] **71897/18**

[Barker's **lawyer** in London was Charles Douglas Medley (1870-1963).]

[Saturday] Jan 29. [1916] 11-30 PM. At the Shaw's – in the country [Ayot]

Today seeing my lawyer – one comfort – the whole business can be got through in a year or less once L will make a start – but as to that no progress. She has been let know I am here if she wants to see me – that is the best – not to say I want to see her. If I say that she will conclude I am softening to her. She has it fixed in her mind still that this is a caprice of yours – a fancy of mine – that I shall go back to her – the thing is to get that idea unfixed. I shall do it my dear one – if it takes days or weeks or months – and you will be a little patient won't you? I shall do it if it takes years. – but if you'd not wait for me – well I need never see her again and – what does more freedom than that mean to me? [...] **71897/19**

[Sunday] Jan 30. [1916] 11-15 PM (Sunday night – still at the Shaws)

My dear – my dear – my very dear – oh such a hunger for you all day – you "with" me apart from my thinking of you – in the way you sometimes are. A blessing to be able to talk. The Shaws both of them so good and wise and helpful – I am glad of good friends Charlotte wanting to get your books to read to learn all about you she could – they both so glad – so glad to be getting me free (please God) of L. so ready to be glad about you – so impressing upon me that I must not persuade you to anything rash that you might regret afterwards even a little – because of my fear of losing you. Oh my darling – is the time going to be long – But I feel so sure – you'll be a little patient won't you? [...] **71897/20**

[Monday] Jan 31. [1916] Grosvenor Hotel [London] 7.PM

My dear one – today your cable forward from Boulogne – for which I thanked God. At four o'clock I saw L. a quiet interview – not long I felt as cold as any stone. She – it's amazing – I'm sure she was feeling it deeply – has been feeling it – One can tell by her face – but yet – not a genuine word did she say or a genuine thing do the whole time – She apologised for things she had done – the letter to AH –

and setting a detective on us – she did do that but only for a day or two – just before I left America with her in June. Then she spoke of various ways out – I couldn't talk or argue – indeed I had nothing to say – she never got near the root of the matter at all – She didn't mention your name – didn't say even she'd start to divorce me – but she obviously will. and I think quite soon – as I said there is nothing else for her to do and she sees it – But – she's amazing – she weaves words and situations and does not – in talking to you – face the facts at all. How utterly impossible any reconciliation between us – oh I think even she must have felt – It may all need a little more patience yet – till she comes through this unreal "tragedy queen" mood – mind you she makes it real to herself and as I say – suffers badly I'm sure. When she gets through that – she will do the thing – the only thing there is to be done. ¶ Of course I hate hurting her – who would not but I feel so cold about it all really and deep down the feeling that even if only she and I were concerned – it must end – God knows I wish I had ended it sooner – never begun it – that was my crime – let me take any punishment for it I must – but I know that only worse would come of not ending it now ¶ Instinctively do you see – I write to you as a friend   one who will just judge me at this moment   I have done wrong in this matter my dear – marrying and not loving – and there is only a cruel way of setting it right – well I must take that way. I know I must – again I write apart from you – Judge me for that – and oh dear Helen – help me through the rest of my life – to be wiser – steadier – more really kind – some good – I will try. **71897/21**

[Archer Huntington (**AH**) received a series of **letters** from McCarthy, see pp.228–29.]

Boulogne [Monday] Feb 7. [1916] 5-30. (lunch time with you dear one).

[...] I question myself time and time again whether I have done and am doing the wisest thing about L. She reproached me that I had not come at once to England to talk to her about it. Yes – if she were the being she thinks she is that I should have done – in both senses

– but then I think she has been more impressed with the finality of it (my intentions) than if I had come and been "nice" over the business. Shaw I told you – was against my seeing her at all – because he said she doesn't want to believe it is final and will take any excuse like your talking to her as a proof that it isn't – he also feared that if we began to row she might make herself unpleasant to you – or try to. I think the interview I did have did not run either of these risks – but then it wasn't a real interview – I mean a real talk in any sense – I did tell you – nor did I feel I could make it one. The difficulty is I think she _is_ really convinced about me – though she may still pretend not to be. She is probably not in the least convinced about you – and therefore is perhaps holding on – holding her hand or planning to because she thinks you may tire of your "caprice" Well – I must leave things for a week yet I suppose [...] **71897/30-31**

[Wednesday] Feb 16. [1916] midnight. Boulogne
[...] To know that you are coming – that lifts me up – and it seems so natural and right too – so in the order of things. I'll have to pull things through with L. There'll be bother but I know I can. She is getting better of her hurt – she was hurt badly   badly at first I feel sure – in spite of the touches of falseness that might run through it. I am sorry – you wouldn't have me not sorry   But I can feel nothing – rather a grudge against her for the wrong things she did – nor a real sympathy with her – however much because of the past I ought to. That of course was always wrong – for always it was like this. Thank God I have attained sure conviction and vision of the future [...] **71897/40**

> [She was now expected to arrive about 8 March. Some of the things McCarthy
> did are noted in 'Archer Huntington's Wife'.]

[Friday] Feb 18. [1916] 10 PM. London
[...] I have to be tactful with her – I hear she is still bitterly angry and hurt – and she must have no chance to vent her anger on you. But I hate being patient and tactful. And then over the very legal

points I have to be. I must not go and see her at her flat. I have to be very careful what I write or say or promise. Now she knows I am in England she'll ask to see me again I expect – and this time the interview may arrive at something. I won't suggest seeing her for that will make her think I am yielding. And up to now this is the difficulty it seems – she will not let herself believe I am in earnest – partly real caring for me – partly pride – partly the sin of possession – oh a deadly sin – So I have to do all I can to make her move at once – not to seem too anxious lest she turn on you – not to seem this – not to seem that – it is all damnable – and I hate moreover having to treat her as an enemy But I know I am right to be patient. I know too that all will be well – It is easier to be patient and I suppose wise now that you are coming – Oh my darling that you are coming   I begin already to jump with excitement. **71897/41**

[Thursday] Feb 24. [1916] 11-15PM. Ayot.
[...] Tomorrow I spend in town – I may see L. Another miserable letter from her today – vaguely pleading. I can't feel anything. Also – though she may not do this deliberately – comes a letter from my solicitor with more money demands. But the mixture is queer   I think I know what will happen – she will go on like this trying what she can think of to stave it off and then – quite suddenly give in. Soon or late she will – I hope soon – even for her sake – for she is genuinely suffering – in spite of the certain falseness there is to it. I still don't quite understand her – I may wrong her – But yet – yet. [...] **71897/49**

Folkestone [Tuesday] Feb 29 [1916] 12.30 [waiting for a delayed boat]
[...] Last night I dined with Barrie – the first time I have seen him since September – for I know him too well (he is one of my four or five real friends) to see him without telling him or to tell him anything without telling him practically all. Which I did and he was most understanding. L. has been coming in to see him lately (they are neighbours) he thinks now to find out if he knows –

wanting to consult him (which is strange – or am I stupid? For she has always professed dislike of him) But immediately he said he must speak to her and insist on the one thing she had to do – start proceedings at once   And from other things I hear she is on the edge of that. It irks me badly – this having to work through other people but really I cannot do otherwise while she is hostile and absurd. I cannot go and see her – for legal reasons. And besides – I know the thing to do is to make her feel by other ways than protest – that all is over. Don't – don't think I am shirking – it isn't that a bit. If she had been reasonable I could have reasoned but this is the way now. I know and by those who have seen her I am strongly advised so too   It will come right my dear. [...]
71897/57-59

[He returned to America, to arrive again in England in July.]

Friday Aug 4 [1916] 11PM – <u>5PM</u>. [Ayot]

[...] tomorrow morning I go up to see L.M. I have let it be delayed like this on purpose – no need to explain all my reasons but I think that has been wise – and oh God make me wise tomorrow with a true kind human wisdom and let me win <u>now</u> what I must win to live or care for life. And let that breed some rightness in her. Poor wretch I know that in a twisted way she is torturing herself – even though she is acting it partly – partly she is hurting herself – pretending to one motive when possessed by another – a vague rebellion only against the inevitable – but one does not want to hurt people – one hates it   But this hurt must be – and six months ago I was sorry and blamed myself. Now – make me wise in what I say and do – just that – to win clear now   Oh – and we all <u>all</u> need forgiveness for so many things. So make me clear-sighted to see all the false part – but not harsh over the true You know all I want to be and how rightly I want to do things even though they've not be done so to me – worse – far worse my dear to you – I want to do all things rightly – to win that way – But to win and now. [...]
71897/131

[Saturday] Aug 5. [1916] 11PM – <u>5PM</u> [Ayot]

[...] this morning I went up early and had a long interview with L.M. Chaotic - unreal as I knew it would be - and I said little - tried only to say the right thing. It is early yet to say what the immediate - definite result is   It can only be to the good I think - for she must see more and more - be unable to avoid confessing the inevitability of it all   Never a word about <u>not</u> divorcing me - just talk about what a mistake I am making - just a repetition of her inability to do it <u>now</u>. How long that will go on God knows. She is - without doubt - torturing herself - and for that I'm sorry - oh you understand - even that I should be the excuse for anyone going on torturing themselves. But apart from that it is all so <u>unreal</u> - words - phrases - all false - and the things done false   One must try to understand even that - but of course it only makes one feel harder and colder than ever. Oh how I wish - and its for her sake too   that she would cut the knot without a minute more of this - and yet again all I say to myself is Hang on - be patient - I won't write any more about it dear one - nothing to write. This is I suppose the inevitable process. [...] **71897/132**

Thursday the 10th I think [August 1916] 9PM – <u>3PM.</u> [Gordon Square, London]

[...] Beloved - I've had the letter sent on from Miss Nellie D as well A.H. having heard again from England - that I don't understand and it troubles me - not to understand   Was it an unsigned letter from L.M.   And I fear you had a bad scene - oh my dear how I want to spare you and cannot - and how good you are. But I'm glad he knows - that nothing has been kept from him [...] **71897/138**

[**Nellie D**: Helen T. Dickinson (1875-1958), a school-teacher from Virginia. She was not of Huntington's social rank but an intimate friend and from early on privy to the relationship with Barker. She secretly conveyed communications between them and acted as chaperone for their meetings. Huntington told her on 22 July that her husband had received an **unsigned letter**, implying it was from McCarthy.]

Sunday Sept 3. [1916 with the Wheelers in Kent]

[...] Now about L.M. She is still shirking the matter. I think that accurately describes it. My judgment as to what she'll ultimately do remains the same – and the two or three people I discuss it with agree. I get depressed and desperate of course at the delay. What I have to consider is whether anything I do now hurries or hinders the outcome. I saw her – at her request. I waited till she did request it so that she might have no excuse for thinking I was making any advance to her (That sounds ridiculous but I am dealing with an unreasoning unreasonable being). It was to all appearance a purposeless sort of interview. I'm sorry to say it but she was "acting" all the time even though she was acting to herself. She mentioned your name several times but I of course never did and never replied to her as to that. The course of the talk was – "Did I really mean it – was I sure I wasn't making a mistake? She was still suffering from the shock of it – I must give her time – at any rate she wouldn't divorce me till the end of the war (that was queer!) Why did not you and I go away together if we were really in earnest? And after this had gone on spasmodically for an hour or two she abruptly went. [...] Wheeler who is most in touch with L.M says – She is hurt and humiliated and until the sharpness of that feeling has died down she will nurse it and do nothing else. He says – She finds herself an interesting figure and likes to have my "intellectual" friends (Barrie and Galsworthy and the like) begging her to move (she thinks they "looked down" on her before though God knows they're not cads! – and never did) and as much longer as the novelty of that lasts she may not move. Nor while she can go on saying to herself that this is a passing infatuation of mine – that you are not serious about it and simply regard me as a sort of conquest. She thrusts at him the plea that it doesn't really matter to us or we should go away together. I have explained to you (somewhere in my diary) that this was till lately the only recognised way to a divorce in England which gives her the chance to say such a thing [...] **71898/9-11**

[The **two or three people** were probably Barrie and Wheeler and perhaps Galsworthy. Shaw was by now compromised. Knowing Huntington's fear of scandal, Barker emphasises that he never mentioned her name. Barker's lengthy explanation of American and British divorce laws is at 71897/121-23.]

Sunday morning [17 September 1916] 11-30am – <u>5-30am</u> Gordon Square, London

[...] For L.M. – granting the thing she is – and one has to grant that – the thing she has shown she is – well I suppose it is hard for her to make up her mind to it and one must still give her time. My God what else <u>can</u> I <u>wisely</u> do And it was (you know) a sudden complete separation from what seemed to her everything – my fault – a great fault – for letting it seem so and I suffer for that – and you [...] **71898/69**

[For this **Gordon Square** address see p.83.]

Tuesday morning [7 November 1916] 7am – <u>2am.</u> [Bloomsbury, London]

[...] <u>Again</u> I'll have to post this letter with no definite news for you – oh my dear. I discover though the reason of the delay (at least this is what it seems to me) L.M away in the country – returning today – her chief adviser – apart from her lawyer – away somewhere else – not returning though till next Monday. It sounds incredible doesn't it that they should just "play" around like this but they just "indulge" themselves in it – and we are at their mercy of course – my Lawyer and I – as far as that sort of thing goes – as long as they have any sort of reasonable excuse. Nothing free and generous – right up to the end! L.M's lawyer's difficulty and he has been privately frank about it to my man – is to get her to be reasonable and businesslike – She just says 'Do what you like' and then we he attempts to do it – makes this demand and that – it is all the money question – and it has to be proved to her what is possible and what is not   Oh – patience – patience I say to myself I have need to say it. And you so good dear – so patient – with <u>me</u>. [...] **71898/226**

Saturday Nov 16 [Saturday was 18 November] [1916] 7-15am – 2-15 am. [Bloomsbury, London]

[...] We have got another step – after 5 weeks!! And I said in my cable 'a few days'   Did you smile then – or have you smiled –

grimly since at this 'beloved optimist' Well – ordinary men could have got to this point in an hour even lawyers I should think – should have thought – in <u>five days</u> But all the time – to speak brutally – it has been with her lawyer "You want something Pay for it!" I thought I had at the start offered all I had and promised all I safely could However – by dint of asking impossibilities and keeping silent for ten days at a time – taking the line of "All right – you're in a hurry are you? we're not" they have been able to make my man amend the offer to suit them better The amounts promised (that I didn't mind – as long as I could – I thought – safely earn the money in the future) and the method of giving it her – that when you boil it down is really all it has been. Well – now they have agreed on that – last Wednesday – that is the 'step' And now her man sticks on the question of 'Security'. But here again he is asking for what I haven't got. He has me at the end of my tether and now has I suppose to be convinced of that. I told you – vaguely – I think that the war plus that New York and Greek play theatre business hit me very badly Of course I always was quite a pauper in a manner of speech – those two things make me one almost in fact. I pledged the few securities I had to the hilt to pay the debts and now that means repayment And it is almost desperately comic to hear the lawyer talking in an airy way about 'money' for all the sums in question are ridiculously small – but if they were millions it would be the same. Where money is concerned one either has or one hasn't and whether it's a penny or a pound makes no difference to that. Well, he's been persuaded at last that I haven't got any wealth up my sleeve – that I really did offer all I had. Now he's talking of Security – which means – frankly – that he wants me to go to my one or two reasonably rich friends here and either borrow money from them or get them to guarantee I should pay it. Well – one doesn't <u>do</u> these things That is to say I talk about them quite candidly to Barrie and Shaw – the two people "indicated" we've no false delicacy of that kind with each other (at least I talk quite freely to Shaw Barrie is a little Scotch and "queer" when money is talked of) and – of course – it is obviously a sort of blackmail and one just has to say No – on principle this is wrong – you (the lawyer) must not by threatening me try and raise money out of my friends – And so – almost in so many words – we have said. And when he is convinced we mean it – he'll give way on that point – as he has given way on the first – and that I really think <u>will</u> be the <u>final</u> step. No – I won't be optimistic until it <u>is</u>. ¶ Meanwhile I'm going to see if by "ringing the changes" on the various things I have done already to raise money in a purely business way – I can raise yet a little more   And if – of course – they really do mean to let time slip away (that is the weapon they argue with!) I shall be brought to doing anything I can honourably do or honourably ask my two friends to do (and it is good to have these things "open" with them from the beginning) For of course there comes a point when you have to use a highwayman's weapon with a highwayman – or rather when you have to recognise his power – if he has it – to hold you up ¶ There my darling – in one way it is all pretty beastly – as the end of something which has – in spite of its mistake – been after all a thing of "life" – of attempt at "life" anyhow. On the other hand it is so openly and simply sordid that it does not touch one at all   Don't think for a minute that I am being "hurt" over this. And I know you won't think for half a minute that I am troubled by the purely money side of it   I'm just anxious to do what I can and only keen to have it done, in the right way – oh for everyone's sake (I don't like even now to think that she – even through her lawyer – is degrading herself) And it is odd – how cheerful I have been and glad this week at having said "No – this is the right thing I'm offering and the wrong thing that you are asking and you can't have it". And yet – you know what it costs me in delay. But somehow I know just what you'd be doing and wishing me to do [...] **71898/241-43**

[**New York and Greek play**: the productions were given at Wallack's Theatre, New York (see Time-line for details). While the season was critically successful, it lost money. After Wallack's, Barker and McCarthy organised an ambitious, expensive tour of two Euripides plays, *Iphigenia in Tauris* and *The Trojan Women*, performing them in the sports stadia of five eastern university towns. **pauper**: Compare Pearson 1951: 84: 'he had never known the distress of mind arising from poverty ... He was on velvet from the start', and other such unsubstantiated claims.)

Extract from a note from H.H. Asquith to Lillah McCarthy, dated 8 December 1916

[...] we must try to meet sometime next week; it ought to be easier now, [...]

Your Devoted HHK **THM/182**

[It would have been **'easier'** because Asquith had just been ousted, two days before, as Prime Minister. The language of this note implies an emotional, if not sexual, relationship. It is not clear when it began, but Masefield writes on 8 October that 'A[squith] (as we know) is furious with H[arley] for his breach with L[illah] (who lets A hold her hand)' (Masefield 1985: 17).]

Friday Dec 15 [1916] 12-15am – <u>7-15PM.</u> [London]

[...] at five o'clock to my lawyers and I was there "served with the papers in the suit" – that is really beginning you see. [...] **71898/277**

[The **suit** for restitution of conjugal rights, the first of two, was heard on 19 April 1917.]

Sunday [17 December 1916] midnight – <u>7PM.</u> [Bloomsbury, London]

Beloved – still the days seem endlessly long and amazingly short! And all I know now is that I want you – in every way Helen my dear It seems as if I must make a new beginning and had nothing to begin with but your love – and that given by having you there near me – part of my life – part of me [...] **71898/278**

[They finally married on 31 July 1918.]

5. Enlisted As A Soldier

The army to which Barker was conscripted had been created by Lord Kitchener as Secretary of State for War from August 1914 onwards. Various accounts of life in it can be sampled in overviews by such as Messenger (2006) and Simkins (2007). Some were written at the time and some, as in J.B. Priestley's 1962 memoir *Margin Released*, recalled many years later. Barker wrote it down more or less as he experienced it each day. And from the start his point of observation was distinctively unusual. In terms of rank, as an officer-cadet in the army he had to begin as a private, on the bottom rung, but outside the army he was equal to and friends with the cultural leaders of the country. In his club, which he could still visit on time off from barracks, he hobnobbed with generals. He took orders from the army but participated in conversations that critiqued it. Even more distinctively, he observed with the very special eye of a good theatre director. He was able, first, to look at every activity from a sceptical position outside it and, second, within what we might call the production process of the training regime, he was always alert to what made that process useful and efficient or, more likely, not.

If, then, we compare Barker's observations with other famous accounts we see some key differences. To begin with, he was writing two years into the war. The men around him were conscripted, unlike the volunteers of 1914, and the early enthusiasm for war service had turned to hatred. Ian Hay's fictional version of army training in his novel *The First Hundred Thousand* (1915) is imbued with that enthusiasm, being cosily sentimental about the interdependence of the army structure and so oily about royalty it glistens. The narrative often works to position the reader somewhere above, and separate from, the privates, who are in general seen as fairly simple folk.

Nonetheless Hay's novel does echo real-life accounts of adjustment to life in the army, with its forced mingling of social backgrounds and professions and its initially chaotic arrangements for accommodation and eating. Kitchener's newly organised and expanded army drew up detailed protocols for training for battle, with standardised regimes of drill and physical exercise, but it lacked both trained officers and equipment. Hay makes comedy out of the difference between what is supposed to happen and what actually happens. By the time Barker was writing much of the early chaos was sorted out. For him the comedy was to be found in the doing of what was indeed supposed to be done.

Barker used some of his observations as the basis for a short story about being on watch duty, 'Picket – July 1916'. Although it was only published in 1919 (in *The Sun* [New York]), it was written contemporaneously with his training (despite its title) and only a thin line separates its mode from that of the letters. 'Picket' allows itself a characteristically fanciful elaboration of his conversation with the horses, while the letters are more consciously – and necessarily – brisk, witty and angry. What he says about training will be familiar to historians of Kitchener's New Army but it's said with the attention to detail and effect of the creative writer.

Huntington spotted this quality (of course) and her comment forms a useful preface: 'You say you can't think and can't write – and I was amused when I read it because all the time you were giving me such a true, vivid picture of <u>Barrack Room life for a gentleman soldier</u>. I could hear it and see it – and smell it – and – more than that – know how it made your mind work – and how it made you <u>feel</u>' (71914/186).

....

Monday [Wednesday 10 May 1916 Williamstown, MA, USA]

[...] today I know certainly that I'm being called back to carry a gun – to leave you again for a little (and I haven't <u>seen</u> you again yet) And I'll try and write something for you for every day [...]
71898/291

[The Military Service Act (January 1916) introduced conscription of men between 18 and 41 but excluded married men. These were included in a second Act passed on 3 May. Barker had been in **Williamstown** since the end of March, having arrived in America around 20 March.]

[Monday 24 July 1916] 11PM. <u>5PM.</u> [Ayot]
[...] to the War Office to see the almighty Adjutant General. He was most pleasant. He has power to give me three months furlough and perhaps he may but only perhaps - Meanwhile I join the army - apparently as a private - which is right - and not foolish in a way. However that I have to start to see about tomorrow. Then down here to the quiet country (that at least) an evening of reading and a little talk - a walk through the Park - and here I am [...] **71897/114-15**

[The **Adjutant General**, Nevil Macready, had unusually liberal views for a military man, and a taste for amateur dramatics. Barker had dinner with him in France in February. The **furlough** was to be used for a lecture tour to the United States, to raise money.]

Wednesday the 26th [July 1916] 6PM - <u>Noon</u> with you. [?Hotel Russell, London]
Well - my beloved - next week I shall be enlisted as a soldier - a private in the artillery to start with - then a cadet to be trained - and so it begins. I don't pretend I'm cheerful about it - for it is not a job I can do well - apart from my intense dislike of the whole business - still it's all part of the general present folly of the world. I'm not so wise that I must be exempt. [...] **71897/116**

[The Army Order of 21 August 1914 laid down a six-week training syllabus for the **artillery**, with artillery training schools established in 1915. The requirement to train in the ranks before getting a commission was introduced in February 1916.]

[Thursday 27 July 1916] Hotel Russell London 10PM. - <u>4PM.</u>
[...] I'm wondering what the army surgeon will say to me tomorrow - what he'll pass me for - I could have done a piece of more or less justifiable shirking and have got a cadetship for home service only - but I thought somehow - (<u>you</u> know how and why) better go for the whole thing - put myself in their hands anyway - quite freely. I made my choice as long as I could make it - and I think it was a

right choice. Now the law tells me it is 'up to them' – well let it be. But I look forward to four months of mitigated hell – a life I loathe learning to do something I can't – kept from doing something I can – away from you. Well – my darling – but it is a road <u>to</u> you – and God knows and you know I'd travel a far worse one that that. **71897/118**

[The Royal Artillery had three sorts of home-based unit: training, provision of mobile artillery, and provision of coastal defence. His **choice** was to take a path that could lead to deployment at the Front. The **four months** detail came from the 'Instructions' he would have received after he was 'selected' to join the officer-cadets. In fact, as he says, they were all pushed through much faster.]

London Aug 2.   [1916] 4-45PM – <u>10-45am</u> [?Hotel Russell, London]

My darling Well – I am now an enlisted man – for the time of the war and six months after – to be sent abroad when needed – the whole thing. As democratic a process as one might wish – that is in theory and partly in practice – though I fear the fact that I got through all the forms and ceremonies between 11 and 12 this morning and 3 and 4 this afternoon was due to my being what is called a "gentleman" And when the man who put me ahead of my turn with the doctor scrabbled his hand for a tip and secured half a crown – he was so impressed that he called aloud "Pass Mr Barker through there" Through – is through the most nondescript crowd of loafers and mysteries that you could imagine. The <u>medical</u> examination was thorough if not strict – and you'll be pleased to hear that I passed in Class A – all fit (though my own doctor had said he wouldn't pass me) And many of the others they ought on the face of it to have turned down – a good few I think they did. The rest will make soldiers of a sort – I shall make a soldier – of a sort. And of course – done in the right way this – National Service is the right thing The doctor was a good man and treated them all like fellow creatures as far as I could see – the clerks were common – civil enough They have to pry into your private life and delicacy is of course them but they do their best. The officers quite courteous – at any rate to me – and I think to all the rest. We have our virtues as a nation. Make us a real democracy – put the snobs and parasites in their place – and we can stand by France – and America can stand by us. And we may mean well for the world yet. God send it – and send that we may see it together my darling [...] **71897/127**

['**Gentlemen**' officers were becoming increasingly rare, with wide concerns about the lack of gentlemanly conduct in new officers (Messenger 2006: 313-14). **Half a crown** is two shillings and sixpence, the equivalent of about £7.37 today (2021, National Archives Currency Converter). In this context **mysteries** seems to mean men of uncertain status or quality. Standards of **medical examination** were highly variable and often done in a rush. Hay describes 'the Medical Officer' as a 'hardened cynic' (1985: 52). Barker's **own doctor** would not pass him because he had a history of illness: the letters of this period speak of eczema, indigestion and chronic tiredness.]

[Monday] Aug 7. [1916] St John's Wood Barracks – 5PM – <u>11am</u>

Well – my darling – here I am. I won't write what I think or feel about it. I'll just tell you the days – and you shall judge. I arrived about midday and spent an hour or more getting into my kit Then I was sent to a stable and told to groom a horse – poor horse – he didn't like it. I watered him – he didn't want water – then bugle's went and we fed him – that he answered to. Then – being rather filthy and smelly – I had an apology for a wash. Then came dinner – enough – but rather messy – served in an inconceivable muddle – all the men very jolly and talkative – they are mostly boys and it is a sort of holiday to them. Then I had to change and clean up some more for a parade at two o'clock. I washed in a basin I shouldn't have washed in – to the loudly expressed horror of some soldier – I answered him softly and he repented him – and said he mustn't be hard on me as I was so ignorant. He even suggested that some one would help me carry my very bulky kit away "as an obligation" I think he meant to oblige me. Then at two – we paraded in the sun – took off our coats and did gun drill

which consisted mainly of numbering off – and doing it again – and running up to a gun and back and doing it many times over. Then I was sent for to see the Colonel – and there was some muddle and I stood in a porch for two hours – while a Sergeant Major asked my name occasionally – and boredom and various pains in the legs and back bade fair to overwhelm me. Then when the two hours were over it seemed the Colonel didn't want to see me after all – so I was sent to tea   And now I have been allotted a bed It is in a great loft and rough to a degree – but clean I've no doubt. There are twenty four of us here – but at this moment – thank goodness only four – one man sits and cleans his boots – one fat man dresses slowly and sings comic songs – a boy opposite puts on rough clothes for stables – and I sit and write to my dear love. They don't seem a bad lot of men – gentlemen mostly – this is the way they train them for commissions now. In an hour I shall be allowed out – and till midnight I believe – (thank God) I hope and hope for a letter from you For the rest – for this "life" (what a word for it!) I must just hang on – set my teeth – and – oh my dear – my dear – we'll win through and to each other. [...]
71897/134-35

[Barker joined "B" Reserve Brigade of the Royal Horse Artillery, based in **St John's Wood Barracks**, Ordnance Hill, London NW8, just to the north of Regent's Park. Simkins (2007: 198) quotes various recruits in the chaos of 1914 complaining about food, which clearly did not improve much. **numbering off**: Calling out your place or number in the rank of soldiers. The **Colonel** was Lieut. Col. Frederick George Glyn Bailey ('Colonel' being used as title for both ranks).]

[Tuesday 8 August 1916] The barrack room 7PM – <u>1PM.</u>
I have just finished my days work – the room thank God is quiet. What have I done – Can I remember 8-30 gun drill – much rushing around – 9-25 paraded for physical exercise – more rushing around – 11-30 stables   an hour grooming and watering – hard work – but this morning I had an amenable horse. Lunch – and half an hour breathing space. Then a lecture on gun mechanism – Then a lecture

on the points of the horse – then another hour of stables – then half an hour working at the gun mechanism – and here I am. Oh – sometime there came tea – the only eatable meal here. At least I have not tried dinner yet. Bad food or throwing it on to filthy tables – which takes away one's appetite more. Last night I went to the club and dined in solitude and civilisation tonight I must dine with Barrie (Enter a corporal-cadet who starts to sing) Your two last letters darling that I always carried with me I have had to put away with the others now – but your clock – our clock is by my bed – in my despatch box by day – I open the lid at night. Don't think that foolish – but – no dearest of all you are not far from me but such a different world [...] **71897/136**

> [The travelling **clock**, as a gift from her, acquired deep emotional investment: he often kissed it at night, as his only link to her.]

Wed. the 10th [actually 9 August 1916] (Barrack room) 1-45 – 7-45
[...] The diary of my days here will begin to bore you. At 6 this morning – riding – under a sergeant whose delight it was to swear at us – use foul language and make foul jokes – I find that hard Then breakfast and washing and shaving. And then I think – gun drill – much pulling of heavy guns around – then physical exercises – then stables (something else there was I think – but I have forgotten it –) then lunch – and this blessed pause – (Enter four or five cadets – arguing – my last vestige of brain has therefore gone – Oh beloved – You are still sleeping are you? I bend down and kiss you. Dear – dear <u>little</u> Helen – gentle – my own – gentle Helen. Wake happily – and the world beautiful to you – you make it so to me dear – my soul is not in this hole – but away with you – Love me I love you.

6-40 – 12-40 And what more? Gun instruction – Lecture on gunnery – stables – an hour of carrying sacks of chaff and sweeping and shovelling – and I have cleaned myself and made my bed and cleaned my buttons and my boots – and now I may get out and dine – but I mean to have a bath too – Dear I can't collect my thoughts to write – my head is all muddled – and the worst sort are in the room shouting and joking – jokes! But I think of you – beloved – ah there's a moment's stillness – and I have found a quiet room here – blessed be heaven. ¶ Sweetheart – till I can write again – I love you.

Thursday [10 August 1916] 4-15PM – <u>10-15am</u>

Beloved – wonder of wonders an empty barrack room and fifty minutes before 'Stables' – and I only have to have tea – and clean my buttons – so I won't clean my buttons I'll write to you. [...] **71897/137**

[Several accounts of training tend to focus not just on the long days but also on the sequence of different activities, which for most forms of employment would have been an unusual rhythm.]

Thursday the 10th I think [August 1916] 9PM – <u>3PM.</u> [the Lee Matthews' house, Gordon Square, London]

[...] two things will happen – I shall get salted down to the physical fatigue and I believe after a few weeks they run one less hard – an hours riding and two hours hard work in stables would be enough for me as a rule – add gun drill – and signalling and physical exercise and a few lectures in the barrack yard – but I shall come through all right   If only they wouldn't <u>all</u> swear (nearly all) and use foul language (most of them) – and if the food and rooms weren't filthy – but that is such a tiny part of it – I have grown soft and pernickety I dare say. [...] **71897/138**

[William **Lee Matthews** (1861-1931), wine merchant, company director, and chairman of the Stage Society in November 1917, was married to Muriel de Selincourt (1867-1938). They lived at this time at 32 Gordon Square. Simkins (2007: 195, 207) quotes recruits from middle-class or religious backgrounds being horrified at the obscene **language**.]

Barrack Room Friday [11 August 1916] 4-15PM. – <u>10-15am</u>

Not a quiet room yet – the orderly cleaning belts – one cadet working a Morse instrument – a genial ruffian who has been in the life guards and is now working for his commission – various other men wandering in and out. I've had an easier day – but not a satisfactory one. Gun drill at 6 – a lot of bullying and little work – breakfast – riding at 8.20 – I had a bad horse this time and did not improve him by my riding. Physical drill – Stables – but few horses to do – lunch – a lecture on the gun-breech – in the boiling sun – standing there an hour – a lecture in horse management conducted by N.C.O's who know nothing of theory and so make us read out of a book which we can more quickly buy and learn. Silly. Oh – at midday we were paid – marched up to a window – our names shouted out – the money slammed down – you salute once before you get it and once after. But my name was not down – so I got nothing. Dear heart – such a noise I shall go to tea – write to you later. [...] **71897/139**

[Hay (1985: 44-51) tells how an inexperienced Second Lieutenant gives a bad lecture and is saved by a Captain who effortlessly engages the class. Later (p75), while lectures are normally regarded as 'fatigues', those given by 'generals and staff officers' returned from the front are viewed as invaluable. Barker here describes non-commissioned officers (**N.C.O's**) but, as we see from Letters 7, unlike Hay he has little affection for the military hierarchy either.]

Saturday Aug 12 [1916] 6PM – 12 <u>noon</u> [?St John's Wood (SJW) barracks]

[...] today they have precipitated my destruction by inoculating me for typhoid and I feel like a sick-cat. Never mind. What opinion have I about the business so far   I do <u>not</u> like it – it isn't my job I loathe the surroundings – though four or five days has blunted me – I've made it – to the indecencies (some of them) For the one or two good men here I'd do anything – to make their work easier by getting on – for they do work whole heartedly – patriotically – if narrow-mindedly – for quite unselfish ends   Beyond that – I feel I won't let myself be beaten by any damned artillery course in the world. Diary - oh the same as usual - I dined last night at the Garrick with Frampton the sculptor Sutro the playwright and Albert Rothenstein - which seemed funny - then back to the barrack room. If I must confess - sleep is the worry. I cannot yet get more than 5 to 6 hours try how I will - but this I'll settle down to I expect. The only new thing added is sword drill - merely drill and intensely stupid - So that you may swagger at the barrack gate when you mount guard. [...] **71897/140**

[George **Frampton** (1860-1926) was a member of the New Sculpture movement, committed to naturalistic representation of the human body. Apart from writing plays, Alfred **Sutro** (1863-1933) made translations of works by his friend Maurice Maeterlinck. Barker produced his translation of Maeterlinck's *The Death of Tintagiles*. **Rothenstein** (1881-1953), an artist who designed the costumes for Barker's 1912 production of *The Winter's Tale*, anglicised his surname to Rutherston in 1916.]

The Barrack Room. Sunday morning [13 August 1916] 9-15am – 3.15am
On week days everyone rushes about - on Sundays - slackness was never slacker. One lies in bed till 6.30 - think of it. Then "stables" at 7, then breakfast - then Church parade. But I was inoculated and have a bad arm and leave from all parades for 48 hours So when they are off to church I shall dodge out and down to the Shaw's - into the blessed country for the afternoon and make them hear me Morse code and drilling and flag-wagging [...] **71897/142**

Garrick Club. Monday Aug 14 [1916] 7-45PM – 1-45PM.
[...] Today - oh today I have been moved from Squad F. (the lowest) to Squad E which means that I have done no "Stables" and only do them once tomorrow - and indeed it has been an easy day - though with rather more than its usual allowance of abuse and insult. I am getting a little used to it - adjusting myself to this army standard of manners which - quite frankly - treats a man as a brute to be tamed

– partly – partly to be made rather more brutal. It is curious to note how an instructor – an N.C.O. deliberately sets himself at a first drill to cow the men and break their spirits – so that they will be easier for him to deal with   Once today I suddenly thought I must be <u>mad</u>. For we stood round – 24 of us in a circle on the parade ground and did what is known as re-drilling – drilling each other, each one drilling the remaining 23 – so that we shall be able in time to drill the men – a very necessary thing. But in an hour we only got through two commands (and a half) – shouted out quite sense-lessly over and over again – and as senselessly obeyed – while they seemed to have no meaning whatever. And – this is the sort of thing I suppose I can naturally do – doing it <u>naturally</u>. But I was entirely stupid and confused and was abused and jeered at with the rest. What sort of way is this of making officers – who to command their men should be individualities. Once again I resented my own being flattened out – tomorrow I shall be glad it is For as I said that is the first rule in the Army <u>You are nobody</u> (a cure for egoism – in <u>that</u> – good no doubt). [...] yesterday I went down to the country and the Shaws were so gentle and affectionate G.B.S. met me twelve miles off in the car and went back with me to the station – and Charlotte mothered me and put me to bed – for I was truth to tell rather sick and bad with my inoculation. [...] **71897/142-43**

[Priestley 'found the sheer repetitiveness of parades and exercises hard to endure' (1962: 94). Barker was right that being able to drill men was neces-sary: lack of training in the new officers was a regular concern (Messenger 2006: 313). He was also right about the **first rule**: several accounts speak of losing individuality in the army. He thought he should be able **'naturally'** to respond to commands because he had worked as an actor.]

Wed Aug 16. [1916] 5PM – <u>11am</u>. [?SJW barracks]
[...] Up and out by 6 – a "lecture" on horse management! We stood rather chilly in shirts and trousers while a Sergeant took us over the points of a horse for the second time. He said all he knew in ten minutes or so – then had to fall back on making us repeat it. I hope that particular waste of time does not occur again Then breakfast

foh! I loathe the messy food (That's petty of me – it is not a hardship – but it is quite unnecessary. Women would not tolerate our piggishness) Then physical exercises. Then gun drill with the 18 pounder guns – at which I distinguished myself by stupidity – then rifle drill – at which I was just as stupid – then semaphore at which I was more stupid still – my brain appears to have stopped. It may be good for my character having been a leading person of sorts for some years to find myself suddenly set back to this – and indeed – honestly I don't resent it – but I doubt much whether there is anything like the makings of a good officer in me. I lose my head hopelessly when I am shouted at – and it is all shouting and hurry – most necessarily so <u>half</u> the time. There is brought home to me a thing I always knew that I am a being with an aptitude and a sense of quality – but not <u>able</u> – Well darling – you know that too. But I'll stick to this and try to be content if I master only the rudiments and not think it waste of time (I don't think that in the sense that <u>I</u> matter) nor waste of material – no I <u>do</u> think it is that. Then – blessed happening – we were given a half holiday – so characteristically that a cricket match might be played – and we might (the non-players) look on. But at that I stuck – have taken my half holiday by having a hot bath [...] **71897/144**

['**foh**': A variant of 'faugh' (but my reading is uncertain). The Battery at St John's Wood had been re-armed with **18 pounder guns** in June 1915. These were QF 3-inch 20 cwt anti-aircraft guns.]

Sunday [20 August 1916] 11-30am – <u>5-30am</u> [Ayot]

[...] Outside there's the garden to be seen full of flowers – beyond a cornfield almost yellow – and gold in the sun – when the sun will shine – beyond that fields and trees – a very English – mixed – disordered landscape. The table is thinly covered with letters and work. I have been pegging away at elementary gunnery. Battery angles and Quadrant angles and aiming points and fuze indicators and such like. The head-work is strange enough to me – all mathematics. But I feel I can get on to it pretty quickly. It is when I have to pull a gun about in a hurry – being shouted and sworn at that I am done. But even that may come. Having started in Squad F (the lowest) last week we were in E and now next week a lot of us move up to D That is not God knows because of any excellence on our parts but they are hurrying us through   To move up from D we have to pass an examination though [...] **71897/146**

[**fuze indicators**: The time-length of an artillery fuze or fuse will aim to set, for example, the height of burst, and is therefore part of the mathematical calculations that control the operation of the guns. The **hurrying through** was to address a shortage of officers.]

Monday Aug 21. [1916] 9-30PM – <u>3-30PM.</u> at the Garrick –

[...] I ought to tell you "things". Today I ve been put up another "Squad" – no real merit for I am a very fool – and it is perhaps good for me to be counted a fool having been counted as "clever" all these years   But they want to get us on and get rid of us. Today then this new squad drilled outside the barracks for the first time – at a place – Primrose Hill – and little boys stood around and stared. We must have looked quaint for we were doing "driving drill" – that is driving the horses and guns about with neither horses nor guns nor wagons – just ourselves trotting and walking and learning the evolutions   Picture me – <u>very hot</u>   In many ways being treated as a schoolboy turns you back to a schoolboy. [...] **71897/148**

[Called 'the intellectual actor' by Beatrice Webb, he was also caricatured in the press as 'Professor' Barker. **Primrose Hill** is to the east of St John's Wood, on the north of Regent's Park. Practising without equipment had been standard from the start, because of shortages. Hay (1985:32) describes the first days in barracks of a 'newly-joined subaltern' as 'very like one's first days at **school**', after which the subaltern grows up. For Barker the army produces precisely the reverse effect.]

Tuesday [22 August 1916] 5PM. – <u>11am</u> [SJW barracks]

The Barrack Room – changed today and a little more crowded than before – but I'm a little more used to it and I've got myself stuck under a window. Tonight I'm kept in barracks   I'm "attending on Picquet" – which means that I have to carry the dinners to the guard room and fetch them beer and their blankets to sleep in. Isn't it <u>comic</u>? One must just think of half of this life as comic. But today has been a heavy day – gun drill – riding and in the afternoon – out through the streets and into Regents Park with the guns (or rather wagons) for the first time – for the first time publicly a soldier – and that seems comic too.   But as I have night duty I am off the last parade – a lecture on horse management which will not be a lecture at all but a weary Non Com making us read things out of a book (I can pick it up from someone's notes) So I sit writing to you darling love – and opposite me the room orderly – burnishes and burnishes my buttons and spurs for picquet duty – such burnishing and polishing you never saw – and if I were going on guard – he would spend another hour at it. By rights let me say <u>I</u> should do all that – but it is winked at that the room orderly for 5/- a week – looks after me in such ways – and a blessing it is – and as I do <u>not</u> mean to remain a private soldier – that "pipe-clay" discipline I shirk. Poor orderly – he is back to the army after 18 years service – and loathing it – the barracks full of such men – they fought through South Africa – and now the army means (here) nothing to them but "spit and polish" ¶ Oh – my dear heart – how mad it all seems Something good – some credit may be in belonging to the machine (I'm so stupid in the head dear – I can't write "thoughts") – credit and good I mean in doing a humble part in a big thing – But the thing itself so against all reason – so uncreative – and the whole machine and method – therefore – monstrous and ridiculous. We keep good tempered mainly amongst ourselves – which is a blessing – nobody I think pretends they <u>like</u> it. Thank God for that – if war is at least getting unpopular […] **71897/149**

[**Non Com**: NCO or non-commissioned officer. **5/-** is 5 shillings, about £14.75 (2021). **'pipe clay'**: Traditionally used for whitening items of military uniform, thus pipe-clay discipline is like a version of spit and polish. **South Africa**: The Boer War of 1899-1902, which Britain fought against the Orange Free State and Republic of Transvaal. Men who had done their time were recalled in 1916.]

Wednesday [23 August 1916] 4-30PM. – <u>10-30am</u> [SJW barracks]
The Barrack working room – where we have lectures and where there are books (a first rate history of the British Army J.W Fortescues – into which I dig for 5 minutes at a time) – where there are few men as a rule – but a telephone that rings distractedly. A devil of a day my dear one (oh my dear dear heart – what it is – what joy and strength and peace of soul to love you and be loved by you) – but not degradingly so – except for an absurd business called re-drilling – in which we stand round in a circle on the square and yell out long strings of commands to each other. A stupid way of learning the job. I could get them all through it twice as well and in half the time – but a suggestion?! – never on earth. Otherwise – gun drill and riding and gun drill again and more gun drill to come – and a lecture (what bliss to sit at a table and <u>understand</u> something). And then we went out on Primrose Hill and pretended to be a battery of guns manoeuvring – ran around with strings in our hands and learned the signals for the movements   But last night! I attended picquet and laid the table and carried the dinners – many many journeys across the Barrack square and then all the blankets – and fetched the beer – and by nine o'clock – two hard hours at it – I was dead! And tonight I am a picquet. I pace around the stables from 6.30 – 8.30 and then from 12.30 – 2.30 and then please God I get to bed for I'm to be up as usual tomorrow at 5.30 What a life […] **71897/150**

> [John William **Fortescue** began his multi-volume history in 1899, with parts published in 1910 and 1915. The **'picquet'** or 'picket' was the duty of keeping watch. Messenger (2006: 320-21) quotes several complaints about perpetual drilling, but Barker, who knew how to rehearse, finds peculiarly galling the practice of **re-drilling**.]

Tuesday night [29 August 1916] 8-30 – <u>2-30PM.</u> [?The Garrick Club]
[…] I look at the decimals and Trigonometry I have to master – and then my heart fails – as my head will I expect. Still! Today – one of the officer-instructors – a cockney rather rough tongued fellow –

but a good sort and a good instructor – risen from the ranks – called me out to do something and in the middle of doing it asked me if I were G̲ B. So I said "Yes sir" whereat he said "Good old Sport" – which was comic – but pleased my small vanity. Still it is right – that absolute loss of all personality in the army – and I'm glad to find that I have not resented it at all. And they are right too in that they bully everyone impartially. **71897/154-5**

....

Up to here most of the extracts in this section are from Barker's 'diary'. Since Huntington would only get this sometime after the events it describes, Barker summarised his position in a letter (below) which could be taken to America by Nellie Dickinson the next week. Although this letter offers an overview, I keep it in the date sequence partly because it serves as a summary at the point where Barker's training moves from London to Trowbridge, and partly because of its tonal contrast with the diary's emotional directness.

....

Sunday Sept 3. [1916 with the Wheelers in Kent]
[...] There is the diary for you of course – but that will take you long to read and will only seem a confused account of things written from day to day ¶ First dear one my being in the army. I am a Cadet-gunner in the Artillery – it means that I am training for a Commission. To do that now one has to enlist – one is technically in the ranks – they train you for an officer – if you don't satisfy them you are put actually in the ranks. (But probably I shall) The training time is four months and I have been at it just a month. They seem to be hurrying us through but all being well I should complete the training and receive the Commission late in December ¶ Then I shall apply for 3 months leave to come to America and give my lectures – it is a choice between that and bankruptcy   I saw the Adjutant General whom I knew slightly before I joined and he agreed that I ought to go – and as he has full power in that matter

there will probably be no difficulty – probably – though of course no promise was or could be made. (There will be gaps in this letter dear one. I was hauled out at that point to "look at the garden") I hope then to be in New York about the end of December for a fortnight or more – then I go to California and the middle west – returning in March – for a few days – then back to England and probably to France with a Battery of guns – and so on till the end of the war and six months after. I shall be able to get shorter periods of leave. I may be employed in "special service" The war I do think will be over next year. But on that one mustn't count. ¶ At present I am in the Royal Horse Artillery with horses and 18 pr: 3 inch field guns but I have asked to be trained for the Garrison Artillery, which means the big siege Howitzers This is wise I think for anyone over 35 who has had no experience of soldiering. You do less galloping around and more head work – and though I am not good at the head work yet I am very bad at the running around. So from St Johns Wood Barracks in London where I now am I am being sent to Trowbridge in Wiltshire where the big guns are and there I presume I shall finish my training ¶ My dear I won't pretend I like it – the whole thing is as you know "foreign" to me and in a sense obnoxious to me – the life very obnoxious indeed. And I shall never be good at it – for I cannot be good at what my heart isn't in, but I shall be less bad at this I think than at any other part of the regular army work. And I have thought is right – you'll understand – not to bring interest to bear to get myself given anything that might seem to be a "softer" job – like administration or propaganda. There came a suggestion or two – and I was tempted because – frankly – I think I could be of more special use doing anything but this. That however is their affair (there are hundreds of men in the same case) I have asked for my 3 months leave – which I know I am right to ask for – it isn't a favour merely. But I'll <u>ask</u> for nothing else – you agree don't you? **71898/6-8**

[**garden**: Christopher Wheeler was a keen gardener. **Trowbridge** is in the west of the county, about 8 miles south-east of Bath and just over a hundred miles from central London.]

Tuesday [?5 September 1916 SJW barracks]

Today – and it is a Tuesday too – I had the first touch of real exhaustion gun firing – for we drilled properly with a six gun battery – every man doing his job – every job and expert job and the whole thing going forward with a rhythmical swing   I was in it at first and then standing watching it – and – oh of course – standing there I thought of you my dear and the joy you would have had with me in watching a thing well thought out and well done. With artillery of course one loses the more sinister feeling of fighting – the cruder brutality isn't there – it is all machinery – the death is dealt three miles off and more. Still one thinks of that – I thought of it as I watched   I'm glad though before I leave this place and start in another to have had one hour of intelligent pleasure and satisfaction – only one. The rest – well one is rushing about and there's <u>some</u> comradeship and most of them mean very well. But it is the negation of all life to me. When a moment pause comes I shut my eyes – and you are there and another life and far far different things – another service of life. [...] **71898/42**

Thursday Sept 7. [1916] Midnight – <u>6PM.</u>   [Gordon Square, London]

[...] I have been on leave and rushing around to get things done and business settled before I leave for Trowbridge. But – the drilling and exercise has knocked my eyes a bit funny and I have to get spectacles and pass another visual test and that may delay me till Monday <u>and</u> I have been sent for by the Intelligence Dept of the War Office today and spoken to about another job – so that I may not go at all. That I'll see in a day or two. **71898/21**

[Friday 8 September 1916] 4-45PM – <u>10-45AM</u> [Gordon Square, London]

[...] Behold me my darling in a large pair of spectacles. But really I shan't wear them much   I believe I saw quite enough and these seem to make everything just too sharp (is that a parable?) But I am now passed – a little grudgingly as fit for an artillery commission – and now it seems I may not have one after all for I have been sent for by the "Intelligence Department" The transfer hasn't come off yet though I am told it will. But I never believe in Departments doing things till I see them done. I had some qualms yesterday. Should I stand out against it and ask to be allowed to go on with my "barrack square" Because I suppose it is what many people will think a "softer job" I know it won't be – because of course I can and shall work far harder (in my sense of work) at a thing I know how to do than at a thing I'm not very hopefully learning. But then I thought – and think – here is something by training I'm fitted for and can do fairly expertly – which looks as if it may lead to something I can do very expertly indeed – it is common sense of them to put me to do it and of me to do it – I can be keen on it. [...] **71898/59-60**

[By **'barrack-square'** he means the officer-cadet training.]

[Saturday 9 September 1916] Midnight – <u>6PM.</u> [Gordon Square, London]

[...] Diary my dear – I went to the Barracks this morning for the third time to report – with my spectacles and passed by the Doctor And I found I was down for Guard tonight – 24 hours in the guard room and standing at the gate two hours at a time with a drawn sword! Did you ever. But being posted to Trowbridge I escaped and then I got leave so that I go to Trowbridge tomorrow. And if the "Intelligence" job comes off I shall only be posted straight back again. For the rest I've worked at my article walked backwards and forwards from here to the club – came back earlyish to meet a favourite nephew of this house – a young fellow – one year at Oxford – two years at the war – all through Gallipoli – waiting now to be sent to France or into the Flying Corps – loathing it – they all do that have tasted it – just setting their teeth to get through – 22 he is – and what he has seen! It seems as if every relation of the Lee Matthews was fighting or had been killed or wounded. She told me today how she had to take the news to her youngest sister that her husband had been killed (one of my company he was two years ago) She said the girl came in after a day in the country – her arms full of flowers and she had to tell her. And after a bit she said "Well – I'm thankful he proved he could do well (he'd been mentioned in despatches I think) for he feared he couldn't. And that was all. But the break down came later. Oh my dear such a country as this is – battered [...] **71898/62-3**

[The **article** is 'The Promise of an American Theatre', which he finished the next day. The **favourite nephew** is probably Mark Jocelyn de Selincourt. Muriel de Selincourt's **youngest sister** was Theodora, married to the actor Guy Rathbone, who was killed at Suvla Bay, Gallipoli, 21 April 1916.]

R.G.A. barracks Trowbridge. Monday Sep 11. [1916] 5PM. – 11am.

My darling – this place would amuse you! If I have to stay here I shall like it better than S John's Wood for though it is rougher in some ways it is quieter   We study more and run about less. They have tried to turn a little barracks into a Cadet school for 250 men – and the consequence is we live and work in outhouses and stables and tents. I am not put in a tent but in a room – but I have to sleep on the floor – a mattress of course. At present I'm sitting in an outhouse where there are tables and papers – the greatest degree of repose and privacy there'll be. But the men – the majority of them are older and quieter. There's a Major in command – a fat person and a humourist and his adjutant and Sergeant Major stand by to laugh at his jokes but he is a jolly sort I think – like a great school master – indeed we're all like school boys and I like the "new" boy – and he has been pleasant to me and interested to know what I'm going to do ¶ We don't get up till six which is something – Then we either have to clean the rooms or do physical exercises. Then we breakfast and though there is an occasional gun drill – it seems mostly lectures after that – not very easy stuff – at least not to me – mathematics and construction of guns – but I daresay I shall manage – Oh but isn't it queer? ¶ We hardly get out of barracks at all – and again the lack of privacy will be the hardest. ¶ This shed is filling up – men and men and men – talking and working. But you are here beloved as I write to you [...] **71898/64-65**

[**R.G.A.**: No 1 Officer Cadet School Trowbridge, Royal Garrison Artillery. The **Major** is probably Montagu James Raymond, a solicitor from Wimborne.]

Tuesday the 12th [September 1916] 1-30PM. – <u>7.30am.</u> [Trowbridge barracks]

[...] Reveillé at six – a great difference to 5.30 washing and shaving under difficulties for it was hardly light – even out of doors Then physical drill but in the middle I was called out and excused physical drill – I believe on the score of my advanced age! I'm not sure though that I shan't get up to it – for I shall be woke – and it brightens you up in the morning – the body of you that is. Then a bath! (luxury) and breakfast – and it is a joy to me that the meals are quiet and the men quiet and the whole thing more civilised That does make such a difference – then lectures – then to finish the morning "knotting and lashing" – learning to tie knots of various sorts – under the direction of a Sergeant Major with the strongest Irish brogue (Why is an Irish brogue attractive?) Then lunch – more British Empire at my table – a man from Zululand – one from East Africa and other like places. That's interesting – that is <u>the</u> interesting thing about this war – and will be perhaps the most important for the future. And I do – I <u>do</u> begin to wish America were in it – quite definitely **71898/65-66**

[**my advanced age:** Barker was 38.]

[Friday] Sept 15. [1916] 12-30PM – <u>6-30am</u> [Trowbridge barracks]

[...] today I got hauled up by an infant Subaltern because I was five minutes late for breakfast. So I said I had risked having a bath (my chance after the first parade) and it had taken too long   And he debated silently whether he would give me "extra drill" on Saturday (he had given it to two others) and then said he would 'think it over' Oh – isnt it funny. But – the mathematical business is serious. A lot of these men – actuaries-accountant walk through it – while I stare hopelessly. I'm going to send you one of the forms – you'll see! [...] **71898/29**

Saturday [?16 September 1916] 11-30PM. – <u>5-30PM.</u> London. – at the Lee Matthews's

[...] A day of strange contrasts   Up at 6 and washed and shaved as I could in a crowd of cadets washing as best they could and cleaning and scrubbing the barrack room – which task I should have been sharing but that I had leave and was catching the 7.30 train which I did – and so to London finding myself with a young and innocent cadet who pinned himself on to me because he said he did not like being alone – a naif grown up schoolboy But he showed me his examination paper (just past)   the examination I may have to do in two weeks – and it seems impossible I ever should – though it is simple to him. Then to London and my Tailors to get my cadet-officers kit then to my club – then to the Intelligence Dept at the War Office and there they tell me that I am being passed on to them in a few days – Heaven send it – for I display <u>no</u> intelligence at Trowbridge – but I shall not believe this till it happens. Then to my uncle's – he is a school-master and I tried to make him help me in the mathematics but – mainly by my bad explanation of things he was flummoxed too – so that was hopeless Then back here Mrs L.M. playing Beethoven and following it with a long discussion on aesthetics! Do you know – beloved – I <u>feel</u> nothing – it is thinking of the Beethoven – a sonata I love the D minor I think – makes me say that   I can think and very clearly and I recognised the thought of the music – but all my feeling waits for you and hangs on you [...] **71898/68**

[**Mrs L.M.**: Mrs Lee Matthews (see p.83 above), a member of the circle around Sturge Moore, which regularly discussed aesthetics, and a musician who worked on the choruses for Barker's *Medea* in 1906.]

Tuesday the 26th [September 1916]   8-30am – <u>2-30am</u> [Trowbridge barracks]

[...] yesterday our squad 45 of us marched out to an enormous field and stood round it learning to "shout orders" to each other accurately   shouted about 20 in two hours. You'd say any child could do it – learn it in an eighth of the time. So any child could (And yet there were two mistakes made!) And then back to barracks for a lecture on Driving bands – an hour taken over twenty minutes work. And then lunch – And then a two hours lecture on the slide rule given by a nice boy who knows a little about the slide rule but nothing about lecturing so most of us were as much in the dark as ever (I have to finish in pencil) Then tea – then in rather noisy barrack rooms writing up our notes. Then I had my bath and rushed out to get my hour out Then dinner and I would take my walk – and be alone with thoughts of my beloved – but only a short one for I had to come back to work – till 11 by the light of a candle in a class room. Then to bed – up at 6 – quite dark – but not thank goodness cold – parade and rifle drill for half an hour (badly done) breakfast much cleaning of boots and buttons – These lines to you – in 10 minutes off to "pass orders" again – round a field [...] **71898/80-81**

[**Driving band**: Band of soft metal around an artillery shell.]

Thursday Sep 28. [1916] R.G.A Cadet School Trowbridge Wilts 5PM – <u>11 am</u>

[...] I am being sent on Monday to Weymouth to learn Coast Defence. This means that I'm placed among the older men and shall not be – as things <u>now</u> are – sent to the front. I'm doing as I'm told without comment – partly because I made that the rule – you know – partly because I think that 'special' job may still come off – a thing I'm suited for – so that it will not matter either way – and if I feel or find I ought to go to the front I can always volunteer and arrange it [...] **71898/93**

[The **'special' job** was in Intelligence.]

Saturday. [?30 September 1916] [Adelphi Terrace, London]

My darling – I write to you much about the army – the little corner of it I see and the thoughts it gives me – repeat myself too I expect. ¶ I am struck by its comradeship – I have received more kindness and help – quite simply given from men met by chance in these barracks this last 8 weeks – than in 8 years I believe from people I've run against in my own work. Most from the men of my own age who are undisguisedly disliking the thing most And they work the hardest what is more. Are they especially kind to me I wonder – you remember I told you how people had been knowing (without knowing it) that you loved me and that we were apart!! Well – kindness there has been. And there's a good spirit in the thing – emulation without competition – (oh what a vital difference) – a place for everyone But the thought and method of the system deplorably poor (Nobody would learn anything at Trowbridge from what he was taught – alone). Much much for us to talk about and evolve – an army of peace – that must be the world's ideal. [...] **71898/98**

London Oct 1. [1916] 3PM. <u>10am</u> [Adelphi Terrace, London]
[...] Let me write "practical" things now for a bit. About my leave – I think I shall get it – almost surely I shall. But the reason for my being given it of course is to give the lectures and earn and pay that money And as they last from January to March – I must ask for leave during that time. <u>But</u> – if you want me my dear one I can get over. Three months (the maximum time they <u>say</u> they can give) would cover (by the time I could hear from you) a part of the lecture time – I'd get the others transferred – I'd manage somehow [...] the lecture plan so far is that I remain in the East (in and about New York) till Feb 10 then to California working my way back to Chicago by the middle of March. Then – if my leave is ending I must go almost straight back to England. But much will depend on the war and on what sort of job I am doing. To finish with this – I am not quite happy at being sent to Coast Defence. I haven't asked for it but I believe they have done it to me as a sort of favour and it is supposed to be "safe" (But I am passed for General Service). But if I get this Intelligence Department job – that would be another matter – it would be something I could specially do So I think it best to hold my tongue and go to Weymouth – I shall learn a lot more gunnery there. If the "Intelligence" thing matures – well and good. If not – after my leave I can easily volunteer for foreign service and I shall know more about the whole thing by

then. As to when the war will end no-one can tell. No-one thinks this year - most people do think next - and that's all there is to say about the chances - no-one <u>knows</u>. [...] **71898/87-8**

[Much of this was said, more briefly, in a letter hastily written on 28 September to catch the post (71898/93). The slightly redundant explanation for the **leave** may imply that a secret purpose had already been suggested by Intelligence. For **Coast Defence** he was sent to No 4 Officer Cadet School, Weymouth at the start of October.]

Wednesday. Oct 11. [1916] 11-30PM – <u>5-30PM</u> [London]

[...] Oh - beloved - but isn't it marvellous - just at the time when my lawyer is getting to work and may want me here - here in London I am sent for today and commissioned after all this five weeks of waiting - just when I need to be here. For I know there may be difficulties still but if there are - if there still are even when you read this - oh don't doubt Helen - just see how it does all move to its appointed end. Tomorrow darling - oh my darling love I'll tell you all about my commission and my new work - real work for me I hope it is to be - and other news. [...] **71898/151**

[The **lawyer**'s work and **difficulties** relate to his divorce.]

Thursday Oct 12. [1916] 11-30PM – <u>6-30PM.</u> [London]

[...] Here I am settled I think then for a little in London in the Intelligence Dept - really interesting work - the most interesting possible I suppose to me - hours - anything I please 9 in the morning till 12 at night seems possible - a perfectly charming "chief" - and (mainly) people around that are human and real - oh so different - the mitigated nightmare of these past weeks - well - well it hasn't been bad they have shown me much kindness in their way - but what a way! Description of my days - in a sense I shan't be able to write you now - it's all office work - and the substance of it of course not discussable - but thoughts will come again now [...] **71898/152**

[The Secret Service Bureau, or Secret **Intelligence** Service, eventually became MI6. At this point there were 60 London staff. For the **'chief'** see p.52.]

[Sunday 22 October 1916] 3-30PM. – <u>10-30am.</u> [Ayot]

[...] I'm glad I went through even such a mild "gruelling" for the army as that was. I learnt – not always what they thought I was learning but a good many things besides for my soul's good. And you don't think me less your soldier now beloved – that I sit at a War Office Desk in the Intelligence Department and really try and set my brains to work. Oh – they were beastly those barracks – and I'm glad I'm through with them (I suppose I am) – but – it was right to do it. [...] **71898/197-98**

....

Once Barker began working for Intelligence his lecture tour of America was used as a vehicle for gathering information about support for Germany, ideological and material, in the towns he would visit. This is clear from his letters, though Smith, who is a little muddled, says he was watching 'Indian anarchists' (2011: 71). Use of lecture tours for propaganda had been regular since the beginning of the war (Wright 1978) but I can find no evidence for Spence's assertion (2004: 520) that these were 'pro-British talks' (for lecture topics see p.4). Gale (2020: 122) claims that the information-gathering would be assisted by Huntington: 'His new relationship with a married heiress gave him access to wealthy Americans'. Actually her circle was in New York and he was in towns which she couldn't even place geographically, let alone know people there. Neither Spence nor Smith nor Gale seem to have read Barker's account. He arrived in America on 1 January 1917.

The next three letters were written to William Wiseman (1885-1962), head of station for British Intelligence in New York, who oversaw a network of agents (Fowler 1969). The schedule had been discussed with Wiseman in London in November.

....

[Tuesday] Feb 20. [1917 Hotel Muehlebach, Kansas City]
My dear W.
Iowa City Iowa. 'Seat' of Iowa State University. 3000 students men and women. But a pretty place. Amount of interest in 'our affair' may be gathered from the fact that I spent an hour and a half at the Faculty Club, guest of honour – asked to talk & plied with questions – and not one mention of the war – and it would have seemed fatally obvious had I dragged it in. In private talk before and after with a 'Professor' or so we glanced on it. I gathered that if they were pro- anything except pro-let me alone they would be pro-ally   I certainly think there is neither German feeling nor German propaganda. It might be worth while if opportunity served to launch there a little Democracy or Autocracy literature. That is the only line on which to touch them [...] **[WW MS 666 1: 6: 163]**

[Thursday] March 8. [1917 Palace Hotel, San Francisco]
[...] There'll be a boat I presume on Saturday the 31st but apart from instructions I'd be glad of your advice as to how best to travel. For my own affairs four or five weeks in England will suffice. If you still want me back you'll be settling it with C. If I could know before I leave that would be convenient – But for the one note I sent through you I have of course not written to him at all. But you'll understand how glad I'll be – if it is thought well – to work under you – and he – that I don't want to leave his job unfinished. However – more important than my protestations – I'll get orders.
[WW MS 666 1: 6: 164]

[The **affairs** are the preparation for the first divorce suit. **C** is Mansfield Cumming.]

[Thursday] March 15. [1917 Hotel Rainbow, Great Falls, Montana]
Dear W.
Portand Oregon   Seattle
Not much to say about either. I interviewed P's men in each place

They both seemed capable chaps. I gathered that as far as anything which could interest us was concerned matters had been "quiet" for some time – general sympathy with the allies. No German "movements" – even the little propaganda they keep going in the German press does not amount to much. At Seattle Charles W. Frye the only rich and prominent German remaining (two others having lately died) and he apparently took no interest in the affairs of the Fatherland. No sign of German movements to Mexico or S. America – nothing noticeable about the shipping. ¶ This much from P's people. I had only a few hours in Seattle – and in Portland met mainly newspaper men. [...] **[WW MS 666 1: 6: 165]**

[Gale (2020), following Smith (2011), says Barker's activity in America was espionage. The letters suggest he was gathering gossip, rather obviously, from those he met and taking reports from agents in the field (**P's men**). This is pretty low-level 'espionage', if it is at all, and it is a little over-sensational to describe it as such.]

....

Back in England Barker continued with what he regarded as the boring 'office-boy' work of scanning files. He had indeed been recruited, according to Cumming's diary, to take charge of the records of the organisation (Judd 2000: 351). Of more interest to him was that he had to read numerous newspapers on a regular basis, for their international reports. Such intelligence gathering was not limited to newspapers. In spring 1918 he tells Huntington, at length, about a dinner given in London by his American friend Paul Cravath, an 'Atlanticist' who was pro-Ally and supported increased US defence spending (Roberts 2005) and who was by now Legal Adviser to the United States Treasury. At the table were an Italian Deputy who had just been released from imprisonment by the Bolsheviks for trying to supply funds to anti-Bolsheviks; the extremely right-wing ex-naval attaché of Tsar Nicholas II; an American lawyer who had advised Woodrow Wilson; a Frenchman concerned about Russian financial interests – and himself (Texas Friday morning 7am.). Conversation was largely about international tactics in relation to Russia, which was Barker's special Intelligence area (the Bureau was at this stage organised into geographical units).

This dinner was perhaps not unusual. There is mention of various such meal-time meetings. Russia was discussed again at a lunch with Hugh Walpole, head of British propaganda in Petrograd. But too many guests remain obscure: who was the 'American Russian' man and what was the 'Icelandic-Finnish' lunch? About one, however, we can infer a little more. In spring 1918 Barker was seconded to work for Wiseman, now in London. Wiseman had a direct line to President Woodrow Wilson, via Colonel House, Wilson's close advisor (Fowler 1969), and his move to London may thus be significant. Certainly from this time Barker seems to have more to do with various American contacts. In particular he started meeting the *New Republic* journalist Ray Stannard Baker (1870-1946). Baker's actual work in London was to report directly to Wilson on 'the state of radical opinion and organization, especially the attitude of labor in England' (in Martin 1973: 166). A close connection between Wilson and British radicals was increasingly important to their shared aims of ending the war with a just peace settlement (as against the punitive British militarism which they felt, rightly as it turned out, would lead only to another war). Barker dined with Baker, and then gave him lunches where either Beatrice or both Webbs were present. This is an interesting moment of overlap between Barker's personal and military life. His friends the Webbs were central figures in the labour movement and told Baker of the extent of 'progressive thinking' in Britain (Baker 1918). Which prompts a question: in asking the 'progressive' Barker to facilitate a meeting between his friends and Baker, was British Intelligence, even while the government pursued victory by military means, in fact enabling the work of an American agent who was committed to, and sought to strengthen, his President's policy of peace-by-negotiation?

The last we hear of Barker's military service is this, written to Huntington:

Friday morning [late spring 1918] 7am. [Gordon Square, London]
[...] One little thing has just happened that will amuse you – plus a tang of something <u>not</u> amusement.   The Propaganda Department wanted me to make one of a small committee – W.A. H.B. Irving and

myself to draw up a report on the possibility of sending dramatic companies to neutral countries – very good propaganda if well done worse than useless if not   The 'request for my services' went through the usual official channels and had to go up to Powers that Be beyond my Chief. The particular Power that resents my presence on his section of the globe (quite impersonally – for I've seen him once in my life never even spoken to him) said 'If you lend him you can't take him back' Whereat my chief said he was dashed if he'd lend me. And that's that. But it is a good instance of what we call War Office methods. Three days work on it – not more and I happen to be about the best – well almost the only expert opinion that is to be had – on the theatre side of the job. ¶ Oh and I finished yesterday among the Jugo-Slavs the Czechs to be quite correct – Our Czech expert said I <u>must</u> attend a meeting for forming a Readership in Czech at Kings College That's all right – The Czechs do these things from a political point of view – but we must keep our own eyes open and our own wits clear about that and education in becoming good Europeans – that's a real service anyhow. I thought it was to be just a public meeting and that I should sit at the back and applaud But behold – I found myself round a committee table – moving resolutions and making suggestions. I wanted my dear one there – the discussion would have bored you – it bored me! but you could have watched with me the light failing and falling so queerly on the faces round the big table – the odd English 'academic' face – always an exception and never a 'type' – and then the Czech 'heads' so different. I have let myself in for asking the Duchess of Marlborough to go on the Committee for raising the funds   Asked for suggestions I protested they were leaving out both women and Americans [...] I laughed at myself as I came back   your own dear 'office boy' sitting on commit-tees and having his opinion asked [...] (**Texas**)

[**Powers that Be**: Cumming had two bosses, Reginald 'Blinker' Hall, Director of Naval Intelligence, in the Admiralty, and George MacDonogh, Director of Military Intelligence, in the War Office. There was friction between these two offices. In April 1918, in the House of Commons, Billing (see p.119) named the Director of Theatrical Propaganda in Neutral Countries as J.T.Grein, the founder in 1891 of the Independent Theatre Society. **WA**: William Archer, drama critic, translator of Ibsen and friend of Barker. Henry Brodribb **Irving**: an actor, eldest son of Sir Henry Irving. The reason why someone in Intelligence had to attend the meeting was that the **Czech** Thomas Masaryk was already a lecturer at King's. Masaryk was strongly pro-ally, was well networked and had operated in Russia, and the British wanted to cultivate a Czech alliance. Barker may have been the one chosen because, following his work in America, he was used to being around academics and he knew a lot about Russia. It is also the case that he knew the American agent Ray Stannard Baker, who had links with Masaryk, but the extent of his involvement cannot yet be established. **Duchess of Marlborough**: The American Consuelo Vanderbilt. Coerced by her mother into a loveless marriage motivated by rank and money she committed herself to philanthropic causes.]

6. Nation and War

Wednesday morning [19 January 1916] 10 o'clock. Hotel Palais d'Orsay. Paris

[...] I travelled from Bordeaux with a jolly young French officer. As soon as he saw my Red Cross Brassard he began to talk – about the war – "Just the same as ever at the Front" here And "The English must change their methods if anything is to be done" The French say that outright now – but it is easily said – and – a nation can't change its methods in a year or two – no matter what the stress. More and more I see it and know it – not a question of army organisation – but of thought – of way of thinking. True. I suppose some really great commander, with a "piercing" and commanding mind – could inform his underlings for the time being with a different spirit. But I don't know – Wellington – who brought order out of chaos for us once before – with him it was a matter of years – four years of Peninsular fighting I think it was – perhaps only three with Wellington – and he had a smaller task - 50 - or 60000 men only to handle. Here's a question of a million and more – and behind them a nation to organise – with habits less simple now than they were a hundred years back We can only win this war on what we are – and have made ourselves up to the time it began – many virtues we have but buried in laziness of mind – and "fatness" of nature – the keener more masterly people – doing pioneer work for England in the outlying Empire – and apt to be passed over and forgotten by the self-seekers at home – the finer minds at home either blunted in their efforts to make impression on the great crowd or turning in on themselves (Meredith!) discontented that they who really love England as a whole – should be understood by a few thousand out of the millions – too proud to complain of it [...] **71897/3**

[**Brassard**: armband. George **Meredith**: poet and novelist much admired by Barker, became increasingly crippled and deaf in old age.]

[Friday] Feb 18. [1916] 10 PM. London.

[...] London has looked hideous today but last night with its lights out but a bright moon shining it was quite beautiful. But I shall be glad to be away from it – to shake free of it as it is now   collect my thoughts   do my work. I think I see how and why we have failed in this war (indeed I have always seen it – I'm a part of the failure!) for though we win we shall in a sense have failed. Nor have I much hope now that this war will end war. Perhaps we as a nation in the next generation <u>can</u> end war by preparing ourselves in – so to speak – a super-war way. And that sort of preparation – not mere drilling – is what we have to bend our backs to in the time to come. Patriotism – a matter for hard thought – not for shouting. [...] **71897/42**

Saturday [?May 1916 Williamstown, MA, USA]

Dear – a thought came to me the other day – among those thick Berkshire Hills – that is perhaps worth having   I was wishing that England could really keep altruistic over this war – and then it struck me that perhaps altruism was not in itself a sufficient power to <u>win </u>anything   I think this is true of both nations and people. You may be disinterested as long as you sit still – but action of any sort must enlist your whole being if it is to be worth while. So one should not be too down on that sort of egoism – it is perhaps neces-sary for achievement.   How the victory is employed – that is another thing. And indeed it is one of the tests of greatness – the fine unselfish use of success. You'll detect how the thought flows back to personal things. **71898/122**

[The **Berkshire Hills** are in Massachusetts; **Williamstown**, in First Berkshire, is in the northwest of the state.]

Wednesday [12 July 1916] Midday – <u>9-50</u>   [on board the 'New York']

[...] Who else is on the ship - do you want to know? I speak to very few. A white haired woman - doll beauty in her youth - no maturity - now grown fat - you know the type. She has her chair near mine   I "soignéd" her into it and wrapped her rug around her. She wasn't used to being waited on she said pathetically. Had lost a son in the war. So I sympathised and then for a quarter of an hour had to listen to muddleheaded and rather poisonous nonsense (since if you have suffered [how much?] there is nothing you cannot say)   It came in her mind to the fact that when we get into Germany – the officers wouldn't be able to "hold" their men. Good God – does she really wish English soldiers to have rape and murder on <u>their</u> souls. Well – I suppose she just doesn't think at all. [...] Oh – and Australian woman "I think you know my cousin" I don't! What is it in Australia that seems to turn – well nearly <u>all</u> the inhabitants into blazing cads! <u>with</u> cockney accents.   New Zealand doesn't   Mystery of Geography. [...] **71897/77**

[Thursday] August 3 [1916] 11PM – <u>5PM</u> (Ayot)

[...] In town – and most of the time with Masefield – who is getting wound in folds of red-tape in his endeavour to go to France – where he has been <u>told</u> to go – and write this book on American hospitals So I went round with him a bit and that made it pleasanter perhaps – and for me to have him to talk to. But we were both depressed at the red-tape – at the Casement execution (he had written in vain to Asquith about the Irish situation and the effect on it) – and worse at the calculated meanness with which Newton (Under-Secretary for Foreign Affairs I think he is) had put abroad a tale of German's shooting Irish prisoners because they had refused to join Casement – no evidence of it at all – but just done to counteract public opinion. For the man personally no mercy need be shown – but what is one life more or less in these bloody times. But that is not I think how to view the matter. If you must kill a man to prevent him preying on Society – well do so – But not kill him for vengeance – And do not let a Nation revenge itself on a man by killing him – a man who can say with any show of truth that he belonged to another and an oppressed nation. The measure of a people's greatness is the measure of its magnanimity. We are safe in Ireland – Casement's death can make us no safer. We should be above vengeance of that sort I think – not for his sake – but for our own. Well – it is done. God send no further evil from it.[...] **71897/129**

[Sir Roger **Casement** was a British diplomat whose politics became anti-imperialist, increasingly supporting Irish republicanism. In 1916 he sought German military aid for the Easter Rising in Dublin. Following his arrest the British government released excerpts from his diaries which detailed his homosexual activities – which could be seen as **'preying on Society'** – and thus helped curtail support for his cause. He was hanged on 3 August 1916. H.H. **Asquith** was Prime Minister 1908-1916. Thomas Legh, Second Baron **Newton** was Assistant Under-Secretary.]

Sunday. [?early August 1916 with the Shaws in Ayot]
One has to face the fact that war – however righteous it <u>may</u> be – does coarsen the moral fibre of a nation. I pass by the vulgar inanity the theatre has been reduced to here and the sights I see in the streets and some shop windows. But the Sunday papers! The mass of incitement to hate and the lowest sort of hate which is now served up to the unthinking sort of English man and woman – saddens one. It seems as if they thought that the only way they could get them to go on fighting was by rousing all their worst instincts of greed and cruelty. <u>Is</u> that true? Whatever is said about the real things we are fighting for is hidden now in senseless boasting   And it has its effect. I hear men talking now about killing Germans – as if that were an end in itself. And (educated men – W.J. Locke the novelist last night) about the British Empire <u>against</u> the world. As if that were a desirable end. One must not overrate the meaning of all this – But one must not shirk it. We are right – you and I – to hate and mistrust war as war, my dear. **71898/26**

[William John **Locke** was also a playwright.]

Tuesday. [?15 August 1916 SJW barracks]
The war oppression is at its worst with me now for I am caught in the machine of it and that claims every bit of my mind and body

that it can. My spirit it doesn't and shall never claim. And so I shall never be a good soldier I fear! ¶ The spirit of re-action in England troubles me. All war leads to re-action – it is in its very nature – all militarism does – it replaces the spirit by the letter   it is a short cut to everything that Democracy with its horrible faults and confusions as we have it now is a long way to. But we must go the long way – We must always go the long way – patiently. War breeds impatience in all things – violence   I note at St John's Wood – the cadets and soldiers – under strict discipline all day – once free of that having less <u>manners</u> than the veriest street arabs – except for those who are old enough to be conscious of the tendency and resist it ¶ No dear we must work until we get the discipline from within – outward and visible sign of inward and spiritual grace – for our nation   <u>one</u> nation – that we love. [...] **71898/35**

Thursday [?24 August 1916 SJW barracks]

War – war – I write you nothing else now! I don't want to – but – one is caught in it. The toll of young men it takes is so awful Not only of the very young men but – for instance – I hear that the three young Dons at Oxford the best Scientists they have had for years have all been killed leading infantry troops And that is a particular wrong – apart from the general wrong I think. For if they had died doing their own job it would have been one thing – one would have felt sorrow at loss but not anger at waste. And that again is a thing that war runs to – waste – waste all the time. Here in England especially we have not learned to think of a nation as anything but a crowd – and civilisation is – isn't it – the tendency to abolish crowds and substitute for that chaos of humanity a cosmos – with each soul fulfilling its true function. And religion is to me – the faith – that every soul has its function – can make itself – by fulfilling that first – a worthier one to follow   The clear eye sees men – not masses. [...] **71898/36**

[Human relationship to the '**cosmos**' is a crucial element of civilisation as articulated by J.A. Hobson (see p.156). The opposition of chaos and cosmos also featured in the value system of Gilbert Murray.]

Friday [?15 September 1916 Trowbridge barracks]
Everything I see proves the truth of a thing I said early in the war when people were talking of the wonderful effect that fighting had on a nation "In war a people doesn't change – it becomes 'more so". That may be true of every crisis. But I see it in individuals and newspapers – theatres (alack I am ashamed!) politics. For good and evil **71898/40**

Friday. [?13 October 1916 London]
Today – it was a Friday – I write this the next morning but it seemed natural to say 'today' – I was taken by my chief – a duty lunch – he also on duty taking someone – to the Savoy Hotel I had not been there since before the war – in fact the last time I think was a lunch with the German Ambassador there! I think the place emptied during the first months of it all but now! It is packed. And every other hotel in London is packed and every "known" restaurant the lunch as luxurious as ever – as much and more money flowing. What is one to make of it? We shook our heads but we were there and so were dozens of other soldiers. It is done for the soldiers people would say – those home from the front who want to be made to forget the horrors. But is it? I don't think so – and does it make them forget? I'm sure it doesn't. No the horrible thing it looks and seems to me is that the old luxury loving spirit is quite unchanged – has learnt nothing – forgets and will forget the war and its meaning and its <u>cause</u> (largely in the last analysis <u>this</u>). God forgive me a harsh judgment – but it makes me afraid. [...] **71898/163**

Wednesday. [?18 October 1916 London]
My dear – It is troubling me much the things that certain people of the soldier government class are saying about America here. Of course there is the war-soreness. And as to that and the part America is taking and refusing to take what they say is mild compared to what you say – and I understand. But they add to it such stupid mean foolish ignorant things which betray such a lack

of understanding of anything America is or is trying to be – national prejudice and the snobbish pig headed English form of it at its very worst. That's – not unforgiveable because I suppose it is no use ever saying that one can't forgive ignorance – but very tragic – and yes it is unforgiveable for they (this sort of man and woman ought to know better). It must be got round the two countries must understand and meet and work together – honestly – honestly – I see no safety for the world but in that England must travel far and I won't deny I think America must travel a little further along the right road and they must find and know their common purpose. If one dare say such a big thing (and why not) I'd say that our life work yours and mine – must be to help towards that We may say that – secretly – to ourselves – and then do simple things Yes? **71898/170**

[A parliamentary debate on 17 October 1916 about America's attitudes to British cruisers patrolling its waters (to protect trading vessels) expressed considerable hostility to America, much of it led by Admiral Lord Beresford.]

Thursday. [?mid-October 1916 London]
[...] I have in my mind this question of nationalities and especially the small nationalities and their rights which we are supposed to be dipping Europe in blood for. You know – nobody loves the Belgians (the French loathe them) – or the Swiss or Dutch nor the Irish – when they are insisting on their nationality. And that I believe is the important point. England Russia America – Germany – these are big enough for their national feelings to represent a world-tendency – one can feel enthusiasm about it – or the reverse But it is really the tendency the purpose one should be enthusiastic – patriotic – about. Only when the small nation stands for something bigger than itself do we sympathise. Athens stood for culture but she made a mess of government. When Holland stood for religious advancement and freedom she meant something Inasmuch as Ireland stands for more than her own "parochial" independence we stand for that too for her sake but the parochialism repels us – oh too big a subject. [...] **71898/166**

Tuesday. [?24 October 1916 London]

I am amused to find myself a constant champion of America – and she needs some championing over here from time to time. England – poor dear – is very sore and strained and unreasonable – and when she won't think of anything else she remembers the unfortunate 'too proud to fight' as if it were the national motto that a hundred million people had solemnly subscribed to. I suppose that even if I didn't love America I should be championing her because I love you (there is an extra readiness to take up the cudgels I can't deny) But I do love her and I do begin to understand her problems which people here mostly don't and don't trouble to. But what amuses me is that you bemoan her state to me and I defend her here. While I bemoan England's state to you and you – do you defend her? Perhaps you don't need to dear – but you will for there are going to be some little excusable things done in her name and France's before the war is over – and even when it is over I fear. [...] **71898/184**

[The quotation is from a speech by Woodrow Wilson on 10 May 1915, asserting the ethical importance of America's commitment to neutrality.]

Thursday [?26 October 1916 London]

Masefield back from France and the American hospitals and ambulances there.   Rather down on American "indiscipline" in the work. That I have to own to – as far as I have seen it – but it is a virtue as well as a vice. Admiring French men – down – very very down on French women. Then I say Nonsense – you can't condemn a sex wholesale any more than a nation   Truthfully I know nothing of French women but I do guess that anyway – those you see most of will least represent what the rest are like. ¶ But it was odd – as we were talking (no but a little later) – there was turned on the small son's gramophone – a Palestrina Mass Oh – amazing music – spiritually stimulating – almost exciting – music if ever there was (and perhaps it should not be exciting) but true music of the spirit only to be heard at all if one's spirit listened. So then I said – And Italy in her most decadent days produced that. These sweeping judgments of countries and peoples are nonsense   History is much more interesting than that. I'm not a big enough man to discover the truth of contemporary things – but I do think I can read history – a little. [...] **71898/185**

[**Masefield**'s article on a night with the Field Service Section of the American Ambulance was published in *Harpers Monthly Magazine,* May 1917.]

Saturday [?28 October 1916 London]

These Reflections of a Soldier have caused a certain amount of talk – and indeed they are worth reading   I think his accusations are true – though of course not all true of any one person. And his thought as to why and wherefore is good.   It is one of the tragedies of this war – perhaps an inevitable tragedy in any war – how one can lose touch with the original purpose. The dyer's hand subdued to what it works in   And how one's sense of values alters. Perhaps we fussed too much before – well not too much heaven knows but from the wrong point of view   the more bodily security point of view – about human life and suffering   But now – we read of a thousand deaths and never turn a hair – and nobody seems to shudder any more at the trench horrors – they want the horror piled on horror now and are only moved to a sort of callous amused disgust even then. That is true It is deeply true that they are <u>bored</u> with the war – bored sick with it – and this Newspaper picturesque writing – is a frantic attempt to keep the nation inter-ested – as apart from obsessed   It really is – and as the nation is bleeding to death under it – it's <u>horrible</u> [...] **71898/186**

['**Reflections of a Soldier**', although unsigned, was by R.H. Tawney and was published in *The Nation* 20 (21 October 1916). Tawney shared similar targets with Barker: sentimentalising of the war, misrepresentation of soldiers and culti-vation of a hatred not shared by those actually fighting. The language of his attacks on illusory ideas and the newspapers that spread them is very like Barker: 'you have chosen to make to yourselves an image of war, not as it is, but of a kind which, being picturesque, flatters your appetite for novelty, for excitement, for easy admiration, without troubling you with masterful emotions. You have chosen, I say, to make an image, because you do not like, or cannot bear, the truth'. The image of the **dyer's hand** has its origin in Shakespeare's Sonnet 111.]

Wednesday [15 November 1916 Ayot]

A heated argument with Charlotte Shaw today which – though I yielded to temptation – one does and shouldn't – to argue for victory instead of the shere discovery of truth – yet was interesting I pursued truth single-mindedly enough for that. She has lately "got" religion – of a peculiarly irritating kind – I chaffed her about being a "spiritual snob" – Mystic Holiness out of the <u>East</u>! – you know! That War only came about because men <u>thought</u> wrongly of things So far I agree. Indeed so fervently do I hold it that to have it argued from that – Therefore one should stop fighting now! Would the Germans? No I loathe unrealities even more than I loathe war And the tragedy of this war is that it forces us down to a lower plane of life – one we were struggling out of – in order that future generations may struggle better we <u>hope</u> But we are forced (have forced ourselves if you like) down to the lower plane. That <u>is</u> the tragedy and to shirk it is unreal – and – subtly – would prevent us – if we don't accept the descent from beginning to climb again. [...] **71898/251**

[Thursday] Dec 14. [1916] 11-30am – <u>6-30am</u> [London]

[...]Things about the war should I write – just to show I haven't lost the sense of all else in the world. The peace offer must be a beginning. We shall say No to it there seems no doubt.   But then we shall have to put down what we're prepared to say "Yes" to – and that will be a gain – it will restore a definite purpose and put a definite term to things – fighting after that will be more business like – less fierce in one way. It is a first step – and all to the good however it seems to fail now – the peoples must begin to face realities and see what can and cannot be. [...] **71898/276**

[The '**Peace** Note of Germany and Her Allies' was sent on 12 December 1916.]

Friday-Saturday [22-23 December 1916] 12-45am – <u>7-45PM.</u> [Bloomsbury, London]

[...] I have pictured you too raging at Wilson's Note. An ill day's work that of his   I fear it will put a coolness between England and

America that will take long to cure. That cold pedant mind of his. Suppose England said All right we can agree with Germany – she only asks us one thing in return for all she'll give us – a free hand in South America – and as you trust to her protestations as to the rights of smaller nations – you'll feel quite safe – ! What a temptation to make that reply. I try to understand and be tolerant but this Note – does defeat me – I know how you're feeling – I can hear you. [...] **71898/281-82**

[On 18 December 1916 Woodrow **Wilson** issued a note to all the combatant powers asking them to state their peace terms. It seemed variously to compromise British war aims or liken them to Germany's, to threaten and create divisions among the Allies and even to collude with Germany.]

Tuesday [23 April 1918] 7-45am. [Gordon Square, London]

[...] Think – those damned idiots of Germans are straining every muscle (I deny them nerves) – putting thought and <u>lives</u> into another desperate effort to achieve – <u>what</u>? Nothing at all   The simpler spirits among them know it the common soldiers and the lesser spirits (wherever they are!) know that they won't get to Calais or Paris – that they won't smash our armies – and even if they did the result would still be nothing.   The war would not end – we should never sit down to an unrighteous peace.   Even Russia – armyless – navyless – foodless will almost certainly start fighting again next year – if not before.   Do they think they can beat us?   It is so curious as I say – put it to the 'simple' soldier and he knows no result will come of it (I'm talking of prisoners) but of course he adds "Ah but they <u>tell</u> us – "   And so the thing goes on because of the megalomaniac's pride and stupidity of the Kaiser and his like – candidates for Hell (elected candidates) Hell being the place of the wilfully stupid the wilfully blind. God forgive us – we had a few of the sort here but here they don't matter.   Mr de Vere Stacpoole (!!) in his letter to the Morning Post complaining that we are a degenerate race   that we have lost the "passion of the male that has made Germany great" Let me do the creature justice I do forget whether he said "great" or "powerful".   Of course what <u>is</u> one to say of a nation that has allowed a set of uniformed "Hoch Hoch" idiots like that to master it – to turn all its cleverness and enterprise and its music and philosophy even to their service? Well – they must be taught their lesson   we must go on and on till they have learnt it. And God knows we have lessons to learn. If we had learnt them earlier – Yes it is true we could have done the job quicker But even now alas we don't seem to know just what the lessons were. People think in a muddle-headed way. "If only we'd been a little more like Germany" cf Mr de Vere Stacpoole!!! (he must have invented it) with his "passion of the male" ¶ No – back my mind comes to where it started (though that's not a good sign perhaps but it does come bringing some sheaves with it) – to where it started at the start of the war. The stupidity of these militarists. We have to fight them with their weapons and beat them at their game – it's no use reasoning with a tiger But never – never forget our own – and our own way of thought and action. I am convinced that the appropriate punish-ment for the Kaiser   the thing that would punish him most – put him most directly in his place is that he should be publicly spanked – on the steps of that absurd Wilhelm I monument in Berlin – by some strong minded and strong handed English school mistress – though there's none you could insult by asking her to do it   But that is the real level of his "achievement" in life – the ill-conduct of a common minded boy at an industrial school who breaks windows (but he has made it Reims!) and tortures the cat and the baby – God help us we know the parallels there – He throws his stones over Europe   But that is the level of his existence. [...] (**Texas**)

[Henry **de Vere Stacpoole**, a successful popular novelist, was a frequent contributor to the war-mongering *Morning Post*. '**Hoch** der Kaiser'/'Praise the Kaiser' was satirised in Whit Cunliffe's 1914 song 'Hoch Hoch der Kaiser'. The destruction of much of **Reims** cathedral on 20 September 1914 by German shelling was regarded as deliberate vandalism.]

Friday [31 May 1918] 7am. [Gordon Square, London]

[...] This Billing case – I trust I am not a vindictive or a violent man but I would cheerfully horsewhip Billing in front of the House of

Commons that he has disgraced That such a cad should exist in England – at least that was my first feeling ¶ But now that he is flattering those lunatics in the box with their "Black books written in German" – really it is like Titus Oates over again (Ah – <u>we</u> can talk history) – I am not sure the wretched thing may not have a salutary effect (though I hope Billing will get a year in gaol for all that – I rather fear the jury though) – for it will show people what is the logical result – the reductio ad absurdum – of talking in this reckless way of Pro-Germanism and Peace-Offensives and "Lord Haldane the friend of the Kaiser" – This is what weak minded people think they mean It <u>is</u> just like Titus Oates over again. **71915/123**

[Noel Pemberton **Billing** ran a weekly journal, *The Imperialist*, in 1918 re-named *Vigilante*, which was part-funded by Beaverbrook. On 26 January 1918 it published an article claiming there was a '**black book**' containing the names of 47,000 British lesbians and gay men being blackmailed by the Germans. Billing referred to German agents on the first day (30 May) of his trial for defamation of Maud Allan. **Titus Oates** claimed there was a Catholic plot to kill Charles II and listed names of those connected. This led to anti-Catholic hysteria between 1678 and 1681. Richard Burdon **Haldane** was Asquith's Lord Chancellor until May 1915, when he was forced from office by a press campaign, led by Beaverbrook's *Daily Express*, based on Haldane's supposed liking for Germany (because he was, unusually, able to speak German, was an intellectual, and was also apparently in the 'black book'). Ironically his thorough-going re-organisation of the army was perhaps the single most effective preparation for war.]

7. THE MILITARY MIND

By contrast with the extracts in Letters 5, these reflect on the culture, structure and mind-set of the army as an institution. Character-istically, observations often begin with a phrase such as 'I was amused'.

....

Friday July 21. [1916] 12-15 – <u>6-15</u>. [The Garrick Club, London]
[...] London – oh a queer place now, much emptier and quieter than of old. One result of conscription is that the horrible recruiting posters are gone. Isn't it like us? When National Service would have been a glorious thing – a big thing – we didn't tackle it. Before the war – long – it should have been a part of our life – as a Socialist I think so – without thinking that it should have been purely military service – or indeed – mainly military service   For in peace that is only an emergency calling (I grant you must be ready for the emergency) and even in war-time it is only a part – though far the greatest part of the national need. But soldiers are stupid – oh I fear there is something in the very nature of soldiering that tends to make men stupid or to bring the stupid men into positions where they stick – obstructing the clever men that could climb by them. We have got a few clever men by the fools – got them to the top – one hopes – and they are sweating blood to save the Country but the fools spoil much of their work for them – and the clever men below can't get by and their hearts are broken in seeing their own work and their men's lives thrown away. That's the state of things I find – it always has been so in war – unless you made nothing but war your business   And from that – we know – comes an evil to all concerned far worse than muddling – however angry muddling makes one. ¶ I seem to do nothing but grumble. I don't mean to (There – it is <u>half past</u> six with you. <u>Darling Helen</u> – <u>Darling Helen</u> – <u>Darling Helen</u> – and as I write it I send you – my heart – all I am and have of strength and purpose and love – my own – my friend –

dear – dearest in the world) No. I don't mean to grumble – but to see good men <u>trying</u> to give their best – without stint – and being thwarted – by dull people and self-indulgent people and blind-hearted people – that <u>angers</u> me. [...] **71897/108-9**

Monday. [?31 July 1916 Manaton, Devon]

England and war crushes everything out of me leaves me hopeless (though I won't be) of any spiritual life or light coming back to her at all   For war – in its carrying out – is not a heroic thing my dear – whatever it may be in its intention. It gets the wrong men on top – the stupid violent men (necessarily) and their coarser side – and the coarser side of all men – <u>and</u> women – <u>no</u> – that's wrong. But this is true – those that were coarse became coarser and are more in evidence – men and women. And the finer ones – become finer perhaps – but they work hard to forget it and hide themselves away all they can – and keep silent   So you see the land it leaves. Not a good land to live in – I am disheartened. [...] **71898/23**

Thursday. [?10 August 1916 SJW barracks]

Reflections on the army! They are already many and various. Much good and much bad in it. The certainties of it are good   There is no cut throat competition – but only emulation – and that makes men happier I think – and comradely. But the unlimited authority – the code which holds a man may be blamed – berated – whether he be right or wrong and must never answer back – is a great pitfall for the natures that are neither naturally authoritative or naturally just. It makes bullies – and in the men abolishes all sense of honesty. They do things well under the eye of the bully – but the truth is not in them. I find myself already going in fear – in the sense that I am prepared to do things to avoid rows and not because I am glad to do them right – when the tasks are useless – as many are or you are being badly taught ¶ With the best of the army tradition you can make fine men – with the worst you make brutes – and as you can't have all good officers and very few good NCO's – well the proportion of brutes is rather large **71898/28**

Saturday. [?12 August 1916 SJW barracks]

More army reflections - beloved ¶ One curse is cheap labour. That is to say you can order men to do anything and give them any amount of trouble over it - and the excuse is that it is good for discipline. This is one of the reasons armies are backward - people are not driven to exercise their ingenuity. This is probably most obvious in the infantry regiments - in the artillery where I belong - you have at least to be ingenious over the machines And the army is at its best when it does - also at least - treat its men as fine machines But then - man is something more than that - and I believe thoroughly that it is possible - even with "common" men to take them a step higher - and granted the necessity for a good machine - and I do grant that and allow the army a legitimate pride in it - you can get a better army I believe by inspiring other men. Idealist am I? I'm glad <u>we</u> are that my darling - it is the only thing to be - better to die disappointed and hopeful that "take things as they are". [...] **71898/30**

Wednesday. [?16 August 1916 SJW barracks]

Still military! At first you resent the absolute loss of your dignity as a human being   You are spoken to habitually as no decent man would speak to a dog. That passes - and you are relieved to find you have no individuality at all. What you ask as you go round the riding school or parade is that your name shall be forgotten   that you shall not even be "Hi you there you - " which is most likely all you will be if you are spoken to at all - Oh <u>some</u> of the men are better - the instructors. But that is really the normal thing among the NCO's. <u>It is wrong</u>. I find one boy here - not a nice natured boy certainly but it is I think a year's bullying that has made him rather a dishonest worker - getting out of what he can unseen - doing the seen things with outside polish. And openly saying that when he gets his commission he'll "take it out of the NCO's". There is the making of the lowest type of officer under my eyes. The older men - among the cadets - keep their balance better of course. But still [...] **71898/32**

Thursday [?7 September 1916 Gordon Square, London]
Walking up Whitehall this afternoon I think I saluted twenty times. Really it is a nuisance being about London in the daytime for it swarms with officers. But – did I tell you – I take rather a perverse pride in being a private and behaving most correctly to an infant of a subaltern – who equally behaves most correctly to me and solemnly returns the salute. But – this is queer – a young cousin of mine 22 – has been through a lot of the fighting – is now all but a Captain – and I must ask him to my club to lunch – for being still technically in the ranks I can't sit down with him in a public restaurant. But in my club I hob-nob with generals! ¶ I have an idea that – at the barracks – they thought I should step out of my "place" if I could. But needless to say I have been rigidly "correct" and lately one or two of the officers have been almost human to me – whereat I am more correct than ever. It has given me an insight into new things [...] **71898/44**

Friday [?22 September 1916 Trowbridge barracks]
It is amusing to find that the one thing which really excites men in the army is their uniform. To begin with the authorities are always ordering trivial alterations – the wearing of a new button or a new badge. And this is the topic of the barracks for days and passions rage high. Why is it? And I have just got my officers-cadets uniform and I am quite pleased Now whether it is the comfort and civilisation of the clothes as compared to the private's (and there's a vast difference) or because my perverse pride in being a private is wearing thin – or whether I have acquired the army vanity quite naturally I don't know (I certainly shall look much more "the thing" in them) But it's interesting isn't it? And I believe you'd like to see me in my uniform wouldn't you? Baby! So there we should be two babies together [...] **71898/56**

Sunday. [?early October 1916 Weymouth]
I said to myself the other day in one of the intervals of this drill they make us do – attention – stand at ease – right turn left turn about turn form fours right turn etc – till our heads are dizzy – I

said "The army is always living in the last century but one and when war comes it takes the killing of a quarter of it to bring it up to date" ¶ Really it is true. They want to make us smart. They do succeed by this senseless drill in making us - jump - half instinctively after a while - through mechanical movements that have no sense in themselves   No - they have found out neither the sensible thing to do - nor a sensible way to do it. That is as far as the human side goes. On the scientific side it seems as if they had got more ahead - but considering their unlimited opportunity of research and experiment I doubt if this is so. No - war is an essentially stupid thing and it condemns the "military mind" which all soldiers (and some of the best) haven't got - to be essentially stupid too (But what else should killing people be - by whatever name we call it?) [...] **71898/102**

Sunday. [?15 October 1916 London]

How it would have amused you - the method of my despatch from Weymouth. I was sent for by the C.O. addressed (jokingly) as 2nd Lieutenant Barker bidden to hurry and buy my officer's badges and get out the kit - to lunch in the officers' mess!! Of course - if you have not felt that semi school - semi prison atmosphere of barracks - at its barrackiest you won't quite get the pleasure of this sudden change. Truth to tell - they had all been very nice to me and it had irked them not to be able to treat me humanly - and now they wanted to. And they did. But <u>how</u> it bored me - their silly stories at lunch about drinking and women - no nothing vile - but full of that deeply vulgar jocularity - a little good talk about their work - that's true. But outside the details of their own job - no real world seems to exist for them at all - And indeed - that was the old army - is the army still - and now the army is governing England - in a way to an extent you can hardly appreciate till you feel it. There must be a new sort of army that we're not <u>fully</u> getting as we believe - and even then it mustn't govern. Not the "soldier mind" **71898/164**

[Messenger quotes John Lucy's account of the 'openly warm' reception he got when being 'dined in' after receiving his commission (2006: 330).]

Sunday. [?mid-October 1916 London]

It would amuse you to see me being saluted - Not the ordinary salute but the other day I was walking past Marlborough House and St. James's and suddenly was conscious of a tremendous demonstration on the part of the sentries – sloping of arms and smacking of rifle-butts and the rest.   So I counter-demonstrated with due formality – And it amused me to feel conscious for the minute of quite a childish sense of added importance at all this.   Now that is all part of the curious quite childish make up of the military mind The good side of it is I think the constant-courtesy and its return (always a good meaning hidden somewhere in these fooleries) but the childish (and God knows one discovers under army rule the dangerous) – side is – that it is part of a constant conspiracy to give rank – as apart from ability – an added sense of importance. A large proportion of generals get to think that they <u>do</u> know better than Colonels – because the Colonels salute them and call them "Sir" – and so on down the ranks   But in the "salut<u>er</u>" it is generally an hypocrisy   he does not look up to the salut<u>ed</u> necessarily and <u>unquestioningly</u> – and there the danger lies – of distrust while you obey. [...] **71898/137**

Tuesday [?16 July 1918] 7am. [Gordon Square, London]

[...] the Offensive has begun again. Oh it makes me rather sick - to sit here making calculations about it while one thinks of what it really means. And if one had anyone really dear – out there. Poor Barrie last night said 'Peter has been put on the Staff"   Usually he gives no sign about the boys. And I with brutal caution felt he mustn't comfort himself too much. But he said so pathetically 'He's attached to a French Division and his new address is at GHQ – I'm thinking that he is safer" And indeed he is. About Michael – <u>the</u> apple of his eye who now has to leave Eton and go practically straight into the Guards he'll hardly trust himself to speak. The Eton boys he says are all keen to go but "This must be the last of the wars"   A General came down the other day to address them about building a hall to <u>drill</u> in as a memorial to the boys fallen in the war. They were polite to the General but there was a great feeling that they would have none of it   No "militarism" at Eton. And when the General said the usual things they only thought him rather a pretentious old fool   No school has given more or lost more than Eton – the casualty list for them is appalling. And still they go and very keenly to 'do the job' But they say we <u>know</u> what this war is like and retired Generals don't. We don't want any 'glorification talk' about it. It is a queer tense point of view for boys of 16 and 17. And those that come back (Peter for one) have got a very clear cold outlook on life and a judgment of people and things. Get all these men away from the army and France and they'll listen rather grimly – or rather I fancy they won't listen to the 'easy-patriot" politician who tries to stoke them up with the usual rhetoric. No – when the older generation passes over things one can see the younger looking at it with a grim and tolerant smile. ¶ Well we're in for another week or two of – God knows what. And I feel in one sense a nothingness because I'm not there – not that in one way I <u>want</u> to be you know darling (I won't pretend that) but I feel Who and what am <u>I</u> that these men should be being killed for me – when twenty years ago it would have been my lot – as it might be now. But all my patriotism must be to be at the office at 9-30. sharp – and push papers through a little better and quicker [...] (**Texas**)

> [My guess is that the **Offensive** was the second battle of the Marne, which began on 15 July. **Michael** Llewellyn-Davies was a younger brother of Peter (see pp.46–47). The visit of the **General** to Eton may have been that of the Duke of Connaught on 10 July, to inspect the cadet corps. Technically his rank was Field Marshal, but he was indeed both retired and elderly.]

8. England

[Saturday 8 July 1916] 9-45PM. [on board the 'New York']

[...] you want to know about the ship? Why I took her instead of the empty Orduna I don't know – to please Cravath I suppose – who has been most kind to me – I can't forget kindnesses – And he was one of God's instruments in my meeting <u>you</u> (for that he'll go to heaven) And kind he still is – but – oh – a Snob – an innocent snob and outspoken – Let people be rich or successful – that's all. Well he has made up one table. A shrewd – twisty faced – kindly capable American – President of a Trust Company or something called I think Bannard. Stuart Wortley – a quite charming – amiable – very British – quite genuine snob (Lady Kinsale – oh yes she was a Mallaby! As you might say She was a Borzoi!) But sensitive and real of his sort. Walker-Leigh – a sham Irish version of the same – talks all the time, knows nothing – gets everything wrong (I have known him on and off for years). Those two talk English affairs and land me in depths of depression – for it is by them – a little better or worse versions of them – that England and her war is being run now   Their spiritual blindness is amazing. And it recalls to me everything I felt in February in France – which made me say – I must keep out of this galley – I can do no good in it. And here I am going back to be put under the thumb of these – oh honourable men enough – of a schoolboy code. But <u>blind</u> – not living in a real world <u>yet</u>. [...] **71897/66**

[For **Cravath** see p.220. Otto T. **Bannard**: President of the New York Trust Company. **Wortley**: Possibly A. Richard Montagu Stuart-Wortley, a lieutenant-general in the army. The **Mallaby** family name was found frequently in Scotland, UK and US at this period. Knoblock uses it in *A War Committee* (1915) but for an 'earnest' woman. **Borzoi**: Fashionable Russian wolf-hound, featured on a cover of *Vogue* in January 1913 and of *Collier's* in May 1913. **Leigh**: Cecil Ainslie Walker-Leigh, briefly an actor before becoming an army officer. His first wife, Decima Moore, divorced him for adultery and cruelty.]

[Sunday 9 July 1916] 12-20 with me – 11-50 with you [on board the 'New York']

[...] Don't think – from what I said yesterday about Stuart-Wortley being a snob that I set myself apart and above him – a pleasant genuine charming fellow. But his thoughts are not thoughts – they are only mental habits – and he himself is not vital – he is only and instance of a Life-habit. It isn't that I'd disagree with him – I like disagreeing with people – when one must – it is that there isn't anything real there to disagree with. **71897/67**

Sunday the 16ᵗʰ [July 1916] 10-15 – <u>5.30.am.</u> [on board the 'New York']

[...] I'm depressed as I approach England – not on personal grounds – but realising for the first time how England has always depressed me – and how little English I am. That's odd isn't it – for in another way I'm very English indeed – in the way I hope that makes you love me the better for it! But the England that I love and do seem to belong to is partly the England of Nature and for the rest an England of my dreams – the England too of the poets and thinkers and the people who have fought for her – for what she should be – so often by fighting bitterly against what she was. But the England of the successful man – of the popular newspaper – of the London club – of the politicians – that can never be my England I feel. Less and less can I be or want to be any of those things or mix in any of those places. So what most English qualities will my dear one love me for? Just as when I was that romantic thing – an actor (romantic!! oh my dear Helen! baby!) I refused to succeed in the theatre as it was. Yes dear – honestly I did – I could have been a successful actor – if 12 years ago I had made up my mind to be. No – never. These are not perversities with me indeed. I have followed and do follow a <u>call</u> in choosing not these things – but others – and the others leading me to you and <u>our</u> life instead. [...] **71897/94-95**

[The irony about acting being **romantic** is a response to her comment 'It gives me a fearful – yet delightful thrill – to think of your having been an actor – as if you had been a gypsy chief! Those are old-fashioned, last-century instincts stirring, amusingly, in me' (71904/49). Twelve years earlier, in 1904, he did five significant roles, including Keegan in *John Bull's Other Island* and Pierrot in *Prunella*.]

[Tuesday 18 July 1916] 10-45PM. – <u>4-45PM.</u> [Cholsey]

[...] J.M. has written a book on the Gallipoli expedition – authorised by the Foreign office – and I have the yet uncensored M.S. to read tonight. He has been shown the official papers and knows the truth about it – and what a truth as far as our rulers are concerned   Heart breaking – these men sent to their death (as usual) by shere official muddling and incompetence – and then – as bad – scapegoats made ¶ My dear – my dear – but I'm depressed about my country. Those who after all cannot travail in thought – going blindly, cheerfully, trustfully out to give their lives – an honest thing to do   Those who can think – not thinking honestly. And those who are trained both to think and feel – letting the moral currency be debased   And you feel every hour you are here – that its lower – lower yet. This is not mere pessimism darling   It is alas I fear the real effect of war – as apart from the ideal effect that a mortal struggle should bring – a purging of the nation's soul. That still remains to do. How? **71897/102**

[J.M.: John Masefield. *Gallipoli* (London: William Heinemann, 1916). Barker implies the initiative was Masefield's and, elsewhere, says it was intended for the American market. Masefield was probably encouraged to write it as part of the propaganda campaign whereby famous authors wrote in support of England's claim to moral righteousness in the war (Wright 1978).]

Wednesday night [19 July 1916] 11-15PM – <u>5-15PM.</u> [Ayot]

[...] Did I say to you that my England was the England of Nature and of the Poets? Oh I felt it so – going down to that quiet ancient Berkshire country. The first feeling of joy I have had in England – since the war began   And then back to London – and to that Red Cross office – Dukes and Duchesses – the clever lawyer the bureaucrat – the politician – the smart woman – (and the patient clients and hangers on) – these people who pretend to govern us while they exploit themselves – I have <u>nothing</u> in common with them - I hate them – if they were England I could learn to hate England. And that feeling will grow. There's Barrie - in flashes - as bitter - and bitterer than I am. It is the common people who are fighting and boys just fresh from school – and many quite simple men – to whom this world of "social graft" is unknown. While this ring of exploiters who should be keen of mind at least to do their share – are still blaspheming patri-otism – yes they are. For not from one of their prejudices and follies and vanities have they really purged themselves. Projected from the plane of England at peace – when they did nothing creative – and it didn't matter – to the plane of England at war – when they still do nothing creative – and England's spirit – insofar as they prompt it – rots under them – and men's lives are thrown away for lack of any real <u>meaning</u> in these <u>parasites</u>. Oh you'd feel it in your bones as I do – if you come within touch of them.¶ This Gallipoli business – JM has seen all the papers. He daren't write the truth he tells me. The Censor would never pass it – there'd be an outcry – the truth would be <u>made</u> into a lie. The truth is – that these men were slaughtered – because at home – where brains should have been keen – brains have been rotted by London – the "West End" – the inner ring of political-social London as it is   No real moral and intellectual fibre. And when they get a man keen highly trained sensitive – set on high standards – when they get him among them – as he must get among them – to be part of the governing machine at all – there's a conspiracy to soften him, to make him think that "it'll do" – to put him a little "crooked" – make him a hedonist. ¶ No – my darling this is not monomania with me. This is the real tragedy of England. And what is to be the end of it I do not know.   We who have to think and imagine – struggling against this conspiracy almost in vain Those who have to fight and <u>do</u> things – being wasted – their lives and energy – because of these – <u>blood-suckers</u>. [...] **71897/105-6**

[The **Berkshire country** was that around Cholsey. Barker goes to the **Red Cross office** because they want him to revise the ending of his book ('I think I shall have to make a P.S. to my book – from the point of view of the critic and not of the advocate. They <u>are</u> irritating' 71897/104); see also p.82.]

Monday. [?mid-September 1916 Trowbridge barracks]

[He quotes an English folk-song: 'When I was gay and in my pride']

Isn't it simple – and in its way quite beautiful? I write it from memory – but that is how such things were handed on – changing in the process. So Murray says of Homer   Well that was the song of a whole nation   These are only the songs of peasants – peasants kept down too to their soil: but even so music springs from them and it. And I think it is the only true way music can spring – from those in touch with reality.   And if we can get our people – all of them – not only the peasants in touch with reality and not shams – the realities of modern life are not the soil necessarily of course – why then we may have an artistic people again – a people happy in expressing themselves. Mayn't we? You know about Spain – my dear – England your grand-fatherland – has its beauties too – and I want you to love the England of her unknown poets. [...] **71898/54**

[Gilbert **Murray** in *The Rise of the Greek Epic* (1907) proposes an 'evolutionary model' of Homer. The importance of a people '**expressing themselves**' recurs emphatically in 'The Promise of an American Theatre', p.14.]

Sunday [5 November 1916 Bloomsbury, London]

I looked in at lunch time to the Arts and Crafts Exhibition. Do you know about it – it's almost the only genuine artistic movement in England? Most of it good – some of it very very good indeed. One was proud for it was real art – real expression and really English. And it sprang from the war – some of the paintings and carvings – from a great and dignified feeling about the war – as far removed from the horrible brawling caddish vindictive newspapers as white from black ¶ Oh I wished you had been there. Some great decorative things – clean and simple – and a lot of clean glad colour ¶ While there is that feeling for beauty and that purpose one need never despair need one ¶ I wish – I wish – my dear had been with me (I always wish <u>that</u>!) but I would have liked to be showing you something that was England's life and a promise of her future – the real England – not the politicians place but the artist's. [...] **71898/140**

[The **Arts and Crafts** Society's Exhibition at the Royal Academy of Arts, London, 9 October-20 November 1916.]

Thursday – Friday [21-22 December 1916] 12-30am Thursday <u>7-30PM</u> [Bloomsbury, London]

Packing! A weird process with me since I have been "living in my boxes" for 18 months – and I shed things all over the place – and wonder where they are – and always carry about a lot more than I want – a bad habit of mine – But I must carry books   fancy being stranded with nothing to read. and I always think I <u>might</u> wear clothes. Besides as an old traveller now I know there is no difference between two trunks and three.   Take either a toothbrush – or take all you want. Otherwise – office! and lunch with a man – Sutro the playwright a good fellow – fond of me I know for which I'm grateful but – no – not interesting   Office! to dine with an old friend – a good fellow too   more interesting – but he is prolixly troubled about the state of England. Well he may be but it is no use being prolix about it.   England either has life or she hasn't. With life she'll win through – without it she'll wither. She has life I believe but I do think that our capitalist class – the exploiters – and they have a tight grip on things just now – that's the tragedy the <u>real</u> tragedy of this war, it becomes a war of property it seems one can hardly prevent it – I think this class of governors is guiding England into paths unnatural to her where her true genius may not shine [...] **71898/280-81**

[If **'living in my boxes'** began 18 months before 22 December, it started around 20 June 1915, when Barker and McCarthy sailed back to England.]

Tuesday [4 June 1918] 7am. [Gordon Square, London]

[...] And as to Sir W.W. they gave him a C.B. yesterday and thereby hangs a tale. My Colonel (not my <u>Chief</u>) told me of it and in a voice trembling with emotion said he was glad. But the emotion was really jealousy of a kind because he is only a C.M.G. (<u>I</u> know – it being my business to know these things because – poor dear –

apropos something entirely different he remarked a few minutes earlier that 'perhaps he had a petty nature'!). But isn't it awful that bits of ribbon can turn grown men into children like this? I suppose an Honours list brings more unhappiness to those left out than a Casualty list brings (God forgive me that joke!). There are two things perhaps worth having in England the V.C. and the O.M. And the OM is a <u>little</u> doubtful and the V.C. may be. Gordon - who had the stuff of a great man in him - the more so perhaps because he was a little mad - protested against the creation of the V.C. on the ground that any soldier who wouldn't earn it if he got the chance ought to have his uniform stripped off him and that you mustn't decorate men for 'chances'. Which is a 'hard saying' but like most hard sayings -- Well beloved we may be proudest that we belong to the great Republic of Letters and - by our works ye shall know us. Fancy knighting Blake or Bunyan - or Dickens or Ruskin or Carlyle Carlyle on one knee to little George V Of course though it was different with little Victoria. If people want to keep Monarchy going they should have nothing but Queens reigning. (**Texas**)

[**W.W.**: William Wiseman. **C.B.**: Companion of the Order of the Bath. **Colonel**: In Intelligence Barker remained a member of his regiment. **Chief**: Cumming. **C.M.G**: Companion of the Order of St Michael and St George. **V.C.**: Victoria Cross. **O.M.**: Order of Merit. **Gordon**: Major-General Charles George Gordon ('of Khartoum').]

9. RACE, CLASS AND DEMOCRACY

Sunday Feb 6. [1916] Boulogne 4-45 (lunch time for you!)
[...] Tonight I go off to dine with the Commissioner – I rather gather he wants to talk to me. The queerest mixture of company here as I told you – the jolliest sort of young Englishman in this morning on his way back to the front – the modern young landlord – administering an estate in the country for the welfare of his tenants but with no illusions about them. Conservative probably with more Socialist ideas than a whole bunch of Liberals put together – the sense of English country in his bones – but with a book of French poetry in his pocket to read on his journey. It would all interest you – and we'll talk – we'll talk. (oh and the whole lot was topped off the other day by the ex-King of Portugal – who now works for the Red Cross and turns up occasionally [...]
71897/29

[The Red Cross **Commissioner** in Boulogne, as from December 1914, was Colonel Sir Courtauld Thomson. The **ex-King** was Manuel II, ousted from power by the revolution of October 1910.]

Monday [?25 May 1916 Williamstown, MA, USA]
[...] I'm not the usual sort of patriot I know – but a patriot I am   I have always cared intensely about public things.   And it was one of the things – one of them – that drew me to you first – that you care intensely too   I have nothing to say to private-minded people and to public minded I forgive much – don't you? I want a country to be able to express itself.   And that implies a great deal   For the "exploiters" who used only to know how to exploit a few at a time now learn how to exploit whole nations and to do that among our democracies – they must first discourage the people's real expression and conspire with lawyers and journalists to put ready-made feelings and thoughts into them   And they don't – then – the

exploiters need to do any genuine thinking themselves. If the people truly feel then they will throw up leaders that must truly think. And you say (I have the letter over my heart now I feel it there) There are great souls in obscure and untrained men – That's a good thought dear one – We must always build on it. **71898/116**

Monday [?May-June 1916 Williamstown, MA, USA]

There must be a great tendency coming in America to "class destruction". Partly the natural re-action against extreme democracy – partly because I think of the emancipation of such a number of "lower" races I have no foolish ideas about "Latin decadence" and that sort of thing I hope. But there is no doubt I think that there are forward and backward national types – <u>racial</u> types rather And certainly I have quite a different feeling towards some of these – squat – big mouthed – low-browed folk I meet to what I have to the roughest English peasant. They're not conceivably intermarriageable I feel – and that is the final test. I am all for class destructions – but founded on any and every other basis than they are founded on now ¶ Fastidious – oh you dainty thing. But I'm as fastidious of you – I boast to be. And one should be. Only healthy with it. And I think we are. A ploughman that's all right – It's the cad or the greasy Jewess with diamonds on her – ! [...] **71898/130**

[Thursday 13 July 1916] 12 o'clock. – 9-20. [on board the 'New York']

[...] At breakfast I only meet old Bannard with his flattened twisted face. He talks to me of American politics (when I can make him) and that is interesting. He ran for Mayor in New York in 1910 – or /12 was it? There is this to note about him – he is but one generation from an Oxfordshire peasant – and an able public spirited man – falsifying therefore all the commonplace political things that people say in England about class distinctions and heredity – but – justifying – I should think – a lot of things they might say and don't. Shrewd – with no fineness – he is I think – Honest – one need not qualify that. Honesty is the same for all. Sympathetic but not sensitive.   Curious and enterprising – but unimaginative. Now we don't want to be ruled by <u>that</u> – there the Tories are right. But have we to take that as the price of getting rid of the Tories – with their shere lack of vital qualities without which all their taste and knowledge count for nothing. Have we to go through the phase of being under these men, till out of them or the mixture of them and the older governing stocks – spring the finer qualities we do want. That is happening in America of course – and the system makes it happen badly. I mean – you are apt to get the worst of such men and not the best. As to England – I don't know. We want to get rid of the lawyers there – with their dead minds. I hate lawyers – unless they are creative lawyers – who rise so to speak – to the constructive poetry of Law. Then they're great. But how few! [...] **71897/80**

[**Bannard** ran for Mayor in 1909, coming second.]

Tuesday. [25 July 1916 ?Hotel Russell, London]

I was amused the other day when I went to the Barracks where I am to enlist. I had a letter of introduction from a man in the War Office to the Colonel – just such a letter as one man would give to another. But because I was going to enlist the Colonel felt he must begin to put me in my "place". So he addressed me as "Granville Barker" though I had never met him before – and he did not rise from his desk and he kept me standing. And the next morning when I had to go again he called me in and called me Barker and kept me standing all the time. Quite courteous otherwise – and of course the situation is difficult   But – isn't it odd to have to do things like that to mark your "position" And more oddly – I seemed to feel only an added dignity because I was kept standing there. Is that how servants feel? The mark of civilisation is good manners – natural – unenforced.   The French have them – we at our best have them.   The Germans have them only as they are taught. [...] **71898/27**

[**Colonel:** see p.81.]

Wednesday. [?13 September 1916 Trowbridge barracks]
In this officer's cadet corps that I am passing through one gets an idea of what the British Empire really means – for there are men from all over it training for commissions. Many of them have been over in France fighting already – if ever people had <u>rights</u> to a commission – (for they have been fighting in the ranks) – they have. And one sees the coming too of an Imperial Democracy – for they are many of them what one would call quite "common" fellows – the old army would never have dreamed of them as officers – "the men will only follow a gentleman" was the cry. Whether we will or not that has to be altered for there are not enough "gentlemen" to go round in an army of 5 millions and more. So I am seeing a remarkable thing – the balance of power in this great Empire (a wrong name for it for it will have nothing in common with an Emperor or King) – in this great Commonwealth shift As a whole the problem is still too big to grasp but one can grasp the tendency – towards a real Democracy – towards such an organisation as the U.S.A. Oh – with great blundering and much wanton obstruction - but I think we can see – and help towards (<u>We</u>) – a future for our race. **71898/39**

Wednesday. [?11 October 1916 Weymouth]
[...] it's about manners it came to me – the idea. I dined out last night with one of the Cadets and his wife and our Lieutenant-Instructor was there – we treat him in barracks with enormous respect. He is a "ranker" – and as far as a dinner table goes – well he just isn't the thing. Not vulgar you know or blatant – but not the thing. Now what does it matter – I mean really how much validity is there in our discomfort when our etiquette is ignored and things make us "shrivel" a little? Well – I discovered last night, watching him that the manners matter just so long as they spring from some real consideration for other people Half the time of course he wasn't natural – he was trying to say the "right thing" – when the natural thing would have been right. But now and again I noticed – I thought – a really wrong thought. There it is I suppose – good manners tell you what you ought to <u>feel</u> for people – and

the best manners aren't the empty form but – at the worst – a reminder to yourself of what you should be feeling (Very trite philosophy)   My real thought though was – that Democracy is upon us – here in England as never before And if our contribution (or one of them) is to be manners to the crowd – it is the meaning and implication of manners we must teach. I'd teach it just as I'd teach the meaning of discipline in the army. No one ever does. [...] **71898/161-62**

Friday. Nov 24 [1916] 7-15am – <u>2-15am</u> [Bloomsbury, London]
[...] Yes I'm a lieutenant – and it isn't <u>very</u> wonderful – only quite convenient   What is better – and really wonderful – oh <u>really</u> – that I work in an office where I am a human being among other human beings. Such a "spreading of atmosphere" by one personality – the chief's. I've seldom met such a noticeable thing. And not in the least because he's a martinet (that he makes it all very efficient) or that he puts on airs of omniscience of kindness He's always asking for advice – and sometimes talking quite foolishly and making mistakes – and losing his temper But he just "is"   something that can't be imitated – and it matters. He is "alive" and it keeps an office of 60 people alive too. ¶   No – you don't address me as Lieutenant!! I'm Mr till I'm a Captain – and that please heaven I shall never be – or the war will have lasted much too long. ¶   Now I must leave your letter for it's 8 o'clock – 3 o'clock with you – my darling and you are sleeping – I put my head down by you and bless you, my darling. The mail goes early today. I must finish this soon then. What to say to you? ¶   The war? Oh there's much doubt in England – much weariness and pessimism – much doubt of our leaders who <u>won't</u> lead. But that's unfair for we're a democracy – at least we boasted we were though it was never true – and therefore we shouldn't be helpless – incompetent   We should be able to think and act in a disciplined way for ourselves We can't and we don't – and we have taken the power from them to make us – taken power from them – can't use it ourselves hand it back to them and they can't use it now. I fear that is true and it is the worst of the picture – bad enough. But we stick to it – and the people who see

their work plain (the soldier's fighting) do it well – that I'm sure. They may save us – but it is all that can. [...] **71898/260-61**

['**chief**': Cumming.]

Thursday [mid-April 1918] 7-15 am. [Gordon Square, London]
    [...] 'The harlot's cry from street to street
    Shall weave old England's winding sheet
    The winner's shout, the loser's curse,
    Dance before dead Englands hearse
And when I think of <u>all</u> that means – sins of luxury – sins of greed – I do tremble sometimes. I've no fear of Germans – I mean for England (personally I sit at home in safety – I've no right even to <u>talk</u> about Germans!) but I do believe that a man or a country – a man in himself or his children – a country in her generations – do have to pay the price of their sins – and all the virtues in store – all the sacrifice (I know that England is sacrificing now) may not suffice to pay. The Lord may be merciful but it's as well not to count on his mercy – he is not sentimental that is certain And many bills have been sent in for payment during this war one can't choose one's time for paying them. Ireland – the bill of the people who had only learned how to make money and now they have had to make 'sinews of war' – even when they mean well in a vague sort of way – can't get out of the habit. The bill of the people who have despised knowledge – oh that is a heavy one – I wonder how many lives we have lost in this war merely because we would <u>not</u> take Education – science and art seriously. I've crossed the channel – how many times on boats full of officers – with <u>staff</u> officers sprinkled thick. We <u>have</u> good men but sprinkled thin – and – here's the point – never known or sought for – never 'considered' their worth not a passport to anything – except a living for them and to have 'profit' made out of them. And now of course but for a very few that have been found or have found themselves they are being wasted and their spirits broken. This isnt personal bitterness – for I know that I happened on my life work in something so far removed from things war-like that though I <u>might</u> have served my

country with all I had – I did make a feeble try but I hadn't been wasted in peace time how much less in war –so I'm content enough – except for a little foolish grumbling which my dear forgives?! to recognise that I am ignorant and go on being an office boy and learning – but every week every day I meet the wasted men ¶ Oh but I'm being very gloomy. Well – my heart there is trouble ahead and what makes me gloomier is that very few people – oh no there must be very many the thing is so patent but yesterday that damned club of mine was 'giggling' away – there's no other word. [...] **(Texas)**

[The verse quotation is from William Blake's 'Auguries of Innocence'. **Ireland** was resisting an attempt to impose conscription by means of a Military Service Bill, which was debated in mid-April.]

Sunday [5 May 1918] 6-40am. [Gordon Square, London]

[...] Crowds of sparrows in the ugly little flagged garden down below (And the people next door I see keep a Belgian hare - poor thing trying to make a burrow - Uncongenial soil!) These ugly little London gardens are the final mockery of the English idea of 'a house and land' - his resolute refusal to be made into a town dweller - a creature in rooms. Even I can remember the coming of the 'Flat' in London - we were some of the earliest dwellers in them - and the strenuous objection there was to it. Sensible logical French who said "A town is a town and the country the country" - And yet - and yet - The feeling for a house and land. I part company with many Socialists just over things like that. Not that I'm a 'Belloc-ian' peasant-proprietor - and I think that France for all it has to its credit side in material prosperity over this - has much to its debit in the national selfishness - self-centredness it seems to engender - reduction of birthrate - to 'fit' the land "dot" to buy the land and the failure as a whole of French colonising   in fact your peasant-proprietor does not tend to make either a world citizen or an idealist (He can carve his god in the end out of a vegetable marrow grown too big and tough for eating!) But all the same it isn't statesmanship I feel to cut a man clear from any instinctive base of his feelings and thoughts. For ages now – oh many hundred years since any of the blood of West Europe ceased to be nomads – as man has felt <u>safe</u> in his bit of soil his citizen self respect has grown on that (The Out-<u>law</u> was always called the 'landless' man) And though now many of us can say 'My mind to me a kingdom is' – and certainly I've no land hunger – I can enjoy other people's fields and forests as if they were my own – as long as there are no Trespasser notices about! (a big 'as long') and though I think that our serious cultivation – yours and mine had better be our brains and imaginations and our garden only for pleasure – still even with us – well Groombridge meant something that a mere flat wouldn't – that a mere 'house' wouldn't (and quite apart from its beauty) – and of this I am quite sure – these stock and share makers of riches have damned our civilisation pretty much living on <u>their</u> brains and imagination – or lack of it! – No I'm not prepared with a 'clean cut' from the 'house and land' gospel [...] (**Texas**)

[Hilaire **Belloc**, poet and essayist, outlines his social ideal in *The Servile State* (1912). '**dot**': A dowry. The quotation in the penultimate sentence is the opening of a poem by Edward Dyer. **Groombridge**: A country house on the border of Kent and Sussex that Barker and Huntington hoped to rent.]

10. MY HISTORY PLAYS

We first hear of a new writing project in July 1916 when Barker was sailing to England to join up.

....

[Thursday] 13 July [1916] 9-20 – <u>6-50</u>. [on board the 'New York']
I've picked up Froude's historical studies – so <u>English</u> – And I read them eagerly for more and more it seems to me that these History plays of mine if I can do them <u>may</u> be – <u>might</u> be my life's real work. Perhaps I'm not a creator so much as a creative interpreter. That would fit. And I know they want doing – because for this re-making of England that has to be after this war must go an imaginative knowledge of her history – such as most people have not got now – such as plays could most easily give them. And dear – I do like to think of it as my life-work because the sort of work it is seems to fit so well with the sort of life we shall like to lead – the groundwork of serious reading and imaginative thought – the leisure for the things to germinate Such day-dream that seems now – But we can bring it true. **71897/82**

> [James Anthony **Froude:** *Short Studies on Great Subjects* (first publ. 1867-82). Froude sees Tudor rule as the key period in English history, when Protestant reformers fought for liberty against the 'darkness' of Roman Catholicism.]

Friday Aug 4 [1916] 11PM – <u>5PM</u>. [Ayot]
[...] Diary – my dear – I was in town all day. First at the barracks to get a uniform – much waiting about but the sergeants and people are civil and kind in their puzzled way – puzzled a little they are at such a creature as I – and others like me I suppose – becoming 'gunners'. And in the afternoon I went to tea at Downing Street following a letter from Elisabeth Asquith begging me to – partly that they have

been good friends to me – and in their way I think really fond of me (but their way is not my way and never can be) – partly I did not want to seem to be skulking here and avoiding people. So I went – found only Elisabeth – had half an hour's "witty" talk with her (heaven help us!). In the Cabinet room there is a relief map of the country the troops are now fighting over. I walked in to see it. That should impress one I suppose – the historic room in which so much of the British Empire has been made – and that miniature piece of country – where it is being made again (one has to keep on making things again) or lost. As I feel over "Greens – Short History of the English People" which I have got and shall take to barracks – as a text book for the history plays that someday will come from me I hope. If I'm asked why – "To see if we can't make it a little longer" [...] **71897/130-31**

[**Elisabeth Asquith**: The daughter of Prime Minister Asquith, reputedly precocious and 'radical' with an interest in organising cultural works. For **Green** see below.]

....

Although he read Froude, John Richard Green's *Short History of the English People* (1874, repr. 1915, Everyman Library) was Barker's 'text book'. We therefore need to know a little about it. My brief account is from Brundage (1994: 80): 'The organizing principle of the Short History is an emphasis on social and cultural history at the expense of political and military accounts.' This history is explored by focussing on the lives of key representative and significant individuals, not necessarily of the ruling order. Important groups included seventeenth-century Levellers and the Saxon freemen. The healthy practices of self-government and 'common deliberation', supposedly 'natural' to the English, were threatened by the rise of oligarchies and social inequality. For Green 'cultural vitality' was as important as 'political freedom'. Intellectuals had a leadership role: the fourteenth-century 'aggrieved masses' needed 'the inspiration of the men of ideas'. While in Froude's pro-Protestant history Henry VIII is celebrated for creating a strong state, Green was highly critical of centralised Tudor despotism and praised instead the new learning and the 'free discussion' facilitated by the Reformation (1994: 82–89). Brundage summarises: 'Informed throughout by an advanced liberalism, the book was markedly critical of monarchy, aristocracy, and the traditional authority of the Church of England' (1994: 121).

....

Wednesday. [?mid-August 1916 SJW barracks]
I've told you haven't I about my plan for a series of History "Panel" plays oh a great number of them   little episodes of twenty minutes each arranged in groups of four or five – with a "Reader" to make the history part clear and connect the plays and point out their unity of idea – a sort of poetical-historical-philosophical narrative running in between. And the plays themselves quite simple. Edward I and Henry III with the body of Simon de Montfort. Wyclif at Lutterworth A Saxon Freeman making himself a slave to pay his debts – putting his head between his new master's hands.   Pepys visiting the Navy and finding all the old Commonwealth names (that they had won victories under) taken off the ships and they being called Royal Charles's and James's and such like – they were to go to defeat under those. I make notes for subjects every now and then – and I must see I don't lose them. Ten years work in this – when autumn is just beginning – between 50 and 60. They must be done with a calm clear mind. Shall we have an American series? Will you think of episodes for that (Franklin's first meeting with his wife?) Does the plan please my dear – my friend? **71898/117**

> [**Wyclif** in retirement at Lutterworth revised his translation of the Bible which Green calls 'the great weapon which ... was to produce so terrible an effect on the triumphant hierarchy' (1926: 244). If the project were to take ten years Barker would be 48 when he finished. His sense that **autumn** was begin-ning came from the unusually cold, and in mid-August very wet, weather.]

Sunday [20 August 1916] 11-30am – <u>5-30am</u> [Ayot]

[...] oh – beloved – how your mind does jump to mine. How <u>always</u> you say the right thing – the thing that illuminates a problem for me. About the 20 minute – history plays. I'd only been thinking – or mostly so far – of their material – and then you say at once – about the Japanese Pillar Pictures – the difficulty of the form (a thing I take real delight in – instinctive delight in a difficult form) and the "few essential lines" – At once, you see – you add a new "value" for me – illumine the thing – make – in this case – (you see!) a "finer" thing of it. [...] 71897/147

> [Her comment was: '**the twenty-minute plays** – a <u>delightful</u> idea – and – somehow it makes me think of what I have just read in an article on Japanese pillar-prints' (71903/97). Huntington shares her interest in Japanese art with many up-to-the-minute writers.]

Saturday [?26 August 1916 Gordon Square, London]

This afternoon I went a few yards out of my way to look at Rodin's Burghers of Calais – outside our House of Lords here now. It is a masterpiece of sculpture – a difficult thing – supremely difficult done with supreme ease – so it seems. I remembered it was just a year ago that I – on my way from Boulogne to Dunkirk – made the car turn aside in Calais to look at it there ¶ Strange – wouldn't it have seemed – to the Burghers to feel that they would be immortalised in effigy in the town they had fought for and in the England they were fighting. History – a wonderful thing rightly thought of. And one is right to choose the salient moments with which to impress people's imagination. They may get thus the key to the understanding of a whole nation's work and worth.   Darling – it was so good that you "jumped" to my panel play scheme – for I want – oh I do want that to be <u>our</u> work – it seems like it to me – as if it suited us peculiarly Science of history there has been but the "art" of history – there is – I think – a little untrodden corner of that – for <u>us</u>. [...] 71898/45

> [Auguste **Rodin's** monument to the Burghers of Calais was completed in 1889, designed for Calais; of the four casts, one went to London in 1911.]

Saturday. [?mid-September 1916 Trowbridge barracks]

Sweetheart – think of the little panel pictures of bye-ways of American history (your share) as I think of them   search for them in English history. And here is one for you. I pick it from the Evening Post which follows me to England. Forts Donelson and Henry were captured in the Civil War through Lincoln sending privately a woman Anna Ella Carroll to report on the Mississippi situation – it was her suggestion and she drew up a full plan – and Grant was sent to do the job. Then (when the job was done) there were discussions in the Senate and the House as to whose was the brilliant plan – and she sat in the gallery listening. But the Cabinet decided it would antagonise army leaders if they knew they had followed the direction of a civilian – and a woman   So nothing was said about that. Her reply was only to hand them a plan for taking Vicksburg and Island 10. ¶ Oh the irony of it! We need – and more and more – to know the truth of history and the little things often shed the brightest light on the bigger stretches. Our job! **71898/52**

[**Evening Post**: *Evening Post* (New York), 28 August 1916, p. 8. **Island 10** was at the Kentucky Bend of the Mississippi River.]

Saturday [?7 October 1916 Weymouth]

Weymouth – a quaint old place. George III used to come here – yes – about the time that you rebelled against me – and the place as a seaside resort grew up round him. And he used to bathe – solemnly – and the populace would gather on the beach to see him – and once – a band played God save the King when he went in and the crowd cheered when he ducked his head. But after he died the place stagnated rather – so the old Georgian houses remain – and the shops and inns and assembly rooms – all very full of 'character' and ugly-pretty to look at. I like their plain uncompromising fronts – though it is about all of the 18th Century I do like – its architecture. But I like that too for its history   Oh – when shall I get to my history work? Have you been thinking of it – thinking of American bits? [...] **71898/105**

[**rebelled**: He refers to the American War of Independence.]

Tuesday morning [31 October 1916] 7-45am – <u>2-45am</u> [Bloomsbury, London]

[...] well I was up and reading after all by a quarter to seven – reading history. There's comfort in that – it gives me vision – and I plan work from it (you know) as one likes to plan and may – work that one sees the beginning of and not the end [...]

Tuesday midnight <u>7PM.</u>

[...] At seven this evening when I left I went to call on Mrs J.R.Green – for I wanted to find out if her husband (who wrote the 'Short History') had left any bibliography or private notes of his own which would be useful for the history plays. Well – he hadn't but she began at once to reel off the names of book after book – out of his library I daresay - or her own (she writes history herself of course) – the sort of book that I need – that would take years of mere searching to find And I seemed to see though I didn't need to see – by her being so quick in the "uptake" how alive the idea was – and more and more I felt There – please God – is a life work – and I came away happy thinking of that – and of you. [...]

71898/214-15

[**Mrs J.R. Green** was Alice Stopford Green (1847-1929), Irish historian and nationalist.]

Sunday night [12 November 1916] 11-45PM – <u>6-45PM.</u> [Ayot]

[...] I woke early this morning – before light – and asked our clock the time. It said half past twelve – that meant half past five with me. I wondered were you still awake and lay and loved you and sent my love to you. And then suddenly an 'idea' came – as they will. About my "history" plays – I'll have I think two "readers" before the curtain – probably a man and a woman and each with a book – a book of the Past and a book of the Future. And I'll do the linking up of the plays and their "explanation" by dialogue And that idea having arrived I went to sleep again [...]

71898/236

[Tuesday] Nov 14. [1916] 10PM – 5PM. [Bloomsbury, London]
[...] I came to another decision this morning about my history plays. I shall tackle first the 17th Century and then I think the 13th get all I can out of those That narrows down the reading a bit. The things are beginning to shape (I believe the dialogue in front of the curtain between the reader's may be quite good I shall let them argue and dispute over the broad aspects of historical questions – point the moral and adorn the tales – and then when they are getting too abstruse of acrimonious – the curtain will go up – or rather the curtains will part – on quite a simple story about people who just went ahead and did their little part – unconscious perhaps of the deeper implications of the time – making history unknow-ingly. Then when its over the 'readers' comment – and perhaps argue again – or perhaps agree this time – and I wish I could write poetry.   But they may have to quote poetry that there mayn't be always a combative mood – and so on leading to the next little play. Do you like it? ¶ Oh but it means much reading – much soaking in the times till you forget you have learned things and they become quite simple. I shan't even start them for two or three years – much to be done before then. [...] **71898/238**

Sunday. [?mid-November 1916 Bloomsbury, London]
[...] I took down my Green's History to see if I could drop across an idea for one of the 'panel' plays (you remember) And I opened the book at random and found – the setting out of the Pilgrim Fathers – and <u>that</u> pleased me – you won't wonder why. And here's the idea. A belated 'Pilgrim Father' who could not make up his mind to leave England with the others – driven away by – let us say – the removal of the Communion Table back from the Nave to the Chancel – that the last straw. Of course the point would be in all the other stories. Then I looked round as to where to make a note of this – and – here's the best place isn't it? Will you remember it for me? And I found a quotation – good for one of my lectures and the point that battling for an art involves self sacrifice (though artists are supposed egoists) and should. Someone writing from England to console the Fathers in the early days of hardship "Let it

not be grievous unto you that you have been instrumental to break the ice for others. The honour shall be yours to the world's end" It has the clear cut fineness of that time hasn't it. A good phrase – and good if we can make the spirit of history so live. **71898/183**

[The account of the **Communion Table** and the quotation are in Green (1926: 508, 513). Barker mentions starting work on the **lectures** in a letter from 16 November.]

Although we have no more of his letters about this, Huntington writes on 28 June 1917:

'I think you've found the <u>essential</u> thought for the 'panel' plays – the growth of the idea of Freedom. It will be the thread to string your separate conceptions on – and will bring unity and beauty out of fragments. I see it all – quite clearly – now – as a thing of significance and beauty – also much originality. And what fun you will have doing it' (71905/247).

....

A COUNTRY ABLE TO EXPRESS ITSELF:
THE HISTORY PLAYS IN CONTEXT

Increasingly during the war Barker, like his friends, was concerned about what England would be like when the war ended. More specifically, the question was about the sort of democracy that would emerge. This question had become pressing for Barker, because the war had produced an England he did not like. This was an England run by the military and controlled by the 'exploiters'. Both were assisted by newspapers that whipped up hatred. For Barker there was another England, which he characterised as that of nature and the poets. Traces of this England could be seen and felt in its countryside, in the work of the Arts and Crafts movement, in survivals of folk song. As against the language of newspapers, the language of folk song enabled a different sort of England to express itself. A country being able to express itself was, then, the key to the establishment of a democracy that was not distorted by the military and the exploiters.

History thus becomes important, because a people that knows its history is more able to express itself. But there is history and history. In John Green's *Short History* (1874 repr. 1915) Barker found a history not of military campaigns and politics but of culture and society, lives lived among the middling sort as well as the great. Green's focus on particular individuals, in all their complexity, provided a dramatist with almost ready-made scenes which through individual acts could exemplify historical moments. Such human-centred and graspable history could facilitate the self-expression of a people.

To aid accessibility Barker devised a mode that was a combination of acting-out and narrating, or, as we might say in a different context, of epic and gestus. Furthermore it only required simple material elements so it could be done almost anywhere. That sort of consideration was crucial for a dramatist who disliked theatre as business and believed that society and democracy could re-build themselves through the making of drama in town and village halls. But this simplicity was very far from a banalisation of dramatic method. If anything it was exactly the reverse. Barker wanted his plays to be like Japanese 'pillar pictures', a difficult form with its distillation into a 'few essential lines' (71897/147). This was the technique of high art in the service of popular democracy, unlike much so-called Modernism. It is a pity that the history plays never got off the drawing-board.

AFTER THE HISTORY PLAYS

Nothing more from him about the history plays has come to light after the letter of 14 November, by which time he knew he was going to be able to do his lecture tour of the United States early in 1917. The three-month tour took him across the whole country, during which time he was also working for British Intelligence (see p.101). Yet the creative work persisted. Huntington was asked to report in detail on the production of *The Morris Dance* and he finished off his play *Farewell to the Theatre*, begun just under a year earlier. Soon after he got back to England he picked up on the history plays again: Huntington responded to a letter about them from late May-June 1917. She also tells us that in mid-May 1917 he was planning a production of *Peer Gynt* (for the Stage Society), which occupied him over the summer, until it was shelved around 20 November in favour of Maud Cunard's idea of doing Byron's *Manfred*. That too was shelved. In late August-September he briefly thought about writing a play about the case of Lieutenant Malcolm who shot a man whom he suspected of trying to take away his wife. But Huntington agreed that this was a bad idea. A new play, *Vote by Ballot*, was staged on 16 December, while he was also exploring options for directing the English translation of Maeterlinck's *Les Fiançailles/The Betrothal*.

But alongside this activity there was another new project. In February 1918 Huntington refers to his 'idea for the International drama'. Although she found it 'ingenious and amusing' there was a problem: 'don't you think you have a tendency toward using your wit and imagination toward solving difficult – sometimes unessential – problems? I mean – don't you think you're sometimes attracted to the path that no one wants to take – just <u>because</u> no one wants to take it?' His idea suffered, she thought, from 'self-imposed difficulties – like leaping from continent to continent and race to race and country to country in three acts' (71912/72-73). While back in summer 1916 the history play project grew from thoughts about reconstruction, eighteen months later Barker seems to have become closely interested in, if not directly involved with, international socialist and pacifist plans for ending the war and building the new world (see pp.213–16). It is perhaps not surprising, therefore, that alongside the potential projects developing during the second half of 1917 and into 1918 we hear about an international play of vast scope.

But we (as yet) have no letters that tell us anything more. After one tantalising appearance it slides away, possibly killed off, as was a previous short story, following her criticism. But that one glimpse is enough to bring into view a particular artistic trajectory that arches from 1913 through to 1919. In 1913 Barker worked with the illustrator and author Dion Calthrop (1878-1937) on a play called

Harlequinade. It presents a sequence of scenes enacted by commedia-type figures which tell the history of theatre from its origins up to the immediate future. In the following year the interest in ways of telling history was developed in Barker's dramatization of Hardy's epic poem about the Napoleonic Wars, *The Dynasts*, staged late in 1914. The history plays project of 1916-17 planned a more extensive historical sweep but delivered in a form which would punctuate and fragment the chronological flow with its significant historical actions presented in twenty-minute units. In summer 1917 this project seemed to yield place to the planning of a production of *Peer Gynt*. Barker had been interested in *Peer Gynt* for several years and although the play is much more of an account of an individual's life than a people's history, what is consistent about its re-appearance here is its formal construction as a sequence of episodes. Both that sort of construction and an interest in large-scale political and historical overview seem to come together in the aborted 'international' play which Huntington describes in early 1918.

More specific than episodic construction is the recurrence of a device used in *Harlequinade*. From the evidence of the writing style this was added by Barker to Calthrop's text: two figures, young Alice and her Uncle, sit in front of the curtain and comment on the scenes which the pierrots act. This device was then re-used for the projected history plays which would also have figures in front of the curtain. These were to be two Readers, who comment on the historical scenes. That narrated commentary, combined with the format of self-contained, as it were gestic, units of action, together begin to work as what will later be called epic dramaturgy.

The interest in finding a form to tell a big story – a story of the history of the theatre, of the history of a people, of international relations – seems to surface again in an immediately post-war project, a dramatization of Dumas's sprawling historical novel of the mid-1620s, *The Three Musketeers*. Now of course the novel is a fantasy, a romance. But into it Dumas inserted particular and recognisable historical incidents, which had direct bearing on its own time, four years before the uprising of 1848. Thus *The Three Musketeers* offered a readily available romance within which episodes might do the same sort of politics as was planned for the history plays. And if Barker were indeed planning to re-purpose an old novel to new political ends – though we cannot ever certainly know, because it seems there's no finished script – it was definitely the case, because he says so, that he was trying to make a new drama that departed from accepted convention.

Below is the opening of the scenario of *The Three Musketeers* (a) (transcribed from Barker's manuscript THM/147/3). This is followed by some notes on it (b) (from a separate type-written letter). These notes demonstrate Barker's thinking about staging devices and effects in relation to episodic – and indeed epic – theatre.

a)
The Three Musketeers.
Draft scenario.

The Reader ...

    recounts the gift of the yellow horse and d'Artagnan's journey to Meung

Scene 1.

    Outside the Inn door at Meung. Milady's carriage waiting. Rochefort at the door laughing at the horse. The Reader has brought one to the point of d'Artagnan riding on and saying "Halloo – Sir, you Sir etc" He draws on Rochefort, is beaten senseless. Rochefort asks who he is. The inn-keeper brings his wallet with the letter to Treville which Rochefort pockets. Milady comes from the Inn ready to start, mounts her coach. D'A. comes to. Rochefort avoids a renewal of the quarrel With a few parting words as in the book Milady starts Rochefort goes off (on horseback) D'A discovers the loss of the letter – berates the host and finally has the yellow horse brought him. He mounts and rides off with the utmost dignity – no one daring to laugh.

The Reader ...

    Takes us to Paris and to M. de Trevilles antechamber next morning

Scene two

This must be an in-and-out double storied scene – Treville's staircase and his cabinet both.

6 minutes

Dumb show. d'A making his way through the crowd – as in Chapter II. Everything passes as in the book – but much abbreviated. And it may be better for Treville's scolding of the musketeers to take place on the staircase and not in the cabinet. But the later scene with d'A should be in the cabinet from which d'A rushes   collides with Athos on the stairs and with Porthos at their bottom   The scene ends

b)

From 'A few explanatory notes' attached to 'the scenario of *The Three Musketeers*'. These notes are in a letter dated 29 June 1919, addressed to Arthur Hopkins, but the name is deleted.

(1) The Reader is an important person and must be a "light weight" able to read not only dramatically but amusingly. He must, especially, be able to keep up the "pitch" of the performance in between the scenes. He should sit at a sort of reversed Conductor's desk on a level, half-way between the audience and the stage.

(2) The Scenery. This will need a good deal of ingenuity. There should be a set of curtains hung about 8 feet up stage, stretching across and so contrived that they can be parted in about four different places. They should be hung, I think, on a slight arc - or at a very obtuse angle. Between their partings the small "background" scenes can be set. These should be little more than rather elaborate screens - of the size indicated by the scene that has to be played before them. The more important interiors which must have three sides and be set "centre" - the Queen's closet, the Cardinal's room, Milady's bedroom, Buckingham's closet - can still be little more than backgrounds - it will be possible to extend the action of the scene in front of them. Certain scenes I have marked to be played in front of the inner curtains as a front scene would be. [...]

[More follows here on different sorts of scenes and a necessary double-deck structure.]

(4) [*sic*] As I have sketched it the whole thing is very long. I have hopes that in writing it I may be able to reduce the time of the individual scenes. It would be unwise to reduce their number, for this would detract from the continuity and spirit of the narrative – and from the <u>narrative-spirit</u>, too, and make it too like a conventional play. [...]

[More follows about what may need to be cut if it cannot be reduced.]

(5) I propose to keep Dumas' dialogue as much as possible and not be afraid of its rather stilted touch.

[In fact he did not keep close to Dumas' dialogue: what he wrote can be seen in the opening scenes of a draft script dated 14 July 1921 (THM 147/4/11). These notes continue with more on the needs of the dramaturgy and casting.]

....

What the History plays and subsequent projects show is that, while hitherto we have assumed that Barker's dramatic writing at this period was occupied by the justly celebrated play *The Secret Life*, beneath the surface was bubbling away a set of experiments working towards a sort of play which, had it ever emerged in finished form, we'd have had to call an instance of epic theatre.

11. 'MY FAITH'

It is not clear to me that there is any single main influence on what Barker called his 'faith'. The one contemporary thinker he cites here at any length is J.A. Hobson. He was a leading figure in the New Liberalism movement of the early twentieth century, as was Graham Wallas, for whose book *The Great Society* (1914) Barker and Huntington shared an enthusiasm. Both of these men had links to contemporary socialists and pacifists. Barker's emphasis on the importance of desire and vitality as against the restrictions of received ideas and legal conventions of behaviour may be fairly regular among Edwardian liberals, but a version of socialism that celebrates desire also has something specifically in common with the political position of Morris, whom Barker admired, as opposed to that of, say, Hyndman or indeed Marx.

....

Friday. [mid-late June 1916 Williamstown, MA, USA]
Oh for a week or more I've not been able to write a word to you here – nor of anything else (I'll confess) except letters to you. There has been on me – on us both dear I know – the strain of this coming separation. And it does seem to deaden one – to rob one of faculties. Well – there's what looks like a little respite – and I do want you to have – oh what a silly substitute even for letters – this will seem. Do you like this I quote it from an article of J.A. Hobsons's ¶ "Man has his place not only in human society but in that larger system of things which we call the Universe. Religious and philosophic thinkers have always striven against the false limitation of the view which regards a man as a mere repository of social activities and duties, owing no regard to those needs and impulses of his nature which transcend humanity – and relate him to the larger life of the Cosmos. This is not an idle speculation or a merely theoretical consideration. It inspires and gives meaning to some of the most powerful feelings which affect human conduct. The delight

in Nature, the sympathy with all the processes of organic life, the central passion of all science, the groping towards some common law of order in the world, and the poetical or mystical vision of a single spirit glowing through the diverse channels of a universal life, of which humanity is but a part." (I didn't think I'd get it all in!) [...] **71898/125**

> [They are to separate because he is being conscripted. Across three articles in *The Nation* in 1916, **Hobson** argued that the Defence of the Realm Act (September 1914) introduced restraints on freedom of speech, publication and meeting which are consistent with those of the Prussian state, thereby turning Britain into the thing it is fighting against. Barker quotes from the third article, which challenges the 'assumption of a suzerainty of the State over all other social relations'.]

Wednesday [July 12 1916] Midday – 9.50 [on board the 'New York']
[...] I am an awful creature of impulse – and I want you to be.   It does not in the least mean a creature of constantly varying impulses. People who think that can hardly have known what impulse is – they confuse it with "appetite".   But the constant impulse – the purpose from beyond – Well you have it darling. It is that which turns you always to your work. And another came when you loved me – you find don't you? – those things are beyond thought – You don't say I "ought" to go on writing or "If I make up my mind to it I do love him."   But you haven't it yet in its proper proportion (No doubt one never can attain the perfection of never having any <u>idle</u> impulse – but only those from 'beyond'). But certainly as between that 'live' life and the 'dead' life which is calculation and taking thought – both for the day and the morrow (It was I'm sure what Christ meant) – the "live" life must determine the main current of life.   That is what I have come to win for you – or rather our love has come that you can win it for yourself. [...] **71897/75-76**

[Friday 14 July 1916] 2.45 – <u>11-30.</u> [on board the 'New York']
[...] What I say about Service for Love and Loveless Duty – I don't want to dogmatise about it – but I don't mind saying it over and over (do I

seem to?) because in the distinction I make to myself about the two things does lie the Whole Duty of Man - to me. I know it isn't quite a simple thing - not so simple as one can make it seem in words. And I don't mean (to start with) to turn my back on duty for it's own sake. But two things I feel about that. It is parallel to study for education's sake   And that does show the same sort of result. We learned things we remember (as children) and things we have forgotten - fruitful things and unfruitful - and even now there is the reading I do - but I do less and less of it (for my time of shere "training" is over) - the reading I do for mental discipline and information - and you know my mind "refuses" it often altogether. And then there is the reading - which my mind accepts. That is fruitful - it at once begets ideas in me. Well - I think that in life too there are the disciplinary things - good to be trained in - as one trains children to be clean   But I think they should never rank higher in one's life than <u>routine</u>. Now a life made up of routine is not life in any real sense at all. And a life of duty is barren. It is a life of good habits - and in that there is no vitality. Anyone can be trained to it as an animal is trained. Convenient for the world - and good for us as a groundwork on which to build - but by itself not life - indeed the very negation of life. And about mere duty - I think it becomes actively harmful if it pretends even tacitly to be more than it is. And often you do get that conspiracy between two people or between one person and the world - the doing of duty with the assumption allowed that some vital impulse prompts one to do it - the acceptance of the service and the return of one with the same pretence   That's the interchange of false coin and their can be no value to it - and yet it is the commonest thing and each keeps up the pretence for the supposed benefit of the other and imagines that only his own coin is false (sometimes) - and - knowing it false - gets to feel that he must pay more and more of it - a vague feeling in him that £10 of duty (false) will be fairer exchange for £5 of love (real) - whereas of course a pennyworth of love outweighs it anyhow - and as what's given and taken are both false together the exchange (in that understanding) is worthless anyway. When I say false, I don't use the word in any bad sense. I think if both parties say - I do - or take this - not in the least because I want to but sherely because I think I ought - well there'd be less harm done. But it is amazing what a lot of false values are created by not saying this – and think how many people would gasp with relief and say "You don't want to do it – Nor do I – Well for Heaven's sake let's stop" For the service so done has <u>in itself</u> I'm convinced no life-value – whereas the smallest service done for love has. It sounds a platitude put that way. But think of the many applications of it in life and of how little one has the courage to abide by one's knowledge of that truth. The thing isn't proveable perhaps. But yet I believe all our experience goes to prove it – to prove that the thing we do from duty only has no vital effect – and only seems to have by the people for whom we do it being persuaded that we do it from love – and <u>then</u> it has no real effect for while we can deceive them or they deceive themselves – we cannot deceive the vital spirit of nature – and it is with <u>that</u> we are dealing all the time – though we tell ourselves we are dealing only with other men and women. No, it becomes a <u>false value</u> – and the world is more impoverished by false values than by actual sin. But the thing we do from love has – in itself – and apart from us after we have done it – a vital effect. Whether one can prove it or no – that is my belief in life – perhaps the only definite one I have – (it is the central one for me rather). You see the distinction between true value and false runs through everything – and you either know it or you don't – you can't explain or argue it – but it is by its enduring (vital) effect that the distinction is shown – sometimes after years. The difference between a good book and a bad one – good verse and bad – good music and bad – there is its present effect on us – and there is the test of time. Now I do believe it true, that to the extent your own life is made up of false values so do you tolerate and try to get nourishment out of bad philosophy – or politics – or art (Of course I am not talking of quite callow people who have had no training in taste or judgment). Though you may pretend to like the good thing being told it is good – that is only (again) the returning of a false value for a value that is false for you.

5-40 – <u>2-20</u>

I think one can argue from art to life. Good art has a vitality of its own – and we who are artists know when we "create" and when we merely make a pretence of creating – and from what the difference comes   It comes from the reality of the impulse in us – the <u>love</u> And we know too how we test living art when we find it – by just that same appeal. There is the authority for thinking such and such a thing is good - so that even if it doesn't appeal to us - we ask twice or thrice or we wait - supposing that it may. I remember I waited so over Brahms music. But I believe I was right not to say I liked it before I really did - believe - I'm sure - I never should really have liked it if I had at first pretended to. No - on the whole what we try and do is to train ourselves on good things - during our training time - which cannot be for ever - and then rely on our inner impulse - our taste - our love - to make us create or appreciate the vital true thing and reject the dead   I know - still we think that we haven't be trained enough in everything - we haven't courage - we bow to mere authority - to duty-appreciation and duty-creation - we mistrust our inner convictions. But I think we know all the time that this is a weakness - that it detracts from the natural creation and healthy enjoyment of art - which ought to be a spontaneous emotion in a <u>trained</u> human being. Well - I do believe that life itself is an exact parallel to this. We must train and form our opinions - our religion of life - under authority partly (other people's experi-ence) partly under our own experience   But training is not meant to last for ever. There comes the time to put it to the test to see if it has created in us that susceptibility to good and evil - which can be our guide in the things that will be to us unlike what they have ever been to anyone before (I write so clumsily all this my darling - but the foghorn is going - distracting me!)   For if that sensitiveness hasn't been created - well I'd as soon be a well trained dog. And if life is not to be a new thing to me - different to what it has been to anyone before - for me to deal with it newly and differently (not on purpose of course - but only because I deal with it freshly) - well - again - the whole world might not be moving forward at all. There is no other proof or means of progress (not - again - in the cant sense of the word). And if I can't believe the world is moving forward - well then I can see no purpose in it or us or anything we do - I'd as soon do wrong as right - I'd sooner die tomorrow - for all the instincts in me - all my power and knowledge - all my love yes - my love for you - would have neither meaning nor purpose - would be a mockery of the cruellest sort and I would pray to die - well I'd see that I did die. ¶ So there is my faith. That one must train oneself - discipline oneself hard - but only do it as one learns

160

the alphabet of a language – not thinking that in discipline itself there is either meaning or virtue   Yes – it is the alphabet of life – by it we can make words. But the <u>meaning</u>   that can only come from within. Training and living are two separate things and to live at all we must live from within. Train all we will – get one's theories right that way – when the question of practice comes it is no use relying on training of discipline and duty then. For from that comes nothing real – nothing vital – nothing belonging truly to oneself. It is only what other people have done and have told us to do. One must decide for oneself by the inner light – which is something transcending all training – all law – training – discipline – all the acquired things will give us understanding of the light – and strength to do well what the light shows us. But the thing itself – in that we must abide by what we are – not be afraid to. For that is the best – inasmuch as it is the only real thing we can be. And our purpose in this world is to add a little atom of fresh vitality to it – something new – ourself – not a copy – or thing we're told. To be our <u>best</u> self – yes – and acquire all the strength and wisdom possible to <u>be</u> acquired. But when it comes to the point – however often (not very often either) it does come to the point – to be <u>oneself</u> and realising that absolute right is not for mere human beings – (therefore they need not fear absolute wrong either) – take the risk and bear the burden of the degree of right and wrong – not question about happiness or unhappiness either – but do the thing that is in one without fear. That is the only true service we can render. [...] **71897/85-89**

[The sentiments here should be contrasted with Beatrice Webb's view in June 1916 that Barker was 'unscrupulous in minor morals, sacrificing all things to the development of his talent or the satisfaction of some artistic or intellectual whim' (Webb 1911-1916 f. 3423-24). For 'service for love' see also pp.191–92.]

Saturday July 15 [1916] 10-30am – <u>6-30am</u> [on board the 'New York']

[...] All that I wrote to you yesterday – that long and perhaps muddled metaphysic. Why? Well – it is a belief that I have worked out for myself, however common to others it may be – and therefore worth writing down because it does express and explain me. That one must only apply training and discipline to live in general – impersonally. But that the particular personal things must come spontaneously – inspiration. That is life for oneself and progress for the world – no other way possible. [...] **71897/91**

Monday July 17. [1916] 8-45am – <u>2-45am.</u> [on board the 'New York', docked in England]

[...] I am too apt to try and overwhelm my main force   It is right to do that I think when the spirit within you does genuinely carry you away – but as long as possible one should try and let the mere law of right and reason by itself prevail.   For there comes the question about law – I do respect it my darling and will – I respect the spirit of it. But – it has always been the biggest question in the world. I suppose it always must be. It has cost the greatest men the deepest travail of mind. When to obey the law and when to disobey   When to trust to one's own discernment of a spirit of law that transcends and contradicts the letter. Against that problem every <u>live</u> soul seems to come sooner or later. I know my own answer. One must give the letter of the law obedience to the last endurable limit until one knows by the fact that obedience to it is unendurable – that in obedience lies death and only in disobedience is life – that the spirit of law one's own spirit discerns is greater than and different from the letter. For obedience to the letter is showing regard to man – obedience to the spirit of right which by great struggle of mind it has been given to one to discern which one can grasp, not disinterestedly with one's brain and judgment (as a judge on the bench does – that again is merely human and literal) – but which one grasps with a <u>purged desire</u> that is showing regard to God – Not to a detached God sitting far off (as to Roman Catholics the Pope sits at Rome) – but to the Holy Spirit in each of us – when by the purging of our souls that is set free to work – in us and for us.   For that after all is the inheritance of Conscience which we get from our Puritan ancestors – you and I. With them the concrete question was whether they should worship God as their conscience would have them or according to forms which they felt meaningless – and sooner than obey the mere letter of the law – though they were the most peaceful law abiding people in England they suffered or went out into the wilderness. And they won that battle for themselves and for the whole world. Thanks to them there are very few spots left where men may not worship by the light of their spirit instead of by the letter of a liturgy – and be the more honoured not despised for doing it. ¶ To us – other questions and other battles. Obey I say until by obedience to a lower law one must break a higher ¶ But we have not come to that parting of the ways yet – I don't think we shall. For we are not up against "law" so much as up against a passionate (and suffering – now or past quite genuinely) and ungoverned – unillumined nature – and it is that I must deal with – firmly – wisely and still patiently – if I can control myself. ¶ But as to the marriage laws you see – all my adult life I have fought against them in the abstract – fought for their reform – they are to me relics of barbarism as they now stand   In marrying I conformed to the letter   I said at the time how much and how little the spirit meant to me. So as individual laws they have never had any sacredness to me at all. Let me be clear my darling – I have told you haven't I – that I could express – or try to – my love for you by kneeling down in the most sacred place and giving you all I had – giving myself to you "till death do us part" Not only did I never want to do that (and when the point arose definitely refused to do it and was married in a registry office) but I never even pretended one <u>could</u> want to do it. But that enlightenment of spirit – through your love – having been given to me – why it would be a bond so different – in (literally) such another world from a legal bond – that the legal bond – well one would wear it just as one puts on ordinary clothes instead of dressing in a toga – convenience to oneself escaping observation – respect to one's neighbours – no deeper moral meaning than that. <u>We</u> take hands, Helen darling. We have taken hands. No – you've said no such words to me – they shall come in their time and place – and to try and put them out of time and place would spoil the beauty of them. But they shall only come when the truth they give utterance to has become a part of our very natures – And – my darling – I do think this truth has. ¶ But now – to follow the Law – as long as law will be followed – until – as I say – it becomes not law – but the breaking of law – [...] **71897/97-99**

[The idea of the 'Puritan' heritage has political resonance. Vernon Lee, a member of the pacifist Union of Democratic Control, and Tom Bryan, instrumental in the formation of the Labour Party, both described themselves as Puritans and both, like Barker, as socialists. The 'passionate' **unillumined nature** they are up against is McCarthy.]

Sunday. [?20 August 1916 Ayot]

[...] Imagination. No one knows what it means who has not got it. We all have it as children. Then the way of the world is to kill it and substitute for it ready-made religion and morals – law. But if we keep it and <u>discipline</u> it – you know my belief – it is the ultimate tribunal – the soul of a human being or a people – the real guide one can trust. With us (thank God) it is first our strength – the bond between us too – and then our gift to the world. We can be proud of that [...] **71898/34**

Thursday. [?28 September 1916 Trowbridge barracks]

What you say, dear, about houses expressing their owners (that has been often enough said) but there's the further thing you say – that if they don't – if the material things they have piled up dominate – what a dead thing their house will be. And that is a deep truth I think. We won't call such a house a 'home' – for that must mean a live thing – I think it must even mean a thing made by two people and their love. You can feel it when you step inside the door and if you can't feel such things – well – "How can we tell them if they do not know?" ¶ But the whole tragedy of the nineteenth century was the creation of wealth and machinery which people could not control – which controlled them It would be the tragedy of this – may still be – for few fight against it. But the war and its devastation may help us few with that fight Long ago I phrased it simply to myself – one must not have more money than one can spend but that only expresses crudely the real thing which is that material things must never be one's master for a moment. One has not so much spiritual power but that one needs it all and all free [...] **71898/98**

[The quotation is from a story she told him when first they met, and regularly used thereafter.]

Thursday [9 November 1916] 7-30am <u>2-30am</u>   [Bloomsbury, London]

[...] Read Plato! Not that I do – diligently and completely – but we'll think Plato a little. And here – I make a shot at it – an interpretation of his doctrine That good in the world is like wealth – it is only increased by being circulated. And while you mustn't absorb good and give none out – become self righteous – equally you mustn't refuse good and happiness – mustn't refuse to seek it – for if you don't receive as you might you cannot give forth your full increase as you should And the test of good – the test that your spiritual machine is (horribly word it has become "machine") – your spiritual self is fully realised (good word "realised") is your vitality. Train your mind all you can to respond to Good and not to respond to Evil. And then your vitality should be a quite unconscious test – that you are taking in all you can and giving out your increase. And I say an unconscious test –because you must do it happily – it is only happiness that other people will respond to. Our 'opinions' differ and we mistrust and argue but our understanding of happiness is infallible [...] **71898/231**

[Saturday] Nov 18. [1916] 7-15am – <u>2-15am</u> [Bloomsbury, London]

Here's a thought for the Puritan Mother in you. ¶ It is true that what is hard and 'agin nature' is in some way good for the soul But it is only one side of the truth – for we were not put in this world to despise it and make it different to what it is – or ourselves different to what we are – by despising ourselves – but to fulfil nature – in the world – in ourselves – to add the spirit to the flesh. But is not one side of that one-sided truth this – that when we who have Puritan natures (for both you and I have them) are to gain a great thing – a great good – we instinctively take the hard path – just to strengthen our souls – just to prove its value and ourselves

165

worthy of it. And we rejoice in the difficulties (in a queer way) – rejoice in overcoming them even at the moments when it seems they may overcome us for we know that if we are worthy we shall win – and if we're not we'd rather we didn't win Yes – we've the courage for that – to believe in the good thing – the heaven we mean to gain so much – that we dare to say "If I'm not good enough to gain by this path – I'm not good enough" That's hard – in the blackest minutes it has come to me. Always I've said – you know it is the good – the thing to win – therefore if you're good enough you'll win – <u>and</u> – oh this final thing – it is comparing the difficulties <u>makes</u> you good enough to win – without them you might not have been ¶ Oh – Helen – oh my <u>dear</u> ¶ 'Nothing by halves' – do you remember I said once – well "Nothing easily" is a good motto too. [...] **71898/253-54**

[This is a response to her comparison of herself (29 October) to a **'Pilgrim Mother'**, feeling that what was hard and **'agin nature'** was good for the soul.]

12. Thinking About Writing

There are three sorts of reflections about the craft of writing: his comments on his own writing; his advice to Huntington on hers, and his responses to the writing of others, from books to newspapers. The advice to Huntington contains most of his views on best practice of the craft. The responses to the writing of others often contain observations about the effects of writing, especially, as with newspapers, the negative effects. Throughout there is the sense that his new relationship with Huntington will make him a better writer, while she much admired his definition of good writing: 'Richness of thought, the drive of emotion, and <u>simplicity</u> of expression' (71905/196).

....

[Friday mid-November 1915] 9.15PM. [Hotel Algonquin, New York]

I finished up the day happy   went for a walk – right round the reservoir singing out loud – and then writing a 'pome'. My poems aren't good   they only echo other people's lines and thoughts but here it is for you

> I shall go out to death so quietly
> There will not be a tremor in the air
> As my soul cleaves it leaving wasted there
> This body of corruption and despair
>
> After a little freedom – happily –
> My soul itself will be dissolved like light
> Obliterate in the solace of deep night
> Joined to the mystery of the Infinite

I have a sense of words – but no power of criticism over that sort of thing – which makes me feel it's never very good **71898/296**

['**reservoir**': Probably in Central Park.]

Monday. [10 July 1916] 9-45 – 8-45 [on board the 'New York']

[...] Damn those houses of yours – I'll have you out of them – out of all the burdensomeness of them. We must live in France – for that is going to be a country of a wonderful revival, during the next ten years or so – and we must breathe its air – while we think about England and America from our detachment. Then when we have settled our minds about things – by working out our feelings and thoughts in our books – well – then we'll see. ¶ Oh – just in time my darling. I was becoming a hack – and you? So dead. It makes my heart ache – you – the most alive thing in the world. [...] **71897/70**

Tuesday Sept 5. [1916] 9PM. – <u>3PM.</u> The Garrick [London]

[...] it's about the books I'm writing – Murray's Greek Epic – I think you said you'd never read it – has beautiful things in it – and the "purple passage" a masterpiece of prose – I wonder if you'll pick it out – the very bit I mean. Hudson – you like him and there are books not get-at-able in America I think. Nevinson – Dip into him only but I like you to glimpse this 'radical' English Mind. The Surrey Labourer – quite an individual rare thing and T E Brown – you may not know (I didn't!) fresh I think (though old) and very very English the narrative poems will keep – but the lyrics you can capture at once. [...] **71898/13**

[Gilbert **Murray**, *The Rise of the Greek Epic* (1907, Oxford: Clarendon Press). William Henry **Hudson**: a naturalist and ornithologist who also wrote about poetry. Henry Woodd **Nevinson**, *Essays in Freedom* (1909, London: Duckworth & Co). George Bourne (George Sturt), *Memoirs of a **Surrey Labourer*** (1907, London: Duckworth & Co). Thomas Edward **Brown**: possibly the posthumous *Collected Poems* (1900, repr. 1909, London: Macmillan).]

Sunday morning [24 September 1916] 11-30am – 5-30 am. (You are sleeping I lean and kiss you) [Ayot]

[...] this morning I had 'ideas' again. You'll read Wells's book naturally – or I'd be sending it you – it seems so natural to send you books

– a sort of poor substitute for talking about them to you. It is good in his way I think – with his usual limitations of artistry which offend one. I am left wondering how much a book's value is lessened by mistakes of that sort. I think – since perfect artistry is 'completeness' – that though its immediate effect may not be much altered – its ultimate life is   It would take long to prove the case – though it would be a very instructive business proving it – discovering how one vital artistic virtue outweighed a less vital artistic defect – but I am inclined to think that it is artistry in the largest sense that gives a book or a play life and makes it survive – go on living after its author has left go of it as it were – for good. And this Well's lacks without doubt. But his thought is honest and vital – and it always comforts me to find that my own thoughts have been travelling with his – for I believe more then that it is the way the world is moving (though I have that egotistic courage anyway). But his final theology in this book – it is all autobiography – all his books are – this love for his son (still only a small boy though) – he never writes well except about things that are actual to him ¶ This is 'calendar' material – whenever any "abstract" thought comes to me I say to myself - my dear's 'calendar' – our talk together to begin her day. [...] **71898/78**

[**Wells' book** was *Mr Britling Sees it Through*, serialised in *The Nation* and published September 1916. It is largely an account of English society's engagement with the war, but it concludes with a lengthy section articulating a religious response to the wartime tragedy. Wells' **son**, Anthony West, was born in 1914; his mother was Rebecca West. Mr Britling's older much-loved son Hugh dies in the novel.]

Wednesday [27 September 1916] 1-30PM – 7-30am [Trowbridge barracks]

[...] I've sent you two books   Do I load you up with books? But it's our way of talking of things in a sense, isn't it? The Masefield Gallipoli you may possibly have (it was written really to be published in America) – in that case you must give your copy to Miss Nellie D when she brings you this. The other little book of verse – quite simple stuff but – to think that does come out of the trenches. I don't think that gives it a fictitious value – it is good of its sort I think we should call it so anyhow It is genuine – some of it made my eyes quite misty as I read. No – with all the evil the war brings (we must not shirk it) – It makes the evil people more evil the fine people finer (and death takes careless toll of both) – and it is making England to sing again – not calculated correct poetry but the simple "song". Do you agree? He hasn't a remarkable mind or anything this fellow (he's a prisoner in Germany now) – but – it rings true and reaches one. I know – oh <u>we</u> and we all of us – know – that true "expression" does only spring out of the <u>real</u> thing – the reality in us which we only find in <u>real</u> life – no – not the outward obvious (I can't write subtle things sanely in a barrack shed – I ought to be able to!!) – but with our life and our self attuned – living whole-heartedly – then without effort – with joy (you know it) the real expression comes. [...] **71898/82**

[The **book of verse** was very probably F.W. Harvey's *A Gloucestershire Lad at Home and Abroad*, first printed September 1916. By this point Harvey was a prisoner. The book is dedicated to 'All comrades of mine who lie dead in foreign fields for love of England, or who live to prosecute the war for another England', a sentiment which would have struck a chord with Barker. It came **out of the trenches** literally in that most of the poems first appeared in the *Fifth Gloucester Gazette*, the first paper to be published from the trenches.]

Thursday Sep 28. [1916] R.G.A. Cadet School Trowbridge Wilts 5PM – <u>11am</u>

[...] About your work my darling – I think always of it Remember "black days" are a <u>good</u> sign – for they mean that you are setting your standard high – they are – growing pains – oh birth-pangs – which only the higher creation feels Just <u>poise above</u> the work for a little – let the thing revolve in your mind until it simplifies itself – turn the focus till the glass becomes clear – in practice – trim back to the fault – prune the dead wood – Oh – beloved – words – and words on paper. <u>Can</u> they help – My spirit is with you **71898/95**

[The thoughts here, hastily written to catch the post, are elaborated in the more leisurely letter that follows below.]

London Oct 1. [1916] 3PM. <u>10am</u> [Adelphi Terrace]

[...] Your book.   I think of it <u>much</u> – you know Don't let the black times dishearten you They are bound to come – I have to face them – (let that comfort you a little) – have to begin every job knowing that sticking places will come – will last for weeks – my brain a knot that won't untie. But – oh my dear – that's when I want to be with you too for I shall be able to help – I understand so well. And I'll be able to free your mind – no – not "distract" it – it isn't that is needed but – free it – strengthen the emotional force that underlies the brain and vitalises it – It isn't that your brain is failing you (bless you – baby!) but one's brain only works creatively because the something underneath – sends blood through it – that vitality. We all lack it sometimes – oh often and can't supply ourselves well I can bring it you [...] You wonder if writing and that world of thought ever seems unimportant to me – ah no my darling not for one minute – it seems more important than ever now I'm in touch with the more actual for I know the power of it more – Don't think me conceited – I know and have tested my own power more I matter a little more than the others (oh vanity!) because of my touch with that world – well I think I do – And I know that the world of thought creates the other – and – we've got to think better and make the world think different – and there's no other way at all out of a repetition of this hell. So that is <u>our</u> job my dear one [...] **71898/88-92**

[The **book** is her novel *Eastern Red*, on which he commented closely.]

Tuesday. [?3 October 1916 Weymouth]

One of our instructors here has risen from the ranks – very much by his own ability – and a quite considerable ability   But he is so overcome by the knowledge he has acquired that he must be displaying all of it – all the time – and so his lectures are the hardest to follow – he manages to make the simplest things appear hard (they have to minister to his own success in understanding them) And it is a lesson to me over my work. If one strives aright it is to make things simpler and simpler – the more one really knows – the easier it is to do it. And I find this by the way in all the machinery we learn about – complex at first – always growing simpler in the later patterns. [...] **71898/101**

Sunday morning [15 October 1916] 10.am <u>5 am</u> [?Bloomsbury, London]

[...] But over your work dear – How does that go? What I <u>do</u> want is that it shouldn't be interrupted I want that badly <u>very badly</u> For you see – you're a worker by nature by instinct – and that – your writing is a part of your life – natural to you – food for life – and yet you've never been able to treat it yet as a main object – you've always had to take it up when you could and put it down because this person wanted you – or that person was coming to call. You've had to work on the lines of an amateur – you who are farthest from that and always have been – Well – that is the first thing that has got to be altered It isn't a question of course of doing more – but of it taking its proper place – of lesser things giving way to it instead of it having to give way. And even now before this can be quite brought about – as we'll bring it – I do want the flow of it not to be interrupted. For that is the only way – <u>the</u> thing that matters – to be able to keep hold – mental hold of a thing day by day until the job is done (unless it asks you for a short holiday from you – as jobs sometimes do. And this book – dear – it is in a way our first book – half way that anyhow – and I don't want it to be interrupted You're 'working' – that's a happiness to you – and it has kept me so happy about you – such a good hold on your real life it is for you to have – keeping <u>you</u> really you – until I come [...] **71898/157**

[My essay 'Archer Huntington's Wife' argues that Barker's encouragement of her writing was a way of helping her overcome her sense of entrapment and alienation: see p.236.]

Sunday night [15 October 1916]   11-30PM – <u>6-30PM</u> [Bloomsbury, London]

[...] I managed a long solitary walk through the country – fields and woods looking quite beautiful with the cold clear autumn light on them – and my brain was alive and I thought – creatively – of a play even for the first time in months [...] **71898/158**

Friday. [?20 October 1916 Bloomsbury, London]

I found in unpacking two sheets of 'Union League' note paper on which I had written out roughly some lines of Meredith to put in your Calendar   Lately - how all poetry has been left out of it   left out of me you'll fear too beloved perhaps   But no - you know - it is always there when one's mind can get into touch with one's spirit so to speak. Meredith's good - pick out the salient things in him very very good - things seem cut out of the rock of the language. I turn always to that poetry - you do too I know.   Not your Swinburne - though he can carve a line sometimes - not even Keats with his flowers - oh but I wouldn't give up Keats! [...] **71898/171**

[He was **unpacking** because he had just moved into his new Bloomsbury room. **Union Leagues** were founded during the American Civil War to promote loyalty to the Union. By Barker's time the Union League of New York was giving money to artistic and cultural causes. He concludes this **Calendar** entry by copying out verses from **Meredith**'s 'Hueless Love', beginning 'Midway the road of our life's term they met'.]

Saturday morning [21 October 1916] 7-45   2-45 [Bloomsbury, London]

[...] My Red Cross book is out <u>at last</u> - and I send you the first copy. Not very much to send you my dear - it is a bit of journalism - and special pleading at that. This war can't be written about in any real sense - perhaps never can be by any of this generation at all. But there are half a dozen bits in it I like and a dozen or more which tell me what <u>not</u> to do again in writing prose. [...] **71898/194**

Sunday. [?22 October 1916 Ayot]

Newspapers, newspapers - one sometimes wishes there were no such things. Of all the instances of blessings men have turned into curses - well newspapers run well in that race   There's a series of articles   on Germany - by an American - one Curtin running through the London Times (so we both must bear the blame) the vilest things. To begin with the man is a cad - and cads shouldn't be let come between two nations fighting to the death – next he's a liar (I trust my instinct) ready with the "lie that is half the truth and ever the blackest of lies" And Northcliffe who employs him – another cad. Oh it comes to that you either have the mind of a gentleman – and the simplest peasant may have – often has <u>can</u> have always – treat him well for some generations (yes we must think in generations) – or you haven't – and if you haven't – well the truth is not in you – for truth must imply a perception of beauty and the fulness of things that is truth – a thing beyond correctness of facts – truth lies in the expression of them. And – how can one tell them if they do not know. [...] **71898/172**

[Thomas **Curtin's** series of articles, many with the title 'Ten Months in Germany', began on 9 October and ran through until 28 December 1916. Barker's view of them was echoed by Masefield: 'This American journalist who has been in Germany is filling me with fury daily. He has by his own confession dirtily betrayed his hosts and those who trusted him, & now influential English papers are printing his dirty innuendoes, suggesting that we should adopt reprisals in bloodiness & dirtiness' (Masefield 1985: 188). Barker **quotes** Alfred Lord Tennyson's poem 'The Grandmother'. Alfred Harmsworth, Lord **Northcliffe**, was a very successful newspaper magnate who pioneered, in particular, the expansion of the popular press.]

[Sunday 22 October 1916] 3-30PM – 10-30am. [Ayot]

[...] Your book. Let's talk. I know just how that happens. One thinks as one writes it – this is the complete thing. And then – as you say – only the skeleton, the plan, there and back one has to go – writing over and over But I believe this. If writing is our real job – our 'natural' job – then Nature works through us in that – and with us precisely as she does over her other struggles towards creation Boys and girls have impulses towards love which they don't interpret as impulses towards creation at all If they foresaw the family life ahead – ! But Nature – having her way leads them on step by step It's the same with our writing. If we knew what the whole job would be like we'd never have the courage to tackle it at all – wouldn't know how to begin. Only I think purely mechanical work is done by people who go from start to finish never turning a hair - nothing 'alive' is given birth to that way. But when you are led by genuine desire - and can only go step by step - Oh it's a strain and you feel that Nature - your inspiration is tricking you - You say, "Why did I ever begin the damned thing?" And you may have to wait. Really Nature has exhausted you a bit by the first creative effort. But presently the desire comes again. That's all that matters - And on you go There may have to be three or four bouts. But as long as the desire lasts - and it will And as it is intellectual creation and not physical - conscious creation not unconscious - you need your critical judgment too - to keep the balance - to mark the periods of effort and rest so to speak. But it does take it out of you and it's bound to. But you have life in you - so much life. I think nobody knows how much but I (I hardly think <u>you</u> know) And, beloved, I want you to work that way - for I know it's the only way. But I want to be there - I must be - so that you can come flinging in to me - you must always have your <u>fling</u> - and say that it's no use and that the wretched thing will never come right And I'll take you a walk - or I'll hold you close and kiss you (I fear I shall always kiss you first of all) and you can pummel me on the chest if you like - and I shall kiss you again - and you'll feel better But never depression my dear one - never that. Because you're alive - all alive - please God you will be then. And till then you must think of that - and be as alive as you can. I send you life and love, my beloved, all I can send So peg away. But I must read the book We must talk - oh - <u>all</u> we have to say My dear - my comrade. ¶ And you're down from the mountains and in New York. Damn New York - at least damn all of it that robs <u>you</u> of yourself and gives you nothing back Furnishing that house. Damn and doubly damn that house - Furnishing your mother's flat - I won't damn that - but I fear my darling that I do take a grim pleasure in your having been angry For one is as right to be angry sometimes as one is to be glad - and as right to show it - not self assertively - nor unkindly but quite simply. Indeed one must be able to show it - must learn to I suppose in such a way that the person one is angry with will see one is right. God forbid you shall ever be angry with me - that I should ever give you cause But if you were God forbid you shouldn't show it   It would hurt of course horribly but it would hurt far more and the hurt would go deeper – if you didn't [...] **71898/200-01**

[The **house** is the Huntingtons' newly refurbished one on 5th Avenue.]

Sunday [29 October 1916]   10-30PM – 5-30PM. [Bloomsbury, London]

Then to the club to dinner – and more depressing things about the war. And I read the end of Esmond for once I meant to do a pot-boiling play of it – and I must think of pot-boiling plays now. **71898/212**

[He refers to Thackeray's novel *The History of Henry* **Esmond** (1852).]

Tuesday. [c. 31 October 1916 London]

[...] [quotes a poem, 'German Prisoners' by 'Joseph Lee Sergeant. Black Watch'.] The signature is the remarkable thing about it – not a great poem of course but that a man out there should feel so and be able to express it – oh how different from these brawling cads in the papers here who can do nothing but spit and wrangle and hate – oh they are a minority of course but they poison many minds a little   And this man who knows and has seen the truth can sweeten them. [...] **71898/141**

[In fact **Lee**, who had been on the staff of the *Dundee Advertiser*, already had a reputation; when a corporal, his *Ballads of Battle* were published in 1916.]

Wednesday. [?1 November 1916 London]

You are my inspiration dear in the true sense of the word Sometimes it works backwards in an odd way – and that is like 'proving' the sum. I have never yet written a thing for you or said one seriously, that you have not shown me in it a better truth – a truer meaning that I, in writing it had known. Yes every time I send you something your comment - inspires <u>it</u> so to speak   And that is my want of you dear – I lack inspiration. A sort of blind striving I have and power and purpose I do think (I humbly think so)   But it is blind – that is I spell out things painfully and slowly and one wearies so at that – one's spirit flags (lack of moral purpose I daresay) [...] **71898/188**

Saturday. [?4 November 1916 London]

[Barker encloses a letter he received from a correspondent wanting to get a photograph of the spot where her last remaining relative died. She was prompted by a section in his book on Red Cross war graves.]

I thought you'd like to see this It made me quite happy for the moment   a useful thing my book has done   And – one mustn't attempt to measure big or little – if this and a few more things like it – is all it does that may be enough. Again one mustn't think that quite literally – but when one is looking for "fame" it is a good thought to let grow. ¶ Indeed I'm often impressed with the idea that a man making a cookery book from shere and sustained love of cooking (Can one love cooking) would produce a finer work of art than he who sets out to show – to show off – that he can write. Yes – that is so – oh altruism! – One ought only to learn from oneself (hard) just what one has to say – and then work and work to say it truly and completely (harder and harder) But the more one can fix on that – the more – yes I think so – will all the little vanities of "literature" fall away. Difficult and the result never what one foresaw (how should it be – when one is discovering) but there has come a virtue into it one could never consciously have put there, which makes it good art. [...] **71898/145**

Sunday night [12 November 1916] 11-45PM – <u>6-45PM.</u> [Ayot]

[...] I'm sending my dear a book – a good book of literary criticism – worth reading I think but I send it because I think one article in it may please you. I had ungratefully forgotten the boy and that he wrote it – and I did not know that he was dead. Oh my dear what right has one to be left alive I sometimes feel – in this slaughtering. So much work cut short.   Well – we must try and do what they would have done   But better work than mine it was going to be perhaps (indeed I think it – glancing at it very good – the articles on Morris and Browning – and I couldn't have done it) and – well I will do all I can. [...] **71898/236**

[The **book** was Dixon Scott's *Men of Letters* (1916); the article that would please her was on him. The editorial note says that Scott died at Gallipoli, before he finished the book: it was completed and published in his memory.]

Thursday morning [16 November 1916] 7-30 am – <u>2-30am.</u> [Bloomsbury, London]

[...] I woke before 6 and our clock told me the time and I lay a little – thinking of you – of you just gone to sleep (I hoped) – and then of work that I ought to get up and do some but I'm depressed about that – I'll own   It is there – the ideas are – but the moment I get them under way I have to break off – and at night – I never could work at night. I'd think – and <u>do</u> think a little that this is a mere excuse but though one can 'get through' things there is the quality of what one does to be thought of. That one can't command quite in that way – Oh but you know – thank God you know and understand just how much is laziness and how much one's not to blame for. Your heart tells you and your own work tells you – oh my dear our double bond – Thank God for you – oh but God bring us together – It is a dull dead life without you Helen – and that's the truth And I'm weary – And you are? ¶ Well I did get up in a few minutes – and made my tea and eat my biscuits – and get out a note book. I have to make a speech today at a reading of a Greek play – oh the Alcestis that Penelope Wheeler (Wheeler's wife) is giving in aid of "Concerts at the Front" It is a little thing I can do for them (the Wheelers) and I want to do it well. So I walked up and down for an hour thinking it out – though it should be but a ten minute speech – and concluded I wouldn't make notes – always better without if one can carry the construction in one's head. That's the difficulty   not to stray into some mental cul-de-sac. However – I'll try. ¶ And from now, every morning I think I must go at my lectures And if I get through that extra act of Prunella and read at history – that's all that is to be expected till – oh till I've seen you and you've given me life again [...] **71898/239-40**

[Barker had worked with **Penelope Wheeler** on productions of Gilbert Murray's Euripides: *Trojan Women, Electra, Hippolytus, Medea* (1905-7) and *Iphigenia in Tauris* (1912). In the last two she was chorus leader. With her own Greek Play Company in 1912 she both acted in and produced *Hippolytus* and *Iphigenia in Tauris* (the company was still operating in 1921). She recited Murray's *Alcestis* to the accompaniment of music by Gluck, played on 'ancient instruments', as part of Lady Islington's 'matinée' on 16 November at 8 Chesterfield-gardens. **Concerts at the Front**, organised by the actor and manager Lena Ashwell in association with The Ladies Auxiliary Committee of the YMCA, raised funds for and took entertainments to troops at the front. *The Guardian* (5 November 1916) advertised this event under the headline 'Mr Granville Barker's Reappearance'. He started on *Prunella* on 16 October.]

Friday [?mid-November 1916 Bloomsbury, London]
Early morning when I write this my darling – and I have been trying to do a little work – and am ashamed that I have done so little   But yet it is something to have sat quietly for an hour thinking of a job and making notes about it <u>and</u> letting ideas <u>come</u> For in our job – with the best will in the world we cannot manufacture.   One must isolate one's mind – get it in touch with whatever imaginative world we're working in – and wait results   Sometimes it is quick and easy and sometimes it is hard and long but whichever way – there is no other plan that I know of To get one's mind and spirit free.   Now that this war office is my mental incubus I know what the problem is – and I marvel more than ever at the work you've done my dear one. Your spirit – that has been free yes – but even then to isolate one's mind – so that the imaginative part of it may have play – and have play <u>connectedly</u> – that is so important. All sorts of good little scrappy ideas may come to one at moments – but they can never be the foundations of work. For that one needs the accustomed room (in one's own mind), the daily visit to it. Even this hour every morning better than nothing in that way. [...] **71898/181**

Tuesday [late November 1916 London]

I don't believe Helen my dear one – that either of us will ever be condemned to popular success!! Success – yes – in the recognition of good work done by people who care good work should be done It would be inhuman not to value that – but not the unthinking popular cry – and for the lack of that one must be glad for it removes a temptation (a subtle one) not to go on doing work for its own sake only – the sole way good work is done. We each know when we do good work and bad better than most people can tell us. You tell me things I don't know beloved (it is the wonderful thing) because you know better than I it seems – the thing that I – and the "beyond" me – am <u>trying</u> to do This is (in a way) apropos my Red Cross book which I think has fallen quite flat. I had one pang about that – no more. Much in it is no better (perhaps not so good) as the hundreds of other books of that sort – but it has half a dozen passages that are worth praise. But the job is done – and I've learnt from it And now the next job. I think one ought to have a prayer ending "Work without end Amen" – for that is the great joy – isn't it – to feel you're <u>creatively alive</u>. But together my dear – for oh I want you in my work <u>totally</u>. **71898/138**

> [**"Work without end"**: Barker parodies the Anglican doxology 'Glory be to the Father', which ends 'world without end'.]

Friday [?19 April 1918] 7-15am.   [Gordon Square, London]

[...] Martin Chuzzlewit – Yes – it has a good grip towards the end but it is far below his real best. Pecksniff gets poorer as the book goes on. He never did recapture the first fine careless rapture of "Warming his back as if it had been a widow's back or an orphan's back – or even an <u>enemy</u>'s back" But Jonas and the murder – that's all finely done. But David Copperfield <u>easily</u> first. Bleak House – Great Expectations and Our Mutual Friend and Little Dorrit for their best bits. That's the cream of Dickens. [...] (**Texas**)

Monday [?27 April 1918] 9-30PM. At the [Garrick] club. [London]

Another flash about Shakespeare's uninventiveness – he started life as an actor and so learnt to interpret not originate – became thus a super-interpreter and an interpreter of human beings instead of 'parts' but always found it natural to interpret and develop character – never to invent stories – I do think that is a sound 'interpretation' of him [...] (**Texas**)

Wed: [?19 June 1918] 7-15am. [Gordon Square, London]

[...] I have been thinking much about <u>our</u> work – I get depressed too – primarily at all the unfinished things that lie around me though I could well be depressed at what they'd be like and worth in <u>these</u> days! – if they were finished   Never yet have I learnt to say the simple direct things that want saying that sink home. But our work beloved is our vitality – our mental vitality certainly and when we are most "alive" we do it and the more alive the more unquestioningly. Not that I cavil at questionings – at incidental questionings – <u>about</u> it – but to question <u>it</u> – itself – is somehow to question life and that one mustn't do. Our writing <u>is</u> our unconscious activity, with you darling heart even more than with me (Children do everything unconsciously then as we grow older we lose the faculties or add calculation to them. I love that we keep and only add 'calculation' to our own gifts. Is that too wide a hole?) No – never fear that I shall give you false encouragement darling. Of course I never look at your work quite detachedly as an outsider would – but there's no gain in that   I stand towards it so much more as I stand towards my own (well – of course) That means that I am rather shy about it to outsiders – should regard it as rather indecent to praise it or to appear <u>too</u> satisfied with it. You know when one <u>is</u> proud of a bit of work one says sort of 'Well there it is – I won't insult you by pointing out the best bits – oh of course there are worst bits too. But if you can't see what's good in it you're a fool! ¶ But to ourselves – well darling – it is as to myself I'm far keener on the doing and to do than on the done – and keen on the bit that wants getting right – apt to say Ha ha! about the bit that <u>is</u> right and then leave it. No – I'll blame myself over your half of our work because I'll be probably <u>too</u> pernickety – critical – partly because I have a nasty carping nature (Have you discovered it?) – partly because to get it <u>right</u> that's always my fuss with my own things and I do fuss too much I miss the whole in worrying about the parts and depress myself – and my fear is that I may depress you. Just scold me if I do – for my sake darling and your own No I don't say we won't question the <u>sorts</u> of work we'll do – but we'll never question our work For to write happily is to write well. We'll dig back deeper then into our life Happy – oh we know But that's not the phrase for life itself. Vital and live we'll be that – please God and that <u>I</u> know – just by loving you dearly dearly I know it – when we're completely together   And from that – quite unconsciously our work will - spring [...] (**Texas**)

13. Aesthetic Pleasures

Monday [?12 June 1916 Williamstown, MA, USA]

I'm so glad that I have spent a time in New England   covered a good deal of it driving and walking. It takes hold of me. Few big houses or slums – a happy mean of living. Oh the old spirit of it is disguised now sometimes with common things thrown carelessly in   But I felt I could discover it for all that – and the meaning – the deeper meaning – that it had – and has. And I could feel a little what you meant when you said you were New England – and I loved it too for that. No. I won't explain. Never again will I 'explain you to yourself' – a vile habit. All I have to do – with you – as with all <u>true</u> life – of which you are a beautiful part – my dear – is to feel rightly about it – to understand. [...] **71898/123**

Tuesday July 11. [1916] 3-25PM. – <u>1-50</u> [on board the 'New York']

[...] I've read – am reading Romain Rolland's Handel – do you know it? Interesting. Written from a full mind. The test – the only test. I find more and more that I cannot read rubbish – or badly loosely written stuff. I read Rolland and think (so you might read it and think too) of evenings we will have of music – not merely idle listening – but of hearing it with our <u>minds</u>. Paris dear – an appartement up there on the hill behind the Luxembourg – someone to play – and we'll find out lots beyond the hundred things one casually knows now – really not much more is it? And when we're in the country – for we'll not be in Paris – so much – you shall have a clavichord Do you know what Bach sounds like on a clavichord – so good – and such fun to play. I see you in the evening – dainty my darling – with very dainty fingers. Such a harmony of life. Such a meaning in it. Creative thought dear   the noblest thing [...] **71897/73**

[**Romain Rolland**, *Handel*, trans. A. Eaglefield-Hull, (New York: Henry Holt, 1916)]

Tuesday July 11. [1916] 10-20. – <u>8-45</u> [on board the 'New York']
[...] Helen – you baby you are beautiful – and you know it! Oh – I see more than others will ever see – but they see enough unless they're blind – blinded by coarse thoughts and feelings (that's blindness) – to see that the whole room you're in is brighter for your being there. That's beauty my dear. It sheds light   I suppose it can reside – that power – in things that people would call "ugly" – it seldom does – though I have seen quite old people with almost ugly features radiate this something from them.   But generally the beauty within models the outside – oh not to Greek features and damask skins and golden hair – in fact if Nature does that it often means that she can do nothing more – well she does it in children often – in fact that is what crude Nature can do – and all it can do. Then comes the other God-like power – which – when human beings have in them an echo of it – we call Art (we have that echo – thanks be to God – in us) and gives the beautiful <u>meaning</u> to the beauty. [...] **71897/71**

[Thursday 13 July 1916] 12 o'clock. – 9-20. [on board the 'New York']
[...] I've never been able to read Hawthorne – so I have picked up The Marble Fawn. What am I to think of Hawthorne? If one comes to him quite young – ?   And is it like an old method in music – that one has to learn to listen to? I don't know. We'll talk of that. **71897/81**

Monday [?4 September 1916 with the Wheelers in Kent]
In the country now I always hear your voice my darling. That isn't merely a phrase – for you have brought me – though I loved it in a way before because of the quiet and peace it gave I only loved it acquiescingly – but you have brought me to go out and meet it as it were – to take something to it myself and so gain something more from Nature for my own spirit. That is a great gift you have my Helen – you are 'attuned'. This – where I write – is an old farm-house in a corner of tumbled country between Kent and Sussex – borders of counties are like that   they have given up trying to be

any shape – the hills have. And the house is old enough (300 years perhaps) to seem to have grown and never been built at all. And that is the right way with houses isn't it as with every thing. We mustn't make them – but put them together in a vital way and then they'll acquire life [...] **71898/38**

Wednesday [4 October 1916 Weymouth]

I've been reading Balzac – les Celibataires – in English – not from laziness but because leaving Barrie's on Sunday I snatched the nearest likely book and snatched this. And – I've read nothing of this sort (or of any other) for a good while – and oh again he strikes me as a great man. A perfect God with his characters – so ruthlessly just – and we know how difficult that is – And seeing things through and through. And again – he always attacks the evil thing – the truly evil – sterility – greed – egoism – and not because they are conventionally evil but because he sees the really evil in them. Over virtues I think he is more conventional – but then it is much harder not to be – and in human life – original value is the hard thing to compass isn't it? Vice is generally a regular thing (that is our test of it) and although it <u>may</u> disgust us we don't fear it but virtues that are beyond our measure – those we almost do fear in people – we prefer the harmless unobtrusive kind Ah we are not free enough and fearless enough any of us. The Law is still a thing of the letter and not of the spirit   But we march towards freedom [...] **71898/104**

> [Honoré de **Balzac**'s *Les Célibataires* consists of a group of three long stories, and in 1843 was published in the collection *Scènes de la vie de province. The Celibates* was published in an English translation by Clara Bell in 1898.]

[Sunday 22 October 1916] 3-30PM – 10-30am. [Ayot]

[...] And you feel that you have only just grown up? Why <u>yes</u> of course and so do I. And as if one hadn't lived at all – and one was just taking breath to begin – With a whole world there – of rather keen soft air and very bright clear colours – Spring colours – nothing heavy – orange or dull red – nothing muddy about them –

and very clearly defined forms. That is my sense of it - such a vivid sense. [...] **71898/202**

Monday. (?23 October 1916 London]

It has become almost a text for us Helen dear one - the point of the first story you ever told me "How could I tell him if he did not know?" It is what you are up against with people over any vital question - though for long you may not discover it. A man goes on listening to and studying music and can talk about Brahms and Beethoven and Bach with the best - but suddenly something new comes - or it may be something old like a folk song - and you discover about him that for all this - he doesn't like music - the thing isn't <u>in</u> him - and there's an end   Whether he has wasted his time or has got any good out of it I can't tell - but you find ever after (and you wonder you never found it before) that you are at cross purposes with him on that point   And so of course in things closer than music. One goes on agreeing and agreeing - for intellectually one can pretend to get anywhere - then suddenly a test moment comes - and you're miles apart. He does not know and you cannot tell him - and there's an end of that. And so it saves God's time when two people only need to hold hands and without words at all they <u>know</u> [...] **71898/169**

[The two relationships, with Huntington and McCarthy, seem to shape Barker's thinking here.]

Monday night - [23 October 1916] half past midnight - <u>7-30PM</u> [Bloomsbury, London]

[...] to the Opera, if you please   Samson and Delila - I had never heard it. Oh - comic! - music with no real meaning or character. Pretty - and I kept thinking not of what it was all about but of Paris restaurants in the 80's and women in bustles and men in braided coats and puffy ties and their "coeurs s'ouvrent à ses voix" all through dinner! I heard it all but it hardly seemed to get inside my ears [...] **71898/213**

[He was taken **to the Opera** by the Galsworthys. *Samson et Dalila* by Camille Saint-Saens (first performed 1877), conducted by Percy Pitt in Thomas Beacham's season at the Aldwych Theatre. Barker refers to "**Mon coeur s'ouvre à ta voix**", a popular aria, known in English as "Softly awakes my heart". He also knew his fashion history: the **bustle** returned to fashion in the 1880s, with its heyday around 1886-88.]

Monday. [early November 1916 Bloomsbury, London]

I have always taken an intense interest in 'opposite windows'. Maeterlinck hit upon one of his really poetic ideas in Intérieur – and to me original too – but you can trace it to something also in French literature can you? Shadows on a blind have a wonderful fascination too. Through a window opposite here about this time in the morning – if I go to look out there's generally a woman's arm – apparently frantically waving a hairbrush. I suppose that at the unseen end of the wave it is brushing her hair   But it seems to me to be a good wave – a better wave than it would be – because she is unconscious and alone. As a small child I longed – to be invisible and able to fly all through the houses seeing people <u>alone</u>. Did you? I think it was the right "artistic" instinct – though the instinct of a very self-conscious child. And yet I don't know that I was in an uncomfortable sense. You know there is sub-consciousness which isn't self-consciousness but a far subtler thing. And we both have that. [...] **71898/147**

[Maurice **Maeterlinck's** *Intérieur* (1895) has a stage setting in which the audience, along with two characters outside, can watch, through the windows of a house, the behaviour of the family inside, who do not yet know their daughter has died. By 1916 Barker had directed three plays by Maeterlinck.]

Friday. Nov 24 [1916] 7-15am – <u>2-15am</u> [Bloomsbury, London]

[...] A high collar you have on – well I'm not <u>sure</u> that I approve. But 18th century things (that's your room) yes – I approve of those – as long as they haven't too many curves to them – and I'm glad there are too many books for neatness – there always should be – it is books that should "disturb" a room and nothing else – and damn the tray of unanswered letters and unpaid bills. Let them lie [...] **71898/258-59**

[The **high collar** and **room** are described by her on 3 November (71903/128).]

Thursday [13 June 1918] 7am. [Gordon Square. London]

[...] The Yeomen of the Guard – !! It is like eating the sweets of ones youth – no thrill but a reminiscent pleasure   You think – how good this <u>did</u> taste and that it was an honest simple taste, and you're glad you haven't lost it The chief dashed us in his car to Hammersmith. He is privileged to drive at any rate he likes and <u>does</u> – and then to Hampstead to drop people – then to Whitehall Court – the drive was worth having – whirling round London – a fast motor has become exciting again in these days of taxis few and far between. **(Texas)**

[Barker had been asked by his **chief** (Cumming) to provide company for a visit to this Gilbert and Sullivan opera, staged at King's Theatre, Hammersmith. Cumming used to race **cars**. The combination of pleasures here exemplifies one sort of engagement with the 'modern'.]

14. Love and Sex

Saturday night [?20 November 1915 Hotel Algonquin, New York]
Do you wonder at all that I had such horrors at the thought of you
and AH. that night? I thought you might remember what I said
calmly about myself in that way when first we spoke of that side of
things. But – I'd let myself think as I did – when I loved no one else
and thought I never should. And besides loving you has changed all
that part of life for me – absolutely – made it a wonderful thing
again – given it back to me as I used first to think of it as a boy. Dear
I must tell you – if you don't realise – that I think constantly –
constantly of ourselves in that way. An outsider would say it was
just the usual thing – but you'll know (because it's you that have
given me back what I thought I'd lost. I remember it coming –
something you said to me in your garden) – you'll know that that
desire for you is for the deepest and most sacred Communion that
could be. There was a thing you never would tell me. I always
hoped – I <u>can't</u> write this – but oh I am so longing to be near you
and tell you – oh my dear, my dear I am <u>yours</u>. **71915/126**

[**AH**: Archer Huntington.]

[Friday] Feb 18. [1916] 10 PM. London.
[...] I said to myself walking back here tonight that I cannot live in
an atmosphere of appetite and passion – only in one of mind and
spirit – those I mean as the dominant – directing things in life   I
don't – you know I don't – turn away from passion – but it is the
instinctive – unconscious passion which is beautiful – consciously
we meet each other in a rarer way. [...] **71897/42**

Wednesday. [?13 May 1916 Williamstown, MA, USA]
[...] we laugh together so naturally, my Helen   It is almost the best
of all I think – to know so to speak that the foundations are so firm

that one can dance all one wants to on the top of them. But in letters one can't laugh (for it's an immediate mutual thing) and we've had very little laughter therefore. But we know – I think – that we belong to each other in that sense too   We're children together. I think of you so out of doors – in some wood with me and glad of little things [...] **71898/110**

Sunday [?18 June 1916 Williamstown, MA, USA]

Do you get times when all your feelings are there – but dulled instead of keen.   One feels so ashamed – at least I do. But I think it is nature's way   after a crisis of emotion – one's physical self has to re-act and rest. And we are too apt to forget – that even in our most spiritual moments we express ourselves only by leave of our bodies so to speak   So we must 'register' the perfect moments and be patient with the poor body at some others. The life of the mind and the spirit that can be constant. But always one must try for the harmony of the three. And it is the thing to be said about love – not in the crudely emotional schoolboy sense – but as one can find it by living and learning. It does in some mysterious way blend and harmonise the three faculties – body and mind and spirit and makes a man and a woman as perfect half-creatures as they can be – and then – the miracle – joining the two makes a whole [...] **71898/126**

> [The image of love as an instinctive search by **half-creatures** for their other half is from Aristophanes' speech in Plato's *Symposium*.]

14 July [1916] Midday – 8-45 [on board the 'New York']

[...] But you <u>are</u> very sweet to look at you know – beautiful – if the word has any real meaning at all. Beautiful – and I take a frank and healthy joy in loving your beauty   to look at you – to hold you close to me – to kiss you – my <u>dear</u> And then <u>through</u> that joy to feel the deeper joy that binds us together – closer than ever my arms can hold you – and they just try to express that closeness and can't (and buttons hurt!) – and kisses try to express it and can't – and nothing ever can or will – but the body – all we have to express with – tries – and tries – and there is joy in that. ¶ My own – I said these should be diaries. Well – there has been nothing to diarise on board. And I said that they shouldn't be too full of simple 'longing' for you. But it's no use – I have to write it down – it hurts <u>too</u> much otherwise. As you read it quickly, it'll seem – morbid? – repeated over and over again? – weak? But remember that <u>days</u> are passing ¶ Our work – and I was writing about that yesterday wasn't I – <u>your</u> work (I think I was – yesterday) before I opened the letter! ¶ Beloved – it comes to me – how long you have stood on the brink of your <u>own</u> life – of your <u>self</u> – and for some reason or other have not plunged in Without me – would you ever have plunged? Even now – oh for good reasons yet – it is with you 'tentative' work – still an adventure – still a thing to be shy about. Oh – no shyness in you in doing it – no silly mock modesty (the blushing amateur!!! none of that) – but as if you still did not quite dare to say – This is my <u>own</u> world." ¶ And yet how plain to you always – and to me as soon as we really met (our first <u>talk</u> did it I think) that it was your world and that your real self was to be found there – could live there and there only. But you sat on the brink – dipping a hand in. Well – I take your hand and say <u>Come</u>. I say it quite confidently – apart from our love I'd say it (so little – so not at all – my Helen – do I think you – did I ever <u>could</u> I ever think you a 'clinging whining woman" (I hasten to tell you that phrase is your own - you telling me not to think it of you – My darling!)). Apart from our love I'd say it – since I know so well it is your real world where your real self lives and can live its best. Still – by yourself it would be a bit of a plunge (worth making Helen dear) But – <u>not</u> apart from our love – and thank God, nothing now need be – it isn't a plunge at all – is it? but from the beginning the natural thing. ¶ And another thing in your letter – that 'Service for love is <u>almost</u> the best. But my dear – isn't it quite the best – Isn't [*sic*] the only possible form of fruitful service? I think so. I think it is a fundamental truth. And I do believe it is given to me to say it to you – The truth is there in you – it must be – and always have been – but overlaid sometimes with other teachings perhaps. No – I won't dogmatise – you will know. Not only will you know but know too just what is truth to you now. But this is truth to me. Service for love is the only fruitful service Loveless duty is barren – however virtuous it may seem **71897/84-85**

[**the letter**: She had written letters in advance for each day of his voyage. The essay 'Archer Huntington's Wife' suggests why Huntington was 'on the brink' of her own life. See pp.213-216.]

Saturday July 15 [1916] 10-30am – <u>6-30am</u> [on board the 'New York']

[...] I like to think that you sleep with your cheek on your two hands. Do you? And I kiss you on the other cheek – and then you turn your head till – oh my darling your lips touch mine. That was the way you first kissed me – I can always feel that kiss – I always shall. [...]

[same letter] [...] "I know a little garden close" – I used to say that over and over to myself – that and other things – while I paced up and down Fifth Avenue – waiting for a word from you – ready to pace and to wait (and determined you should see me. I knew you would – in whatever crowd it was the very first day you came down it) – ready to go on till doomsday. [...] **71897/90**

[He would likely see her on **Fifth Aven**ue because she lived there and regularly patronised Sherrys' restaurant. Such **pacing** was fictionalised in his story 'Souls on Fifth' (1916): see Bibliography.]

Saturday [?2 September 1916 SJW barracks]

The other day a lecture was given to the whole of the Cadets on Venereal Diseases Disguisedly as it might affect themselves – and it does affect them – oh the conversations I hear! – ostensibly that they might be on the look-out for the health of their men when they become officers. A very necessary lecture. Conditions are better in the army They were appalling – one man out of every three affected more or less. At present 40 per thousand always in hospital from that cause. It was an honest straight forward lecture but – full of occasion for laughter – isn't that odd – amazing. I have never been able to laugh at such things – do women ever? Never. But there were certain appeals to honour – for continence – against seduction – never one hint that men were in anyway different to brute beasts never any recognition of some further meaning – nothing said (putting it simply) about Love. Well – how can one tell them if they do not know. But they could know surely and that <u>is</u> the thing to say. A strange hour – I sat and wondered! **71898/37**

[The approach to tackling **VD** by proper sex education was initiated in June 1916 with the first report of the National Council for Combating Venereal Disease.]

15. SELF

Thanksgiving day – and my birthday. [Thursday 25 November 1915 Algonquin Hotel, New York]
[...] I don't want you to think that because of all this I have lost my 'public' spirit. I have thought more seriously over these things than ever before. I don't think England will fail in the end over fighting – though she is fighting wastefully, as she does everything – but I do think she needs brains and imagination – to make the settlement of things – which is what makes for the future a fruitful settlement. And as I have given everything in me to feed that in her I believe that is where my work really lies. If it comes to the question of not being individuals any more but just units to count up – then I can go as a unit. I hate the waste and foolishness of war – but I don't fear it (any more than anyone else does – it is extraordinary – when you get among the firing – even only where I have been – people don't talk or think in the way we do now. They recognize that 'nerves' may go – but otherwise – there is a new standard set and that is danger – and you take your share – just as it comes – without considering that you'll either get further into it or further out of it by your own will at all) I can only do now what comes to my hand – but I think I see the sort of thing it will be a little in the future – unpopular – very – but then I'm used to that. Helen I'm not vain I really am not – self-opinionated (and behind that nervous) but I have always had to fight – never a thing has come easily and it makes one – if one isn't really a great man – sharp and assertive – both faults. ¶ Do you want to know how since you came to me in spirit – my working life has been lifted up. It has been – I seem to have got back the keenness and meaning that I used to have quite as a boy – which lately had been becoming cleverness – such a different thing. Anyway I have done more writing and planning to write these past three months than in the past three years or more – and I do think of a finer freer sort [...] Don't think because of all these long dreary letters that I'm a dull prig. I'm not – I'm quite

nice to live with – more amusing than half the people you have to talk to now. Wouldn't it be a jolly time – oh happy together [...] **71915/130-31**

Tuesday July 11. [1916] 10-20. – <u>8-45</u> [on board the 'New York']

[...] The great will that brings us together makes but a tiny little puppet of me. [...] I have been jealous of the past – but time is conquering that I think. Well it was not always so much jealousy as anger at our wasted time. And perhaps it is not time conquering so much as when you tell me that never – never have you given as you give to me. I know it Helen – as you know it of me.   And whether we should be glad or not – we <u>are</u>   To feel – that though we could not know we'd meet – we always kept hidden the best gifts we had – kept them for each other [...] **71897/71-72**

Tuesday July 18 [1916] 10 am – <u>4 am</u> [Hotel Russell, London]

I note an omen for you if you want an omen – it has a remote reading now though only. On the day I landed – yesterday – the Court Theatre – where my "reputation" was made was sold by auction! **71897/100**

[Barker's co-management of the **Court Theatre** was made possible by the financial backing of an amateur theatre enthusiast, J. H. Leigh, who owned the lease on the theatre.]

Monday [?14 August 1916 SJW barracks]

[...] I think darling how oddly (as we say) it happens that you and I have each – it seems – to go through parallel experience on our road to each other. As I lay the other night before getting to sleep – I thought – This for me is going through the daily round just as Helen has gone through it – a duty because for the moment other things seemed closed and duty was at least duty. And I thought that if I sorted out the needless roughnesses and vilenesses – as you would not either let your spirit be affected by the softnesses – the luxury – then there remained to us both a duty which was at least a training in character. Does this explain why I feel without thinking it on purpose – that this service is a way to you I <u>do</u> A short way – please God – for I want you my dear and my <u>real</u> life – our life of things of the mind and spirit   But – nothing comes unless we earn it I've said. What wouldn't I do? [...] **71898/31**

Sunday Aug 27. [1916] The Garrick Club 12-30PM – <u>6-30am</u>

[...] I must seem to you the greatest grumbler alive. In a flash – (as things do) it came to me yesterday, that my letters – my diary for you – is one long complaint. I'll try to cure that I suppose I <u>do</u> grumble – but believe darling that I <u>don't</u> add shirking to that. I try and plough through. But my difficulty is to do what my brain doesn't <u>want</u> to do – to make it do it. Always till now – in imaginative work – the test has been – do you <u>want</u> to do this. A good and right test I hold, you know, if you discipline the wanting bit perhaps – indeed no doubt the outer discipline will be good for me I think of that – oh – all the time – of the ordeal and test that this is to bring me to you – worthy of you – helpful to you – the best possible Me. That apart from the little use – the very little that I may be in the job. **71897/153**

[The **job** is his service in the artillery: see pp.79-99 above.]

Monday [?11 September 1916 Trowbridge barracks]

Have I told you – I think I have – that I have learnt to be homesick for America? Yes – genuinely and not only because you are there Things in it – not all of it but much of it and more in it I have grown to love. New England – I do think I know what that means and the pride – the rather "dour" pride as the Scotch say – with which you speak of it. I know what that stands for and love it – the independence the stoicism the firm belief in things the light of inspiration breaking through cloud – and sparks from flint. And I understand it – for at heart I remain a Puritan – though I have shed all the outer garments of Puritanism long ago. But we – we see with each other's eyes – (thank God who has given us to each other) and we value the clear keen vision and the self control – and then the more we value – don't we my dear – the force of character – passion – love – thought – feeling that can illumine and break through those bonds. That is our test of worth [...] **71898/46**

Tuesday the 12ᵗʰ [September 1916] 1-30PM. – <u>7-30am.</u> [Trowbridge barracks]

[...] Did I tell you I have one great solace here – At 8-30 when all the day's work is over I can escape – I did last night – and walk into the country by myself (with you) for an hour I did last night – into the dark fields – with cows breathing hard at me – feeling my way a bit – but there was a full moon – giving the country a sort of glow of light through a thick misty sky. But I forgot all gunnery and barracks – and was myself – and you [...] **71898/66**

Sunday [?mid-September 1916 Trowbridge barracks]

[...] I can't call this work in our creative sense – but trying to make it a training for myself – I doubt it's being at all useful to others – to my country. But for many lessons I wouldn't have missed it The rough and ready – but really fine-natured comradeship is good. Especially here – among the older men. Not one but is ready to help – to tell you things – to have a friendly word and a kind thought – oh now I must break off and polish my boots and my buttons. (I <u>love you</u>) ¶ On a real Sunday – in quiet and alone in a room I can finish this. The suppression of self is for me perhaps a good lesson too. No – you are <u>not</u> to take that to yourself beloved one – it is the opposite lesson you must have. But I find my little vanity rising to some mark of recognition of what I was before I was a soldier – and – well I know it is vanity at least. [...] **71898/491**

Monday. [18 September 1916] 1-30PM – 7-30am [Trowbridge barracks]

[...] here I am in the barracks still and buckled down to it – I made a slight dent in the mathematical difficulties this morning – and –

I can do so much better if people are kind to me – well mainly they are – Still – I pray rather to be released from it Although then comes the curious superstition. If I find more congenial work – harder and more trouble it will be but easier to me because I can do it – am I earning <u>you</u> [...] **71898/71**

Thursday [?21 September 1916 Trowbridge barracks]
Roughly speaking I think there are the two sorts of life – the competitive – the life in the crowd – and the observing (critical, contemplative, creative,) or the life apart. And I have no doubt at all to which one our natures draw us. Some of the discipline of the crowd is good for us I daresay – without it we might be narrow-minded egoists out of touch with that other part of the world – and I take my army discipline as you darling have taken your "worldly" life as that discipline. But in the crowd – such gifts as we have don't blossom – we just suppress them and put on our masks – quite good and amusing masks they may be (Oh Helen do you remember the early days – years and years ago when we began to see beneath each others – and <u>knew</u> each other beneath them) Well we both do our best. But as soon as I get alone my thoughts begin to spring and I know that is my real self. But not till I'm with you dear one ("with" you in some sense) are they made really alive by <u>feeling</u> – made truly creative. [...] **71898/51**

<u>**Tuesday**</u>. **[end September 1916] [Trowbridge barracks]**
Your letter (dear letter) tells me that in ways you think I'm like Cavour. Oh – a very duodecimo edition but it pleases me – because I have thought so too – that is always I've had instinctive sympathy with him and his ways. And I've a dominant dash of North Italian blood in me too. I like his realism his resolve to see things as they were – the feeling that neither he nor his reputation mattered if only he could get things done – and his contempt for conventional standards his contented appeal to his own conscience. I think Cavour at the Paris conference and after Villafranca is a big figure. Well – beloved – and I'm not. I've weaknesses – large gaps in me

apart from lack of shere great ability – but one can <u>mean</u> the best – and that I try to do – and to mean the <u>real</u> thing – and so I like you to think I have something of him in me. And it is true of us both – beloved (most things are true of us both) We've taken time to learn what we are but I think we know it now – passed through much 'unreality' which seemed real – which we tried to make real – but we know what is real to us at last – what we mean. [...] **71898/97**

[Camillo Benso, Count of **Cavour** was a campaigner for Italian independence and especially for the expansion of his native Piedmont. He articulated his position on independence at the **Paris** conference which ended the Crimean War in 1856. He fought with France as an ally against the Austrians in the second Italian War of Independence, ended by the treaty of **Villafranca** in July 1859. Huntington much enjoyed reading Thayer's *Life and Times of Cavour* (1911): 'there is much in his character which makes me think of yours – statesman-like qualities they are –' (71903/110). Barker's **North Italian** blood came via his mother, Mary Elizabeth Bozzi-Granville.]

[Thursday] Sep 28. [1916] 8-30am – <u>2-30am.</u> [Trowbridge barracks]

Dearest and best – grey morning rain threatening. Last night a concert. I was roped in to recite – and I felt it would be churlish to refuse. I had got out of it once before. So I flung Tennyson's "Revenge" at them   the only recitable poem that remains in my head. It was curious the harder "professional" touch among all the amateurs – there is something distinctive in it – business like – uncompromising – one tells it at once in pianists The difference is I think that the amateur tries to put all the decoration on (– or in) without being sure that the walls are built firm – the "professional" builds four square and – if he's wise – is sparing of his decoration altogether. I don't recite badly! But it was strange – the old actor's "self-conscious" feeling – which isn't shyness – nor yet vanity (though it may become so) returning for an hour – like a strange ghost. But I did not welcome it (!) and it went. I like to be a mere cipher here – though I'm conscious – to speak the truth that they pick me out rather (though not in my soldiering – God knows) –

and of course I'm glad of the little extra attention I get (I haven't been put on guard yet.) – I think I don't take any advantage of them – no indeed I don't   well nothing illegitimate – I promise my dear one (I see you smile – oh <u>kiss me</u>) – this morning I have begun to let my moustache grow (double association of ideas!) as that is the rule here though it has not been enforced on me yet – still if it is a (silly) rule – No indeed you will never see it – it will be kept under and removed at the first opportunity. ¶ The shed fills up – and men smoke and talk and <u>whistle</u> – vile habit ¶ Another day begins – I believe I am conquering the work here a <u>little</u> – I'm glad of that – I don't want to be a <u>hopeless </u>fool – good at it of course I shall never be – but you mustn't have to own to a <u>hopeless</u> fool in anything must you my dear? [...] **71898/84**

[**Tennyson, 'The Revenge**: A Ballad of the Fleet' tells of a naval battle. The double association with the **moustache** may perhaps be a reference to both Archer Huntington and George Bernard Shaw, two hairy-faced men who made Huntington's life difficult, which is why she will never see it on Barker. But that's simply a guess.]

Monday. [?2 October 1916 ?Adelphi Terrace, London]

Alone in London on a grey autumn Sunday (when I'm writing this) brings me back my early days when I couldn't afford to go to the country (then for years I never was a Sunday here) and I used to take my walk – alone – through the grey green parks or in the grey black streets. And the feeling comes back to me – not thought or definite memory but just feeling – and one becomes again for a little a part of that past time   You get that about places too. But your places are not mine.   My dear I'm glad we've had such different lives – seen and known such different things. Apart from the inner things we bring each other – it is wonderful having completed ourselves alone (really alone always) as far as we can – we meet – and oh how much we have to give – of ordinary things. [...] **71898/100**

Friday. [6 October 1916 Weymouth]

Tonight – the night I write – I wandered round Weymouth – just to find some rooms – just to look at the house – in which I stayed 20 years ago – what an age! I found it – down in the old town – right in the harbour – I remember I had been sent to some cheap "theatrical" rooms   But in the night I was woke – bitten! So I got up and had a bath and went out before dawn and sat on the sea shore – and then went back into the town and found this old house – very "sailorish" smelling fresh of paint – bright blue paint And I spent most of my hard earned salary (only a few shillings) in taking the rooms – so like me. But I had a happy time there – and I remember it to this day. So it was worth while. The bow window of my room looked shere into the harbour   the sails of a boat passing down would almost block out the light. [...] **71898/103**

[**20 years ago** he would have been performing with Ben Greet's Shakespeare and Old English Comedy Company. **A shilling** is 5p; a shilling in 1916 would be £2.95 today (2021).]

Saturday. [?21 October 1916 Bloomsbury, London]

It is 6.30 – or rather now it is near to 7 – and I am sitting at the table in my London room   Just by me to the right is the fireplace – with a gastove which I have just lit – and a gas ring on which I have just boiled a kettle and made myself a cup of tea   A cup of tea an apple and a plasmon biscuit   these are to help me – not get up at 6 these winter mornings – but keep up and awake – so not to waste the two or three hours which will be mine – and yours dear one (and I make very good tea. Then – beyond the fireplace is a washhand stand (savage old English house!) then a large cupboard takes up all one wall   then the corner turns to a door – then a chest of drawers then my bed (all sorts of beds luxuries to me after barracks but this one a good enough sort anyway – then in another corner a queer "Victorian" sideboard – and rough bookshelves over it. Then the window, much be-curtained – for one must show <u>no</u> light at night – and I wish the window were larger and the furniture smaller. Then a dressing-table rather a nice "piece" more bookshelves (the

room they tell me was fitted with them for a member of parliament
- since deceased) and then my table again. On one side of it a
leather box which holds certain letters - on the other a little steel
box which holds things like my passport and Red Cross badge and
papers that matter - and more letters - many pens and pencils and
an ink bottle or two - a certain clock which tells me it is five past
two in the morning. Opposite I only see houses - just like this
house - for this is Bloomsbury - Victorian - plain - severe. But
over the roofs of them there's the top of one tree and the tip top of
the dome of London University - and if I lean out I can see more
trees in the square this street leads to. ¶ So now - can you picture
me - if ever you wake between 2 and 3 - which my darling must not
do - but if ever she does - there I am - and perhaps I'll be writing
to you (I think it is <u>more</u> than probable) and perhaps I'll be
working at a play or an article - and that is writing to you isn't it -
as well. [...] **71898/168**

[**plasmon** biscuits: Now sold principally as a nutritious food for babies. The
certain letters and clock are the letters from her and the travelling clock set
at New York time. The **dome** is that of University College London.]

Tuesday.   [?17 October 1916 Bloomsbury, London]

I wonder if Balzac ever lived in the Maison Vauquer (isn't that the
name of the house in Père Goriot) or if he invented it all. I wonder
because this boarding house I'm in has a touch of the Maison
Vauquer about it - and I have my breakfast in my room! I cannot
sit a meal among the people if I need not. But foolish   I ought to
take the chance of seeing them. But again I ought not to do it for
that purpose. No sight of them will be vision of them unless I love
them (in a wide sense)   But perhaps by seeing them I'd get through
my impatience (it isn't more) and learn to love them. However -
I've such little time to myself these days that I shirk that and if ever
I need a Maison Vauquer I shall have to invent it. But I believe I
have - partly from mere shyness - shirked meeting all sorts and
conditions too much ¶ Which is it you draw on most - imagination
or knowledge - in what proportion do you mostly blend the two -

in what proportion ought they to be blended? Oh well – profitless questions I suppose. One does what one <u>can</u>. [...] **71898/173**

> [*Père Goriot* was published in 1835. The entire narrative is spun out of the ambitions of and relationships between the three main characters who are all boarders at **Maison Vauquer**.]

Monday. [late October 1916 London]

Do you ever get 'brain fidgets'? (I'm sure you do – if <u>I</u> do!!) They manifest themselves in me in what I call the 'Newspaper disease' – an inability to read or think connectedly – a tendency to pick up newspapers at every odd moment and dash through them – in itself a brain rotting thing to do. I've been sick of this – this last week – brought on perhaps by my office work which is to go through files and files and files and make notes of what I find there. But it must be cured. Contemplation and some solid prose. 'Club conversation' of course is another form of the malady. But that I will <u>not</u> be led into. Queer – how even in more trivial things – brain and heart must work interchangeably. Casual talk with – those we care for (by which vague phrase of course I really mean Helen) gets all the added value of our caring and brain-life springs from it. But if we don't care it's just the 'sounding brass and tinkling cymbal' it gives birth to no melody in us – becomes no part of the whole melody of our lives That's it – we don't remember noise – only tunes That's a thought. [...] **71898/179**

> [The **quotation** is Biblical: 1 Corinthians 13.1]

[Saturday] Nov 18 [1916] 7-15am – <u>2-15am</u> [?Bloomsbury, London]

[...] I couldn't get up till just now – I lay with the burden of things on me (does it comfort you to know what a helpless creature I am at times) And I thought and thought of you – and the picture of you was always – lying on that heap of leaves – and I thought I could have seen you from that place on the other side of the wall – and if

I could come along and pick you up and carry you off. But then it seemed that you were so like just another leaf – and how gentle I must be. And there came – and comes – my frightened feeling about you. I'm not gentle enough – am I? – in my letters – in the thoughts they bring – <u>too</u> insistent – too persistent – too disturbing That's my wretched way. I can be different. No I suppose one can't be different to oneself and shouldn't want to be. But I can turn all the weakness of that into strength – all that would hurt you in it into all that will help you – believe that. [...] **71898/ 252**

16. WHEN THIS FIGHTING IS OVER

Thursday. [?early May 1916 Hotel Algonquin, New York]
In these times I have found a new friend who has come to live for
a while in Forty Fourth Street. His name is Bucyrus and he is a
steam shovel. He'd fascinate you - the way he dashes at his work -
puffing - and where there's an obstacle - he snorts and protests. I
can't describe the process how he swings about and digs in - but it
is wonderfully human. And this sort of machinery lifts up my
heart because I feel that it is setting men free from harsh mechanical things - which should be - the setting them free from that sort
of labour - the progress of civilisation - shouldn't it? But - setting
them free to <u>what</u>? That's the devil isn't it. Science runs so far ahead
of the Art of Life. And so one may think - proudly of <u>our</u> work (as
well as of steam shovels) - for "What to make of Life when you have
it" is the problem we're always trying to solve in books and plays.
Are you working when this finds you. My dear I'm proud if you are
- proud because I know there'll be something of me in it. My life
in your work. That's my good thought - darling - helps me often.
And you? **71898/128**

[His hotel was on **44th Street. Bucyrus** Foundry and Manufacturing
Company was a major producer of steam shovels.]

**[Wednesday 12 July 1916] Midday - <u>9-50</u> [on board the 'New
York']**
[...] Darling we must live for some time in France For the next ten
years or so - there is I think going to be a great revival there - a
moral and spiritual revival. Perhaps it is <u>now</u> that she is really
going to reap the fruit of the Revolution It may easily be so. If -
a century and 20 years ago - she had held to her <u>defensive</u> war - and
had been able to shed the viler products of the Revolutionary time
(there were bound to be those) - she would have been the most

glorious country under Heaven. And perhaps – the wheel has now come full circle and after this righteous and defensive war – she may take up her destiny where she left it then   France is the least tainted in this fighting We English were not tainted – but – God forgive us – we become so if we are not careful with hatred and talk of Revenge. No – not the best and the most articulate of us – but there is a substratum of wrong feeling which may make itself felt. Some of the English newspapers make me ashamed. ¶ But anyhow – France for us I think, during these immediately coming years. [...] **71897/76-77**

Friday [8 September 1916 Gordon Square, London]
Beloved – Ideas – creative things – don't flourish in an atmosphere of war – at least they don't in the "training-barrack" atmosphere I move in now – partly because one is too tired I expect – fagged is the word. my brain will do half an hour's work – no more. ¶ But some imagination does spring up. Do you notice how people write verse out in France – and not bad verse either – that have apparently never written before. I do believe that the war will have set many people free. The knowledge that they have taken a share in a great national movement will liberate and dignify their souls. They will feel that the clever-clever politician cannot lecture and lord it over them again This will be true of course only of a minority of people – but everything involving an idea – however universal it seems – is the work of a minority. The new Idea that England will gain and develop after the war must needs be that – the speed of her journey it may depend on the size of the minority – that is all. How dully I write my darling   dull brain – but not dull heart. [...] **71898/33**

Friday. [?mid-September 1916 London]
Dear heart – did I ever tell you that apart from loving you – though it must be a little because of loving you for everything is more or less because of that now – that I had grown to love America too. New York papers arrived for me today – and I had that queer feeling as I looked through them that one has over anything which

suggests Home. America now has its touch of home for me. I do love it much for what it is – very much for what many people in it are – very very much for what – please God – it is to be. I do steadfastly believe that the Future can always be better than the past   I care for the Future more than for anything – what else should one care for in outside things. And such a large slice of the Future is to be America's. And we are to see it my dear one – and help to build it a little – with our thoughts and our love – love for each other which spreads out – glorified into love for the world [...] **71898/25**

Thursday Sep 21. [1916] Trowbridge (in the shed there) 8-30am – 2-30am

[...] Oh my dear the future of this country and Europe and America – It looms large now and ugly – and nobody who is fighting or has anything to do with fighting will stop to think of it – how can they. But it must be thought of – if thought is of any use in guiding things – and if one doesn't believe it is – well – then we have lost faith indeed. And it is no use hoping that things will "come right". The war has killed that easy optimism in me – in all of us I should think   We can make the future right or make it wrong – And I see horrible signs of it being made wrong. So <u>we</u> must think my darling and work with our brains and hearts. We can – that gift has been given us. I can't now – not consecutively (except on Sundays!!) But that's my work – when this "duty" is through   Duty – such a dead thing – but needed it may be to keep the present from "slipping back" – since this is the best we have made of it – from slipping back to worse. But "work" – a <u>live</u> thing for the future. <u>Our</u> work beloved. [...] **71898/75-76**

Monday [?autumn 1916]

If this war goes on more than another year – well I don't know what will happen to those of us who live by our imagination. I suppose our faculties won't atrophy – that we shall have the power of recovery which we look for in the whole nation   But it isn't certain – a nation or a man may be hit just too hard. And the way every-

thing about one is ground into the same mill   Poetry and music –
the two tests of one's imagination being alive – don't you think
have the strangest "taste". ¶   But I keep my faith that we will recover
and recover with something added if – and only if – one has kept a
true mind through all the horror and muddle   kept a clear mind
as to the realities of things   And it is very hard – it is hard because
the nation is more and more given over to people who have no use
for clear thought or imagination either. I don't complain – if they
can do this job   We others certainly can't – for we always denied
the need or its existence (poor pacific optimists!) But after – when
the mess is cleared away – yes I have faith we can "worship in spirit
and in truth" again. [...] **71898/187**

[The **quotation** is Biblical: John 4. 23-24.]

Monday [?9 October 1916 ?Weymouth]

Give them even a little chance and – thank God – ideas do come
back to me again. Yesterday was Sunday and things began fructi-
fying in my mind again. I had a good talk with Lee Matthews
(whose house I go to to rest) about all the Capital-Labour questions
that will have to be settled after the war. People are thinking this
out – busily – a very few. I wish to God I were one of them for it is
what I believe I can do – grumbling again! But there is so much to
be foreseen if we are not to lose in peace all we are supposed to have
fought for in war That the freedom in "a nation" and the freedom
of nations will not come of itself – for indeed in having to fight for
it we have had to destroy it for the time of the fighting and now we
must consciously create it again. And on a basis of greater equality
between those who have and those who have not. If not those who
have not – since they have fought and felt their power – blindly
will blindly revolt – and they – being in the right will win in the
wrong way (no doubt) – or lose – and then we (at the best) shall keep
them only as servants and lose them as <u>men</u> [...] **71898/20**

[The **Capital-Labour** questions were subsequently explored by various
authors in a series of articles in *New Era* beginning in November 1916.]

[Sunday 22 October 1916] 3-30M – 10-30am. [Ayot]

[...] My dear love – I wish you could see England now – realise it – go up and down it a little – see all the good and the bad   both should be seen and understood to understand at all – the good so good – and the bad – I won't disguise it – much unworthiness Much to be made fresh that this tragedy may never come again. I think we do see where as a nation we fail – not all of us see it but many. And I think I see where <u>we</u> fail – we who have been trying to put people right   I think I can see a little where we have been wrong. Oh much to be done – much fighting – when this fighting is over. [...] **71898/202-3**

Friday [27 October 1916] 6-45am <u>1-45am</u> [Bloomsbury, London]

Well – let me write a little about politics too I'm neither democrat nor republican and I can't believe – no one here can – that it will make much immediate odds whether Hughes or Wilson rules the States next. Perhaps that is only that over here politics have disappeared – affairs are past the direction of any party – for that matter past the direction of all parties put together. We talk vaguely of not making peace <u>until</u> all sorts of wonderful things for the reform of this potential hell of a world are secured. But it becomes more and more evident – though this is never said in public – that peace must be made "on trust" – those things will only be secured later – as a consequence and by mutual free consent and good will. Then indeed will come another sort of battle – of conflicting ideas and ideals (there never need – you'd think have been any other sort) and I hope – I <u>hope</u> that our ideas will be worthy. In the main I do believe they will be but there are some very unworthy ones cropping up and the longer the war lasts the more danger (sometimes I think) of their spreading – though again – as they are "grabbing" ideas the evil chances of war tend to smother them. But more do I hope (or as much) that America will be there to have her say – but I much fear she won't be. And though her say would in the main be right one knows – in detail – no, one doesn't know (no better than ours) and she won't, I fear, <u>say</u> it. And shall we over here encourage her to? The feeling isn't what it should be – oh far

far from it. That troubles me as nothing else in politics does. For more and more I see – as I have always seen and said to you, you know – the next thirty years may decide the plan of governance for the world – as far ahead as we can imagine anyhow. And England and America between them <u>could</u> dictate that plan – if they have any plan – any "kultur" to set against the very definite German "kultur" and idea. But have they? And will they become "articulate" in the world sense? And – most important – will they make it a common plan? For – you know – really it is just like a committee meeting. The well-meaning people – if they are only well-meaning – are left behind by the people who know definitely what they want and can say it. And mere obstructive votes are in the end – no use Individuals or nations – we must be positive about something – or we're damned. ¶ So that is our job – to find out what we stand for – and stand for it. Fighting won't settle it – at best it clears the ground for a settlement We have been – in this fighting though the obstructive vote in the Committee – and America the shocked person who won't vote at all (yes – I know the most aggravating of all) Well – we are stopping the German idea. Having stopped it – what have we to put in its place? For if we have nothing next time (and there will be a next time if we don't hurry up and get an "Idea") – next time we shan't stop it – and we shan't deserve to. ¶ There beloved – there's my politics [...] **71898/207-8**

[The Republican **Hughes** was challenging the incumbent Democrat President **Wilson**. In the contest on 7 November Wilson (eventually) won. '**kultur**': Ironically used by the English during the war to mock German ideas of civilisation.]

Thursday morning [16 November 1916] 7-30 am – <u>2-30am</u>. [Bloomsbury, London]

[...] We beat on on the Somme and the Ancre you see   One hopes that it is there will be the definite decision of the war   Very like Verdun! But we can go on and the Germans couldn't   And that may make all the difference – though it may be the only difference. But there are hard truths about the whole European affair to which

England has not woke up yet – and it may be an unpleasant waking I think   I have faith in the mass of the people taking the truth fairly well though whether it is that they are philosophic (as the poets have it) or too stupid to understand it (as the cynic politicians have it) I'm not quite sure (being a bit of each myself?!)   It is the ranters and shouters and vulgarians who will be knocked out of time – a good thing And then recrimination will begin – and the search of scapegoats – that most unlovely trait in public life   A war of exhaustion it is going to be – whatever the ostensible decision is – of that one feels sure   And the recovery – that – the <u>real</u> recovery won't begin at once I feel. First there'll be the old exploiters trying to capture things again It will take a little time before the people themselves – before some spirit is bred in the people to direct them in whatever the new path is that this experience has blazed. It is for us to see what that is and help to point it out. So? Yes. And let the exploiters and the exploiting be – all the talkers and chatterers and profiteers – oh the crowds of them there'll be Let's keep away and keep in touch with the real life – that's underneath that – and above it. ¶ My breakfast is elbowing me off the table. Has my writing deteriorated even a little more these last dozen lines? It's the break-fast. So I'll start my day. [...] **71898/240-41**

Wed-Thurs [20/21 December 1916] 1245 am   745 am Wed: [Bloomsbury, London]

[...] To lunch with Barrie to say goodbye to him. We talked the war – politics and especially America. He was gloomy   well he mostly is but he says Never has he known such – almost hatred of America as there is in England now. I think he exaggerates – and whatever there is I'm sure (and he thinks too) it is unjust and unwise. It may be in a sense it is America's battle England is fighting   but it has been her destiny – she has in one way "claimed" to fight it – She should not ask for help   That is as long as she can win.   But if she were to be beaten and America stood by – then right or wrong I know England would never forgive. For she knows that now if she were not fighting for principle (however much wrong thinking and greed may be brought into the fight – it is to the great mass a fight for principle) – if she chose to make a bargain with Germany she could make one that would leave America absolutely at German mercy.   And if she is beaten – it will be America's turn next.   But never mind – there must not be the misunderstanding.   More and more I am sure of it – England must become a true democracy. America must become a <u>true</u> democracy in another sense and with France – those three – the moral – political future of the world must lie   their way must be the right way – it isn't yet but it is the nearest thing to it I do believe – and the world's way.   We've got to work at that – yes – we two small atoms my darling – our lives – our <u>life</u> my dear must go for that.   Shall it?   **71898/279-80**

[Thursday] Feb 22. [1917 Hotel Muehlebach, Kansas City] [To William Wiseman]

[...] It seems to me a matter of growing importance to try and plant here some centres of English influence. No great result could be expected now   With a war actually on they will of course be for America first last and all the time. But after the war – . Peace may have been made on terms (our allies may force them) hard for American 'democracy' to approve.   We cannot always count on Germany's diplomatic blundering.   It may be of great value to us to propagate a definitely pro-English sentiment here.   That there is not – but I believe it could be created and cultivated – English art and literature already appeal to them more strongly than any other.   English political thought and ideals could be added.   What we need is a press agent. The vice-consul here is no use. [...] **[WW MS 666 1: 6: 164]**

[For **William Wiseman**, and the context of this letter, see pp.101-04, above.]

We know very little from Barker himself about his activities once he returned from the American tour (see p.101). From Huntington we learn that his sister Grace died in the summer and he himself became ill in the autumn, with eczema among other things. He saw his regular friends, and made another one, Apsley Cherry-Garrard

(1886-1959), a member of Scott's Antarctic expedition in 1911-12, at whose house (Lamer Park) he went to write (see letters held by Scott Polar Research Institute). For the War Office he spent much time reading files, to the boredom of which Knoblock (1939) testifies, and complained about being treated like an 'office boy'. About this, in late February 1918, Huntington observed: 'I've been wondering if your association with Mr. G.B.S. [Shaw] might have anything to do with it? However distinguishing and desirable that may have been from a dramatic and literary standpoint, politically it would be the reverse' (71911/98). She might have been right, but nevertheless the office boy's connections with English radicals may have proved useful for some of the meetings he was required to attend or host (see pp.103–04). Indeed there seems often to be a very thin line between his official Intelligence interests and his personal – shall we say intelligent – interests.

Part of his work was to read a great deal of journalism about international affairs, which included asking Huntington about the French press, and he developed a knowledge that ranged from the Balkans to Japan. There was also, however, a particular focus to this interest. When Huntington was in Paris he asked her to buy him works by French socialists and he was also watching closely the activities of the German Social Democrats. Above all, both at the War Office and outside it, he was interested in Russia. In early August 1917 he sent her two pieces about Russia: his own article on Moscow theatre and 'the message to the Russian People' (71906/42). The first, written in spring 1914, was published on 7 July in the *Manchester Guardian's* special 'Russian Number', intended to support British foreign policy to keep Russia on side. In this issue he is one of those who sends a 'Greeting' in which he celebrates the role of artists in freeing Russia from tyranny, underlining that 'the foundations of political freedom should be laid in imaginative expression'. The second text, I suspect, was a document received by the Labour Party's National Executive Committee (NEC) on 10 July: 'A transcript of a speech from Mr Arthur Henderson to the Russian Council in Petrograd on June 9th' (LPA/NEC 10/07/17). (This was circulated to members of the committee, which included Barker's friend Sidney Webb. Henderson, a Cabinet member, was in Petrograd on official Foreign

Office business, to clarify Russian plans for the Stockholm conference: see below.) Huntington liked 'Henderson's speech'. Then in February 1918 Barker sent her an issue of *The New Europe* (for 7 February 1918). In this she enjoyed Alexander Onou's article on 'the Russian Revolution and German Socialism', which she supposed was the reason he had sent it. Onou (1918) likens Bolshevism to 'scientific German socialism' and prefers the Social Revolutionist position as being free of German influence. Many middle-class liberals and indeed socialists shared Onou's distaste for the second Bolshevik Revolution. Barker was one such, explicitly placing himself between the extremes of Prussian and Bolshevik. Nonetheless, as 1917 wore on, what seems to be clear from Huntington's letters is that Barker's interest in international affairs, War Office apart, was driven by both pacifism and socialism.

Back in April 1916 Huntington approved of his statement 'about it's being impossible for any one country to remain isolated and detached after this war. That will be the beginning of brotherhood – do you think it will come?' (71910/169) By summer 1917 she was asking for information about, and they were discussing, various initiatives towards peace. These were, first, the Stockholm conference, intended as a forum for socialists to meet in a way which transcended national boundaries. Proposed by the Bureau of the Socialist Second International and endorsed by the new Petrograd Soviet, it was opposed by both the British government and conservative elements in the labour movement because of the potential inclusion of 'enemy' German socialists. Instead of Stockholm there was a plan to hold a meeting of international socialists in London, to which the Labour Party could present its position. Nothing came of this and on 29 November 1917 Lord Lansdowne published in the *Daily Telegraph* a carefully reasoned letter which argued, in Newton's words, that 'the best hope for postwar security lay in "an international pact", that is, in multilateral guarantees to submit international disputes to arbitration' (2002: 18). In certain sections of the press this was regarded as treachery, though not by Barker. All of which caused Huntington difficulties. On 10 August 1917 she noted: 'You'll be glad that the English delegates are going to Stockholm.' (71906/62) Six days later, referring to the Papal Peace Note (issued on 1 August to all belligerent nations by Benedict XV in his role as impartial mediator), she asked: 'Are you pleased with the Pope this morning – darling? ¶ Oh – don't tell me that you are!' (71906/82-83). Later in the year, receiving a letter she described as 'Défaitiste' – a term coined after the Franco-Prussian war for a policy of compromise rather than prolonged warfare – she burnt it.

But whatever their disagreements she asked him to write about politics, Russia and Henderson and he kept sending her texts. Throughout their relationship he had sent her books as well as quotations from favourite works. They had also followed a programme of simultaneously reading the same material. His selection both of quotations and of books tells an interesting story. Alongside various literary works, she received books and pamphlets by H.N. Brailsford, Goldsworthy Lowes Dickinson, Henry Woodd Nevinson and AE (pseudonym of George Russell). One of the first books he suggested for joint reading was Graham Wallas' *The Great Society*; one of the non-literary quotations he copied at length was by J.A. Hobson. There are specific and general links between these names. Brailsford and Dickinson were both associated with the New Liberal journal *The Nation* (which was read by Barker) and were early proponents of a League of Nations (Martin 1973). Nevinson was a friend of Brailsford and, like him, a suffragist. AE was an Irish nationalist, active in the cooperative movement and, like Brailsford, Dickinson and Hobson, a pacifist. Hobson was a leading figure in the New Liberalism as was Wallas. And both, like just about all the others, were socialists. By the summer of 1917, as Huntington notes, Barker was interested in the radical Liberal and republican, Charles Dilke. But instead of being sent Dilke she received something very much more of the moment.

On 15 August 1917 she wrote: 'I'm in the midst of Appendix III and there are so many things I want to ask you – First of all – whether these are what you, yourself, feel and want? You don't believe – do you? – no – I'm sure you don't – that you are "not at war" with the peoples of Germany and Austria and that the "restoration of the countries which the Central Powers have devastated" should be done at the expense of an <u>international</u> fund?¶ I've made myself quite nervous over your politics' (71906/77). I take it that this was Appendix 3 of The Labour Party special party conference (Friday, 10th August 1917) (Kirby 1983: 278), a document the NEC was asked to circulate to members on 9 August (LPA/NEC 09/08/17). After a process of redrafting, Appendix 3 became the Labour Party's Memorandum on War Aims, presented to a special conference on 28 December 1917. The material Huntington quotes is very similar to section 6: 'Restoration of the Devastated Areas and Reparation of Wrong Doing' (Labour Party 1917). Then, in mid-April 1918, she received a pamphlet called 'Labour and the New Social Order'. This was submitted to party conference on 23 January 1918 and formally adopted in June.

It is not clear how Barker got hold of the texts he sent her. His friend Sidney Webb was more or less the author of each. But it may have been that Barker was himself more closely involved than we know. Certainly it seems he was doing much more than reading about peace initiatives from a distance. At the time when Arthur Henderson was forced to resign from the War Cabinet, on 11 August, because of the Labour Party's support for going to the Stockholm conference, she noted that after weeks of being ill and depressed he was 'alive and interested over this political crisis – "having a good time" over it' (71906/85). Two days later he told her he had been attacked but doesn't specify how. She conjectured: 'Is it about work you have been doing which is being taken as against the continuation of the war?' (71906/100). No answer to her question survives (yet). But in December 1917, and very probably January 1918, he attended Labour Party conference. This troubled her, as did some of the texts he sent. So he explained that, while he gave her pamphlets which he thought were interesting, for himself, 'I still do mightily quarrel with the "spirit" of the Labour people – I think it is too material – too "mob" – But if I don't clearly and sympathetically understand – my criticism will be of no value' (Texas Thursday 7-15am.).

He would not have been alone as a socialist quarrelling with the Labour Party, whether from outside or – indeed – within. His radical views were, as ever, shaped by his class position and history together with his role as an artist. Significantly enough one of the pamphlets he sent Huntington early in 1918, alongside Labour Party texts, was Richard Lethaby's *Art and Labour* (c. 1917), with its socialist viewpoint coming out of the Arts and Crafts movement. And we know that, personally, Barker wanted more emphasis given to 'instinct', 'vitality', desire. As with several contemporaries, the project was not to argue against socialism but to create the proper sort of socialism. In this context we should read his reflection below:

Tuesday [2 April 1918] 7am [Gordon Square, London]

[...] This I can prophesy for you though – the feudal arm is swinging back in Russia and the Germans are aiming now at restoring some sort of a monarchy – possibly two to start with – one in Kiev. But they are up against grave difficulties. Some of the anti-Bolsheviks Monarchists and Capitalists both (you see it is a double problem always – political and economic   the first revolution was the political one the second the economic – 'Down with the Boujooy Capitalist) – some of them would come back by favour of the Germans – or the devil or anybody or anything just to come back – some would if they couldn't come any other way – and the other way they think would open in time but they are impatient and two-minded and I fear will be won over. It is Russia and themselves and they are liable to think that what is good for them personally <u>must</u> be best for Russia   Then there are the men to whom Russia means everything who feel that this is the penalty she has paid for centuries of sinning and believe that with patience she would work out her salvation and return to sanity – more fully herself. Bonch-Bruevitch is one of them (No you'd never have heard of him)   They are two brothers one a General one I think (I ought to <u>know</u>) a Professor of some sort   both anti-Bolshevik but working with the Bolsheviks – organising   one the army one I believe Education   How far they can get with it on the present political basis I don't know (This is the measure of the really important things we don't know about Russia at the moment. <u>Damn</u> the correspondents who write about roughs in the street and 'German Agents' instead of telling us   Of course there are roughs and of course there are German agents – I daresay one man in every hundred thousand is a German agent and right to be shot – but the other 99,999 are my concern) but I imagine that the basis would gradually shift nearer to the Right and that a good deal could be done. There is nothing in the Bolshevik theory that keeps the "Boujooy" out. You can have a Soviet of Doctors or Lawyers – or Cheesemongers or Dukes But of course the peasants and workmen outnumber everybody – and while the representation is so crude it is difficult to re-adjust political machinery Besides still at any readjustment the peasant says – Yes but what you are really after is the land and the workman Yes – but what you really want is to make me a "wage-slave" again And of course in so many cases there is truth in that But much could be done – for already they have found out that they need the "professional" brain and they are welcoming men of the Bonch Bruevitch type who will work patiently and not patronisingly with them. But – . If there did not happen to be a war on – if the war could be finished and won <u>now</u> I believe the thing could be done. If they'd have the courage to refuse German help I believe it could be done. But Germany is selling them Russia at a price – and what a price. Look at Finland and I fear they'll pay it. And then – God knows – Lenin may be right That was his theory – That all revolutions had failed because people had not had courage to destroy enough of the old institutions – that you must begin again from the bottom – and that after destruction you could <u>not</u> rebuild the old – if the old was wrong. Well we shall see and see soon probably now [...] (**Texas**)

['**sinning**': Elsewhere Barker says England must also pay for its sins (see p.139). Mikhail **Bonch-Bruevich** was put in charge of the Supreme Military Council in March 1918. His younger brother Vladimir was adviser to Lenin and based in the Kremlin. Barker's impression that they were **anti-Bolshevik** may have been based on internal Russian policy differences. British agents later in the month were in contact with both men. '**German help**': I presume this is a reference to the treaty of Brest-Litovsk, formalised on 3 March, in which Russia renounced claims to Finland. It was signed by the pro-German Chicherin, to Vladimir Bonch-Bruevich's disgust.]

V

CONTEXTUAL ESSAYS

A young Helen Huntington with one of a series of much loved
dogs (Harley Granville Barker papers, British Library 71901/89)

ARCHER HUNTINGTON'S WIFE

Helen Huntington says that she met Barker at the Hapgoods on 15 December 1914. Barker says he was introduced to her by two people, one of whom was Paul Cravath.

These names are quite tidily connected (and because there are quite a lot of them in what follows, some will become sets of initials). Barker [hereafter HGB] had been invited to direct a season at Wallack's Theatre, New York, by the Stage Society, the President of which was Emilie Hapgood. He was also invited to take on the management of a venture called the New Theatre. One of those who put up the funding for the New Theatre project was his American lawyer, Paul Cravath (1861-1940). Another was Helen Huntington's husband, Archer Milton Huntington (1870-1955) [hereafter AMH], one of the group of six multi-millionaires, brought together by Norman Hapgood, who funded HGB's season at Wallack's. It seems very likely that Cravath, along with the Huntingtons, attended an event in HGB's honour at the Hapgoods. Having met at this society event, Helen Huntington [hereafter HH], herself a regular theatre-goer, accompanied HGB on various theatre outings. By April 1915 they were firmly in love.

THE MACHINE

The network of names around HH delineates the sphere of wealth, power and cultural competence within which she moved. She entertained diplomats and writers and soon after meeting HGB started to engage, at a distance, with his friends. She saw, and commented on, new plays by Barrie and Galsworthy, was delighted to be able to read the proof of a new Shaw Preface and sought out books by Barrie and Masefield. They in turn took an interest in her. Both the Shaws set about reading her books and were apparently delighted to be getting HGB free of his current wife, Lillah McCarthy. Masefield sent HH his sonnets and asked HGB to pass on his book on

Gallipoli. Apsley Cherry-Garrard invited them both to visit. Even the taciturn Barrie 'expresses a wish to have tea with you quite alone as soon as you are there [in London] – I rather think you'll find that J.M.B. is preparing to be put in your pocket. I know the signs' (Texas Monday morning 7am). Although, as HGB warned her, both Christopher Wheeler and the Galsworthys were inclined to be shy, within a few weeks of her arrival in England she was socialising with them.

But despite her intellectual engagement with them, and their readiness to welcome her, on the eve of sailing from America in July 1917 she fretted nervously: 'You must tell all your friends that I am only a poor, dull, old, diseased, wicked and ugly thing – otherwise the shock of meeting me – if we ever meet – will be too great' (71905/95). As late as spring 1918, she was nervous about meeting the Galsworthys: 'Oh – I hope they will pretend to like me – even if they don't! Otherwise I couldn't bear it. I should be ashamed on your account' (71913/209). This is not just shyness. It's a sense that she is diminishing him in their eyes: 'Oh darling – I want your friends to love you more because of me – not less' (71914/153). Her anxieties had emerged most intensely as she lay ill in Paris, separated from her husband and under three months from her final journey to England: 'I'm all sore and aching, Harley, thinking about your life and friends and mine – I've been so stupid not to have realized it sooner [...] I must see you with your other friends – to know whether there will be one corner of your mind which you will keep away from me – lest I shouldn't understand – or sympathize with what was there' (71910/252-53).

The insecurity and lack of self-worth that we hear in these lines characterise many of her letters to HGB. Trying to grapple with them he suggested they were caused precisely by the privileged life she led. He characterised her New York as a 'machine' which made her life 'mechanical': 'nothing left of "you" – for you but your innermost thoughts – oh how well I know it and just what it means to you – how it robs you of yourself and gives you nothing back'. He vented his particular rage on her new Fifth Avenue house: 'I wish to God that new New York house were in ruins or that you meant never to go into it again'. The new house, at 1083 Fifth

Avenue (with enough space for 25 servants) and the 'machine' of which it was a part were damaging, he said, because they necessitated 'social duties that suck the life out of you'. Defending his repeated rants on this topic he insisted: 'the scale of the whole thing – it <u>does</u> suck your life and drive you in and in on yourself' (71898/89).

She agreed with this analysis and knew herself to be bored, alienated and trapped. Nonetheless her powerful sense of social and marital duty overrode any wishes and desires that seemed merely 'personal'. And this, early on, was a major problem. For HGB's first all-too-simple solution to the entrapment was that they both run away together. In England this was the accepted way of triggering divorce proceedings, but it necessarily involved scandal. HH, dutiful and proper, couldn't do it. She was frightened of what that elite New York social circle – the 'scandal mongers' – would think. This fear was shared by her husband. In the summer of 1917, with America now in the war, the Huntingtons left New York for Paris, travelling towards the war in order to get away from their friends at home. Once in Paris they avoided people they knew, turning down invitations. HH was even cautious about telling her best friends what was going on, until HGB persuaded her, rightly as she found out, to trust them. The fear of scandal remained with her until they were married on 31 July 1918. But by then she was forming good relationships with his friends, bar one.

GBS

George Bernard Shaw [hereafter GBS] and his wife Charlotte said they wanted to meet HH as soon as they could, and both supported HGB's separation from McCarthy. So GBS volunteered to help in the divorce process (see p.59). Things went wrong and McCarthy initially refused a divorce, which HH took badly. Nonetheless she remained a fan of GBS's work. He had read and commented on a story of hers, and in late March 1916 she saw a proof of one of his Prefaces, which she admired. But thereafter her husband got a letter from McCarthy which 'began – "I have been told that your wife is about to join my husband in France – " ' 71905/201). HH assumed that it could only have been from GBS that McCarthy got this information. Then in late spring/early summer GBS told McCarthy something that I'm guessing was about HH's inherited wealth (about which he could have easily learnt from HGB) because HH discovered that she had been covertly investigated. GBS rapidly became one of her 'bogies'. In her diary for autumn 1916, while she acknowledged it was an entirely personal view, she wrote: 'your best friend is a man whose private integrity is as poor and mean as his public integrity' (71899/38).

This was more true than either she or HGB realised. Beatrice Webb records on 6 June 1916 that GBS is 'a perfect gossip, elaborating by witty exaggerations the life stories of his friends into human comedies, and sometimes inhuman tragedies. The last of these is the disaster of the Granville Barker marriage. – Barker having become infatuated with the wife of an American millionaire' (Webb 1911-1916 f.3423). This sort of scandal mongering was precisely what HH feared and hated. Early in January 1918, alone and unwell in Paris, against HGB's defence of GBS's impulsive and sometimes eccentric individuality (see pp.39–40), she maintained her position, discriminating between character and behaviour: 'G.B.S.? – I'm not writing bitterly. I can forgive – if – for your sake I must. And I will always try to understand, to make allowance for that mystery of <u>individuality</u> – which is a sacred thing – But – oh – my beloved – as a guide – a <u>false guide</u> for you – I do believe it. I must say it – now that I can say it without anger' (71910/74-75). As a consequence, the Shaws were kept in the dark about the marriage plans. Charlotte was upset about being left out, 'But', HGB said, probably in April 1918, 'G.B.S. knows "why" – no need to tell him'. Charlotte thus would meet HH soon after she arrived in England, but 'G.B.S. shall be relegated to a later date. How long his vanity will stand it I don't know' (in Salmon 1986: 340). As HGB knew, GBS hated to admit to the mistakes he had made.

What he didn't know was the violence of which GBS's damaged egotism was capable. It festered for years in his private letters but then erupted like a boil in public printed form the year after HH's death. In 1951 Hesketh Pearson published the second volume of his biography of GBS. This included a statement, taken from and approved by GBS before HH's death, that accused her of a series of crimes (Pearson, 1951: 149, 159-61). It said she hated GBS's influence on HGB; she hated all writing after 1865, especially GBS's; she dominated HGB, forcing him to abandon socialism and the theatre, making him do translations of Spanish plays and trying to turn him into a country gentleman. All this comes to climax, as it were, in an accusation which emerged from an event held at King's College London on 13 May 1925 to honour HGB. When HH was shown into the same room as GBS, she was pleasant to him. But GBS claims he initially didn't recognise her because of her 'entirely negative' appearance, though he did recognise the 'chains of pearls decorating her neck and bosom' (Pearson, 1951: 160-61). This seeming diffidence about her physical presence sits oddly with what followed. GBS gave a speech in which he took the opportunity to criticise HGB's retirement from the stage. At the end of the event when he stood up to go, he experienced sudden back pain. A friend of his later told him that during his speech HH, seated behind him, had been leaning forward, 'every muscle in her face and body rigid with hate' (Pearson, 1951: 160-61). GBS then came to the conclusion that HH had 'bewitched' him. Far from a temporary aberration, this accusation was nurtured for twenty-five years. In a letter to a friend in 1928 GBS says 'I told her [Lady Astor] the story of the American lady who sat behind me at Kings College on a celebrated occasion, hating me horribly' (Shaw, 1988: 83). Between 1925 and 1928 his memory of the incident at King's hardened into 'the story' and there it stuck until his death, more or less unchanged – and uninspected.

Much of the statement which GBS had Pearson publish is not just unsubstantiated but actually deceitful. We know, for example, that in 1916 he was enthusiastic about the HH relationship, and, very probably, that she admired his work. He presumably also knew, well connected as he was, that she enjoyed the company of Barrie and the Galsworthys. But it wasn't just a matter of misremembering or even downright lying. The repeated accusation of witchcraft is more violent than that. And this prompts the question of why it was necessary to him to say it. GBS prided himself on his attractiveness to women, of which he had repeated confirmation in a series of extra-marital affairs. This pride was one element of a strident vanity, to which HGB attests. HH's criticism of him was a reminder of ancient errors and thus an offence to his vanity. With HH he found himself not only resisted but also looked back at with accusation. Here was a woman, of all beings, prepared to challenge his carefully cultivated self-image. So obviously, for him, she must be a physical failure as a woman, 'entirely negative' in appearance. And being such an unattractive threat to male vanity she must be, according to an ancient tradition of misogyny, in reality, yes reality, a witch.

But while GBS took years to hatch his public vengeance, there was a threat more immediately apparent.

L. M.

The power of the characterisation of HH as, variously, a rich manipulative American, an interloper, or, more primly, Purdom's 'lady' with 'an air of mystery' (1955: 172), is that it can slide satisfactorily into place as the binary opposite of McCarthy, hardworking English actress, manager and star. This opposition convincingly establishes the woman whom in these circumstances has, with caring intimacy, to be called 'Lillah' as the wronged victim. And it's had long-lasting effect. Among those theatre historians who have taken an interest in McCarthy there is an inclination to blame HGB for coldness and brutality. And HH, such an unknown entity, fades from view against the satisfyingly familiar tragedy of the actress celebrity. On hearing some of my revision to this story, one academic remarked, 'I still prefer Lillah to Helen', with all the aplomb of a judge at a beauty pageant.

That binary mechanism is, however, rather more complicated than such profound academic judgment allows. At one pole, HH was as much insecure as rich and powerful; at the other pole the victim McCarthy was also actress and manager.

Everybody who knew her could see that McCarthy was horribly shocked by the news that HGB wanted separation. And all, including HGB, were sympathetic. He himself repeated that he wanted to do it as far as possible without hurting her, though do it he must. But his certainty of purpose was, initially, the very thing McCarthy could not accept. In fighting to save her marriage she was trying to retrieve her husband from what she regarded as a temporary passion for a woman who was merely flirting with him. To other people there was little that was worth fighting for. When GBS gossiped about it to Beatrice Webb the conversation, as she reports it, went thus: 'The marriage was predestined to a bad end: each one of them is an egoist and there is and has never been any intellectual sympathy between them. She is a finely built woman of statuesque beauty and great personal dignity, a good craftswoman in acting, but without the temperament of an artist, and with no intellect and not much intelligence. He is intellectual to the last degree, fastidious in taste and unscrupulous in minor morals, sacrificing all things to the development of his talent or the satisfaction of some artistic or intellectual whim.' It was simply a 'professional partnership' (Webb, 1911-1916 f. 3423-24). In this view of the marriage Webb repeats her opinion from ten years before, when the relatively recently married McCarthy and HGB visited: 'I fear she is ... commonplace, and he has all the appearance of being bored by her after two months of marriage' (quoted in Holroyd, 1989: 2.157). HGB's own view was that it was all a mistake, 'marrying and not loving' (71897/21).

We don't know whether after nine years of marriage McCarthy had any inkling of this, though she did know her husband had fallen in love with someone else. Indeed, in June 1915, as HH understood, McCarthy had promised 'to set you free' (diary entry for 7 October 1916). Even so, in January 1916 his request to separate caused shock followed by grief, rage and vengeance. And she used what weapons came to hand. As theatre historians tell us, Lillah McCarthy was a woman of competence, inventiveness and enterprise. She mobilised a range of tactics to try and protect her marriage. These served three main purposes: first, to manage her own position and image; second, to put pressure on her husband; and, third, to put pressure on her rival.

As soon as the break seemed to be serious McCarthy started cultivating HGB's close friends, such as J.M. Barrie, her neighbour in Adelphi Terrace, even though, HGB says, she previously claimed to dislike him. Some of the effect of this cultivation was sensed by HH in early May 1916: 'At first I was – well, a little bitter that John M. [Masefield] should have so taken the point of view on the other side. But then, immediately afterwards I saw that it was only natural that he should do so – not understanding all the "tests" we have already undergone, nor what kind of person I was – and being told, probably, all kinds of things of me – by L.M.'(71904/ 15). Later in 1916 Christopher Wheeler told HGB that McCarthy was enjoying having his 'intellectual' friends – Barrie and Galsworthy – trying to persuade her to begin the divorce process (71898/11). Much more publicly, on Saturday 15 April 1916, *Vogue* magazine carried a story on the home life of the Granville Barkers, featuring pictures of the house (Court Lodge) at Stansted, near Tonbridge, in Kent. It was clearly written some time in very early 1916 because it refers to the couple having 'been in London this past winter organizing the war benefits' (*Vogue*, 1916: 48b). There are four photographs. Unlike McCarthy, HGB appears in none of them, though one is of his study. The claim that he was in London in the winter is a little over-done. He was there only briefly – around 28 January to 6 February and 18 to 29 February – not much time to organise war benefits, especially since he saw McCarthy just once. This suggestion, combined with his absence from the pictures, makes this feel like a constructed story, put together soon after McCarthy heard about the separation which she refused to accept, a story implying that everything remained normal, with her at the centre of it.

The image of passive domesticity was very different from her actual activity. Her work on the stage continued, which, as HGB acknowledged, would have increased the stress for her. Alongside that she sent him 'miserable' letters, despatched one of her confi-dantes – Maggie Ponsonby – to ask him to stay away from HH for a year and then had her lawyer begin discussions about money. Of course, as a partner in the McCarthy-Barker management, she knew the debts with which he left America. More or less simultaneously, in mid-February, her other confidante, A. E. Drinkwater, hinted to HGB that there may be delays in the process (71897/43). The combination of delay and money demands continued for the next nine months. Meanwhile McCarthy maintained, as she wrote to the

Galsworthys, that she could not believe HGB's desire to separate was true (71898/60-61). Such a statement to his close friends would inevitably reach him, reinforcing the message that she was not going to budge, despite his raging impatience and distress.

The pressure on him was, however, relatively mild compared to that targeted at HH. HGB, who knew McCarthy pretty well, always dreaded that she would take out her anger on HH. He was right. In late May and early June 1915, at the time the Greek plays were performed, HH was puzzled to receive a cable, then a series of phone calls to various people in the house, asking her to give McCarthy's brooch to HGB when she saw him. When HH picked up a call intended for her husband, McCarthy rang off. She seemed to be making it clear that she knew HH and HGB were meeting, and precisely where, and wanted the household to know. On another occasion an anonymous caller rang to see if Mr Barker were dining there that night. Meanwhile, HH read in his letters that HGB was 'being tortured in so many ways – and that I am a part of it' (71901/40). Just before sailing to England McCarthy had a detective follow them. In August 1915 HH's husband, AMH, received an anonymous letter telling him that HH was having an affair. Another was received on 18 October. McCarthy confessed to all of this on 31 January 1916, but did not stop. On 18 February, at the time her father had a stroke, HH says: 'A letter has been received – the kind of letter written last Aug. (I learn now definitely that it was Aug.) in which it is stated that in London no agreement can ever be reached. [...] You shall have copies of the two letters. They are vulgar and insolent, but just at the moment what does it matter'(71911/42). Then: 'Last night another letter came – a rather longer one this time – full of financial details and accusations and repeating the former assertion that no consent to a divorce would ever be given. It was sent through Mr. Cravath [...] I had a hard scene with A [Archer] but he promised me that you should have type-written copies of the letters. [...] One thing I don't understand – in the last two letters L.M. says that she hears a cable has been received saying – then repeating the message. Someone must be keeping watch for her – for, of course, you wouldn't have told her of any message from me' (71913/1-3). The cable was probably about HH's plan to join HGB in France and she may have assumed it was GBS who was 'keeping watch'. A few months later, around 22 July, it happened again: AMH 'was rather upset at having received another letter from England – unsigned – this time' (71903/87).

The sequence of letters, together with the refusal to initiate divorce, gave HH a sense that they were at the 'mercy' of McCarthy, who says she will '"fight to the death to keep you" – and will hesitate at <u>no means</u>' (71902/122). Nine months later, in December 1916, she learnt more about McCarthy's means. In her diary, responding to HGB's letter from 18 November, she says: 'My heart ached for you having to write it – and then I got quite violently sick and cold – to think of all that secret vileness crawling near when I didn't know it – lawyers putting detectives on me perhaps – and that it was <u>true</u> – their doing it. But you are right Harley. I am not a child – nor of an age or innocence to be spared things.' She notes what the lawyers supposedly found out 'wasn't true. My father was not a rich man – at least not when he died'. She herself was 'very far from being a "millionairess"' (71900/14-15). This interest in her money coincided with the pressure to screw a substantial financial settlement out of HGB. But it had another effect. It fixed in place the – always negative – image of HH as the rich woman that tempts HGB. More locally, it worked to keep HH and HGB apart. HH concludes: 'seeing each other is going to difficult [*sic*] – almost impossible. Now we know that <u>all</u> baseness is to be expected of L.M. and the lawyer who is representing her' (71900/16).

Apart from letters and lawyers there were other means. Prior to the first legal suit, the submission by McCarthy for restitution of conjugal rights, heard on 19 April 1917, on 14 April HH saw a newspaper headline: 'I thought this first suit was to be for desertion merely – and that there was to be nothing in it about any "woman".¶ But if she has done this now – what will she do in the later suit?' (71905/69-70). She interpreted this as a 'deliberate "indiscretion"' (71905/197). It may seem paranoid to attribute such publicity management to McCarthy but HH had seen, in her own home – as presumably McCarthy knew she would – that *Vogue* article on 15 April 1916. Coincidentally, it was followed in

November with an issue of *Ladies Field* which carried a photograph of McCarthy, among other actresses, in a fashionable dress she wore on stage.

McCarthy's own management of public discourse becomes more clearly suggested when, in late May 1917, well before the second suit for divorce, HH heard 'that L.M. was to name me' (presumably as co-respondent) (71905/177). Her name would then be publicised. Even after divorce was granted, on 10 November, pressure continued. Around 24 November HH heard of gossip in London: 'I do feel – don't you? – that L.M. will make any mischief she finds possible' (71908/249). Sustained chatter in London about her marrying HGB was, for her, evidence of mischief. We can't know for sure, but McCarthy, manager and celebrity, was nothing if not well networked. For HH, insecure and fearful of scandal, publicity was acutely uncomfortable. Merely a few months before marriage, she asked HGB to keep his communications to her discreet. 'I keep forgetting L.M. and her evil tongue, and her will for what she would call "revenge"' (71910/204-05).

That final revenge, though, was a longer time coming. Even as she was separating from HGB, McCarthy was reconstructing herself. There is a transition, as it were, from the domestic partner in *Vogue* to the independent celebrity in *Ladies Field*. Among the grand friends to whom she took her sorrow and anger was H. H. Asquith, the Prime Minister, and at some point in the latter half of 1916 she began a relationship with him. Not long thereafter, in 1919, she met a leading academic, Frederick Keeble, and quickly was engaged to him, later becoming Lady Keeble when he was knighted. And then – a decade or so later – she wrote her autobiography. Here HGB forbade mention of his name, which scholars have seen as calculated malice, even though he similarly forbade Housman a couple of years later from mentioning 'me personally, the private me' (BM 18 October 1933). McCarthy turned the ban to advantage. Corralling HGB's friends into assumed intimacy her book persistently singles out GBS, who is said to 'have done more than anyone to rescue the theatre from "theatricality"' (1933: 84). For 'anyone' read 'Granville Barker' and his entire career. Not for nothing was GBS's editorial hand put to the polishing of

McCarthy's version of things. But she was not yet done. When two decades later Mr Purdom from the British Drama League arrived to gather information for his biography of HGB, McCarthy, it seems, readily obliged.

The whole shape of Purdom's story, where a mysterious woman lures the artist into her capricious affection, taking him away from the world he knew, destroying the woman he loved – like, perhaps, a staged drama – derives from McCarthy's version of events. By writing it up some forty years later as historical fact, Purdom allowed himself to become the vehicle which, with admirable efficiency, delivered McCarthy's final revenge on her husband and his new wife.

THE MYSTERIOUS TUTELAGE

That new wife, far from being a flirtatious witch, was lonely, creative, insecure, cultured and, apparently in contrast with McCarthy, a woman of developed intellect and sharp wit. Although her insecurities were intensified by McCarthy's machinations, their roots lay deeper. When first he met her HGB thought her lack of self-worth resulted from the necessity of leading an artificial life, of having to pretend to be something she was not. But that analysis, made too early, did not get to the root of the problem. That was only glanced at, merely intuited, when he noted that there was something odd in her relationship with her husband. He called it a 'mysterious sort of tutelage' (71898/263). Over time, as their relationship deepened, she told him more about that 'mysterious tutelage'. At its heart was a very deep fear. Her husband, she said, '<u>terrifies</u> me – that is the degrading truth. Something in him frightens me just as the dark drives certain children into hysterics. It goes back to the very beginning – I don't think I shall ever get over it' (71902/102).

Usually in the story AMH is seen as the nice guy who gives his wife a very generous settlement at their separation, thereby enabling her to support HGB. Considered on its own, it looks a generous act, leading Chambers and Nelson to say he 'certainly did not behave like a typical aggrieved and cuckolded husband' (Barker 2017: 231). But his wife, experiencing his behaviour over a marriage of twenty years, saw it differently. In her diary in autumn 1916 she wrote that her husband was being kind and supportive, offering her various luxuries, but 'only last Summer – he leaped into my room and flashed a kind of electric dark lantern suddenly in my face – just because he heard me speaking to Sonia [the dog]' (71899/68). It wasn't the only time. There were other incidents when he 'burst into my room in the middle of the night, when I was quietly asleep – and began to wave a revolver and shout that there was someone there' and, again, broke down the locked door of her room at Hotel Ritz in Paris, and then again 'when he fought with me to get a letter from an English woman friend of mine' (71901/225). Forcible invasion of her space sometimes included violence against her person. She recounts his taking her by the shoulders, roughly asking her if she's seen 'that man' (71902/87). This looks not too far distant from the typical cuckolded husband ... and his effects: 'I've been so frightened that it's gone into every bit of me' (71901/226).

But AMH was very far from typical. As his biographer, Beatrice Gilman Proske, tells us, he was a most eminent scholar of Hispanic studies, who generously funded institutions of art and culture. His contribution to scholarship was recognised in honorary degrees from Harvard and Yale. And it's that cleverness of mind that HH most noticed: 'I must not forget all the old days and years – I must not forget that it is there. Some of the gentleness he shows is real, I'm sure, but some is only cleverness – and so well thought out' (71908/113). Alongside the physical violence, then, there was the 'cleverness'. Sometimes it was merely surveillance, as when he, being supposedly away, walked silently into her room to see what she was writing. A holiday in Newport allowed her to write with 'no one knocking at the door, no one watching through cracks to see if my light is still burning' (71902/99). But AMH was still in her head. She half-expected him to turn up, though 'he may have just wanted me to think he was going to do so – He has always done so before' (71902/87). Just over a year later, about to leave for France, she looked back on her life: 'I have been so terrorized – designedly? – I ask myself now. No - I don't quite think so. But A. knows me so well - he knows just what things will hurt most' (71905/253-54).

AFRAID OF JOY

He knew her so well because they had been married for twenty years, and being so thoroughly known, a long-term subject of his cleverness, had its effects. Amongst her anxieties about what HGB's friends would think of her, she was disturbed by reports of his conversations with women friends. Even on the threshold of his formal divorce she wondered whether he might change his mind. Much of this may have been suggested by AMH's insights: 'It's when I have it pointed out to me that your love will not last – that I am making myself ridiculous – and destroying <u>you</u> – as well as myself – that I tremble' (71910/111). The suggestion did its damage in two ways. First she knew that her friends were highly critical of HGB, accusing him of financial malpractice among other things (see, for example, 71901/72), so she was making herself ridiculous in their eyes. Second, she was worried that the love could not last because she thought that, as she repeatedly says, she was ugly, old and diseased. Again and again she asks: 'How can you love such a creature as I, Harley? I don't believe you <u>know</u> how small and mean I am' (71910/144). If she writes about her own feelings she quickly apologises for being egotistical.

What we're hearing is a readiness to anticipate criticism. Of this she was conscious: 'It is true, that I choose, by nature, the point of view which hurts me most – but (as you've divined) it's because I've been hurt so much, that, like a dog, I cringe – I don't want anything to take me unaware, as it were' (71908/276-77). The fear of being taken unaware had another effect: 'How foolish and wicked of me to be afraid of joy!' (71910/158). She had learnt not just to be afraid of joy but to blame herself for doing so. This is surely a result of what we would now call coercive control. Its presence reverberates when she says: 'what I dread most is a kind of power of suggestion he has over me – over most people. He does – really and actually – make one think what he likes' (71901/214). When she says 'he is going to break me if he can – and he knows how – he does know how' (71901/193), the tragedy is that she was already broken ... done in by cleverness.

As HGB's formal divorce, and thus the prospect of the Huntingtons' separation, became imminent, the pressures intensified. This included AMH's working on and trying to alienate HH's closest companion, Nellie Dickinson, of whose affection for HH 'and her <u>belief</u> in me' he was very jealous (71908/200). Coercive control now combined with physical violence. 'I hadn't seen the evil side of him for so long', HH wrote in October 1917, ' – and he said many cruel and bitter things. Toward the end I said – "You know how to hit hard" – and he answered – "Yes – I can hit hard – and hate hard and lie hard!" [...] I am ashamed that the old terror of him came over me.' Here bear in mind that she was a short woman and her husband over six feet tall. 'When he looms over me – and points his great finger at me as if it were a revolver, and shouts and threatens – it turns me into a <u>coward</u> – even though I'm not really afraid of him.' She then added: 'I am sorry, deeply sorry for him, because he suffers – mostly in his vanity – a little in his affections – and – (I <u>imagine</u> now and then – perhaps –) from something like remorse. One thing he said – "I <u>protected</u> you always – protected you as if you had been a dog!" ¶ Isn't it astounding – and fantastic – Harley, that any man could say such a thing to any woman' (71908/157-59).

That ability to step back and comment on, indeed analyse, her situation is consistently present. As part of the pressure to abandon her intention to divorce, her husband warned that HGB's 'libertine fancy had turned to me, would be, as easily, lost to me' and 'that I, having lost all my own friends, would have only yours ... and they would naturally (?) disapprove of me' (71908/262). In that question mark the critical intelligence asserts itself, always sharply alert to the indignity it's watching. The reason she didn't talk about HGB to her husband, she explained, is 'because any <u>understanding</u> between you and him makes me feel as if I were just a material object of some kind – the transfer of which was to be arranged and effected by two competent traders' (71907/14). But powerful as her intelligence was, it was up against something much more deeply embedded. After another of AMH's explosions, very late in 1917, she reported: 'I am ashamed that I let such things shake me physically – but I can't seem to help it! It goes back through too long a time – I'm not frightened in my soul really, but my nerves are frightened' (71901/144). Indeed she became physically ill, 'diseased', with stress. Yet at separation, seemingly still attached to her husband, she tried to explain: 'About A – I wish I could make you understand – I wish I understood perfectly myself. But it's like this – I used often to say to myself in those bad years: "I'm like someone going about with a tiger, a tiger who won't let anyone else have anything to do with it at all." Of course now and then I had an eye gouged out – or a limb bitten off – and I was rather permanently hurt – but on the other hand it was <u>my tiger</u> [double underline]! And that's what I felt when A. went away – showing his gentle, caressing side only – those last weeks – I was losing my tiger – turned suddenly – at the end – into a protection against the world. ¶ This sounds fantastic perhaps, but it expresses what I mean in a way' (71910/266-68). This seems to be a classic psychological reaction whereby the victim feels attached, come what may, to the abuser.

And it is to that abuser that Lillah McCarthy sent her letters. Very early on, when she still called him Mr Barker, HH reported that 'Mrs B's letter has made a difficult situation' (71901/139). Around the same time, in autumn 1915, he had clearly warned her of McCarthy's intentions: 'What is it', HH asked, 'that she wanted to do to ruin me?' (71901/145). Whether or not they were designed to provoke abuse, whether she knew precisely what she was doing, McCarthy's letters, always directed to AMH, created, each time they arrived, what his wife euphemistically called a 'situation'. It's hard not to see them as actions intended, somehow, to ruin.

LONELY

As HGB came to understand what a 'situation' might really involve, he became more and more frustrated with the delays in the divorce process. AMH had said that he would never divorce his own wife until HGB was a 'free man'. And HGB knew that for as long as he was not free, AMH would continue abusing HH. It was a machine in which everyone but AMH was a victim. And, because she held the key to stopping it, McCarthy was the one against whom the other victims raged. From a distance HGB tried to help HH, encouraging her to go into the country and to talk to friends, to stay out of that 'damned' 5th Avenue house: 'I want – oh I do want to keep you from being caught in the "machine" once again – all that that damned new house stands for' (71898/155). But HH's only real escape would be not physical but psychological. For that reason HGB spent so much time reassuring her, repeatedly promising his help and devotion, celebrating her moments of self-renewal: 'I am so glad you are visiting people by yourself rather proud for I feel that I have helped to do that' (71897/141). Above all he encouraged her to write. He saw that as a wife she was enacting a required social role, which was shaped and authenticated by a husband, whereas as an author she had her own identity. Repeatedly in the letters he speaks of the joy he has when he hears she is writing: 'you are working at your book – and that is such good news. [...] I think of your work and I'm so happy that you are working' (71898/2). This was no sentimental patronage. He offered to engage critically with her work, and invited her to do the same with his, and in his criticisms he seems to have pulled few punches. What he was in effect doing was to respect and challenge, and thereby to energise, her cleverness and creativity which could then, against her husband's particular cleverness, assert a potency of its own. And it began to work. In January 1918 one day, in the middle of a tea party, 'Sitting there with those people, Harley, I felt <u>surer</u> – safer – than I used to feel – more free from being hurt – or even touched by them. And it was all you, my darling, your love for me. I thanked God for it' (71910/218).

When she fell in love with HGB, HH 'begun to realize how dreadfully lonely I've been for years and years and years' (71901: 27-28). Although she rarely took time away from her husband's domain she only ever saw him for two hours each day. And those two hours do not seem to have been filled with the affection she craved. Indeed she hints that at the core of the marriage there was a sexual problem: 'my life has been tied up with other peoples' secrets – very grave secrets. There are things I've never told to any one – tragic, horrible things [...] You won't think it a history of successive love affairs – will you – or things like that? Though of course sex comes into it' (71901/160). Finding safety and freedom from hurt with HGB, she found also joy in his caresses and kisses, indeed in his physicality: 'I'm so glad you are such a <u>man</u>. I should hate it if you sat – with very white hands – crouching over the fire – and telling anecdotes about Charles Lamb. ¶ I love the <u>efficiency</u> of you – the efficiency of hands as well as brain' (71905/36).

For him too there was a journey of sexual discovery. In late 1915, having returned to the United States to find her again, he asked: 'Do you wonder that I had such horrors at the thought of you and A.H. that night? I thought you might remember what I said calmly about myself in that way when first we spoke of that side of things. [...] loving you has changed all that part of life for me – absolutely – made it a wonderful thing again – given it back to me as I used first to think of it as a boy' (see p.189 for full quotation). It's not clear what happened between the Huntingtons that night but the reference to 'that side of things' may be a euphemism for physical sex. If so, HGB seems to be describing an adult life of alienation from love as sex. What HH understood about his previous life was that 'you had married her without loving her in a complete way, after having had one very real and tragic love-affair with a girl in your youth, that she had been in any definite sense the one sex relationship in your life and that you had been true to her' (71901/196). This is what may have produced people's sense that HGB was emotionally cold. But in these matters it takes two to tangle, as it were. HGB said he didn't love McCarthy. Looking at them both, Beatrice Webb noted they had little in common, so it may also be the case that McCarthy wasn't getting what she wanted from him. Salmon, reviewing the evidence, suggests that the marriage had been 'much more by her wish than his' (1983: 237), a pursuit of the established star actor perhaps. Certainly she had something of a reputation. Constance Masefield warned her husband off 'dining with Mrs. Barker... I fancy she rather loves having bevies of men round her when she is alone, and I don't think it is a very dignified position for the men' (in Smith 1985: 95). Constance Masefield wasn't alone. The picture of McCarthy that HH saw in *Ladies Field* was part of a feature on actresses, actors and superstitions, with commentary by a 'student of the occult'. A majority of the female celebrities say their 'lucky colour' is blue. For several this is associated with intelligence, but in McCarthy's case alone it supposedly means she 'would be much admired by the opposite sex ... It also indicates a warm heart, but a certain amount of fickleness' (November, 1916). By the time this was published, a week after the divorce, McCarthy was seemingly involved in a relationship with another celebrity much more securely famous for his sexual appetite, Prime Minister Asquith. Seen from this angle, the shock of HGB's request for separation may well, at base, have been to her vanity.

If HGB wanted and experienced sex differently from McCarthy it doesn't follow that he was merely 'cerebral' or 'cold'. Indeed he was aware of how his behaviour might appear. In the middle of November 1915 HH tried to break off their relationship because she thought that his caution showed he had doubts about it. Writing desperately, after several unposted attempts, on 24 November he said: 'for God's sake don't punish me by thinking this because I don't try to "morally abduct" you - as it were. It has been another bitter thing to have the suspicion come that you might have been with me now if I'd been the sort of man who "doesn't have to think twice" about things - the so-called "strong" man. But I know that is not what really strong men are - they are the obtuse men' (71898/264). He may not have wanted - or been able - to inhabit the 'strong man' image but the letters throughout are passionate above all. And it is far from a disembodied passion. He talks much of touching, hugging and kissing. Describing moments when she had loved him best, she recalled, in Brentano's bookshop, when paying for a poetry magazine, 'my sleeve went up over my wrist in an ugly way, and I pulled it down - and you made a queer small sound in your throat - a sort of growl - which somehow meant that you loved me' (71902/21-22).

Clearly capable of growling with love, HGB seems to have been closed down, made cold, by the relationship with McCarthy. That relationship, he knew, was a mistake and should never have happened, for which he blamed himself. It may not have been abusive, but just as with HH's, his marriage was entrapped and alienated. From there, as he worked to get her free from hurt, HH was enabling him to rediscover love.

Helen Huntington in 1918, the year when she married Barker
(Harley Granville Barker papers, British Library 71913/40)

MRS GRANVILLE-BARKER

It's a pity that, when Barker's first biographer Purdom looked at Helen Huntington's diary for late autumn 1916, he managed to miss the entries which told him how often she went to the theatre. Both here and in her letters she not only records almost daily theatre visits but also the regular friends with whom she went. One was Amy Corbin, script-reader for Winthrop Ames and wife of the theatre journalist John Corbin. Another was Emilie Hapgood, President, in 1914, of the Stage Society of New York. She also of course went with Barker, when they first met. But even after he stopped going, in 1916, she persisted.

With this clear, the question that remains is, even granted she was an enthusiastic audience member, how come she ended up being her lover's collaborator in actually making theatre? Falling in love with somebody is one thing, wanting to work with them is quite another. What did she have that made the great Granville Barker want to work with her?

I *WANTED* THEM TO HEAR

Let's begin by joining her in the theatre: 'Every seat – even in the topmost gallery was filled – (one had to pay $4.50 [now £79.00] to get one at all!) Ravishment was the expression on every face as one looked down the line of stalls. <u>Success</u> floated in the air like a fine golden dust. One got to <u>hate</u> pretty young girls and scenery and pink legs and coloured lights and "coons" and orchestras'. The show she is describing was a Ziegfeld musical, *The Century Girl*, which opened at the Century Theatre on 6 November 1916. She noted how the audience 'laughed and howled and applauded with the most violent delight', and she particularly objected to a scene where a 'painted harlot [Hazel Dawn] almost naked except for the Stars and Stripes draped around her and a <u>dove of peace</u> on her shoulder appeared as America, with a chorus of '"pony-ballet" girls as our navy' (the dove of peace was especially objectionable because she thought America should join the war). 'When it was over I said in a clear, if not loud voice that I wanted to go home – that I could not sit any longer and see our flag used as a costume for chorus-girls.' At this, she says, the 'fat-necked men' in front looked at her in 'wonder'. But 'I was glad – because I <u>wanted</u> them to hear' (71902/25).

Tragedy could be as distasteful as revue. 'Mme Silvain, fat and soft and dressed in red damask, shrieked and wallowed about as Andromaque until one had to avert one's eyes. And Hermione was like a character in a comic opera' (Comédie Française, October 1917, 71908/106). If the disgust is felt in the body, so too is enjoyment. At a production of *Cinna* (Comédie Française, December 1917, also with Louise Silvain) she took an almost immersive pleasure in 'the great rhythmic <u>waves</u> of Corneille's classic verse' (71914/223). But combined with this bodily response is an understanding of theatre as a practice. At Sasha Guitry's *L'Illusionniste*, which opened at the Théâtre des Bouffes-Parisiens on 28 November 1917, she thought it 'A foolish, immoral delightful play – with a wit and poetry that are Sasha Guitry's own – the kind of thing which doesn't seem worth doing at all – until you realize how incredibly hard it is to do' (71907/57). This is the woman, we should note, who Shaw claimed hated all writing after 1865. There's awareness, as she watches, of the processes and organisation that have created the event. Thus, elsewhere, she reflects on the inappropriateness of most casting: 'so many adventuresses as high-souled heroines, so many fools as cabinet ministers'. Much as one might think that fools playing cabinet ministers is not exactly an instance of miscasting, her point about management practice is valid: 'managers choose – (don't they?) more for the shape of a head, or the set of an eye, than for spiritual quality' (71909/36-37).

This sensitivity to aesthetic effects responds to, and analyses the efficacy of, performance that is non-theatrical, that of a Catholic funeral: 'The whole service had a <u>rhythm</u> to it – like an elaborate and stately dance. It soothed the nerves and senses – but left the heart untouched – I thought – and the priest looked a great beast – as if he lived on underdone beef-steaks' (71915/45-46). That readiness to distinguish aesthetic soothing from that which touches the heart gives her a keen sense of points where performance, for all its beauty, turns itself into commodity: 'I went to see L'Aventurière with Gilda Dartley doing nothing more than pictorial illustrations of the part. Still it is all so unreal – it didn't much matter – I liked the neatness and finish of some of the lines – so cunningly carved and polished – just like the neat little French tables I feed into my house' (71900/8).

That often ironic reflexivity contributes to her alertness to what is going on in the space. At *The Century Girl* she was simultaneously observing the composition of the audience alongside what was shown on stage, and was thus attending to the effects of the staging. Aesthetic effect is, for her, also ideological effect, a mingling seen in her description of *Pierrot the Prodigal*, done by Ames and Knight (opened 6 November 1916, the Booth Theatre): the character Phrynette 'had a huge wig of curly red hair, which I thought very clever, because it gave her an enormous head, always suggestive of a monster, and at the same time gave an idea of physical seductive-ness. And of course those women are monsters – it is hard to believe they really exist – isn't it! To see men only as owners is bad enough – but to see them as buyers' (71899/4-5). As with her response to *The Century Girl*, the theatre's exploitation of women, and women volunteering to be exploited, has the effect of debasing the audience: 'Just back from the Galsworthy play [*The Fugitive*, opened 19 March 1917 at 39th Street Theatre] which I liked very much. Why can't one have plays without the actors though! Always that leading lady with painted eyes trying to seduce the entire audience! Emily Stevens, though she has cleverness, is a very bad example of that. She was just as much of a prostitute in the first act [where she was a genteel wife trapped in an unhappy marriage] as in the last – and much more vulgarly dressed' (71905/99). This resistance to cheap seductive effects, and the question about managing without actors, lie behind a reflection on masked performance: 'I care less and less for the theatre – the awful self-consciousness of it all. I wonder if it wouldn't be a good idea to have all the actors and actresses masked – conventional or symbolical masks. The Chinese do it – don't they? Perhaps if it were all as far as possible from nature and real life – it would be more interesting as an art'. Then with character-istic modesty she pulls up short: 'Beloved – I have to stop or laugh at myself for writing about theatres to H. Granville Barker. Tomorrow I shall pen a few words on military strategy to General Haig probably' (71908/74-75). Despite her mockery of her own impertinence this is the sort of thinking that characterised plenty of other Modernist experiments that sought to break with dominant practices of realism.

Of course Barker actually enjoyed her writing about theatres. Her physical and mental engagement as audience member was something he regarded as a major constituent in a theatre experience: 'One learns, as actor, to demand that the audience too must take its active part of sympathy and understanding.' These words come from 'The Promise of an American Theatre', written in September 1916. By that time, the letters apart, he had had first-hand experience of her as audience because in the early days as members of the same social circuit they went to a variety of shows together: *Tristan und Isolde*, *Lohengrin*, *Tannhäuser*, *La Bohême*, the circus, his productions of *Androcles and the Lion* and *The Doctor's Dilemma*. *Tristan* on 6 March 1915 was of particular significance: 'a <u>part</u> of love began then – one part – not brought about by the music (that was your idea for a play – I don't like it now) but finding itself in the music' (71899/64) (the play finally surfaced as *The Secret Life*, completed in 1922).

The first production of his that she comments on is *The Trojan Women*. Together with *Iphigenia in Tauris*, this toured sports stadia of eastern university towns. Huntington saw it at the new stadium of the College of the City of New York on Saturday 29 May 1915: 'The Trojan Women made me forget my surroundings – everything. It was infinitely better than anything I had expected to see – as a production I mean. And all <u>you</u> – even the thrill in the words – and the almost breathless hush over the audience (weren't you pleased – more than your hopes – by that silent audience?) I liked the things I heard people saying as one came out – and some of them had been crying' (71901/24-25). The memory of the production was vivid over a year later (4 November 1916): 'Oh, those Greek Play days – How far away they seem! But the Trojan Women was a real triumph, dear Harley. People speak of it – still – with a little emotional thrill in their voices, and I think of that bleak windy day

– with the clouds of dust and the clanging of trolley cars – and New York so plainly visible over the heads of the Trojans – and reporters with cameras somehow mixing themselves up with Greek heralds – and it seems a <u>miracle</u> to me – that you – by the mere force of your own spirit with poor material of every kind – could have given us that glimpse of classic beauty and pain' (71903/132).

Her attentiveness to theatre effect was useful when Barker's play *The Morris Dance* was critically attacked, despite audience delight, after it opened in New York on 13 February 1917. He asked for her opinion: 'There was just one moment when I had the slightest suggestion of the <u>macabre</u> – (it comes back to me now) – that was when Morris – having had the piano placed in what's-his-name's apartments – and being there, alone, with Pitman – plays, with a flourish, on the soundless key-board – and says something about a March Funèbre – or the dead March from Saul – I forget which! ¶ Then – I remembered this morning – that the first scene of the 3rd Act (I think) where Uncle Joseph is discovered in a public-house – ought to have been supremely funny and wasn't quite. I wondered if it were because the fun was in Uncle Joseph's boring the people in the public-house with his lecturing – and (on the stage –) the actor was afraid of boring the <u>audience</u> – so rattled through his speeches in order that they might <u>not</u> be boring – when the whole humour of the scene lay in their being so' (71915/85). She wanted to see it done by French actors, with 'each character made more a <u>character</u>', but the actors 'are already above the average – not as actors – but in the way they act – which of course is <u>you</u>!' (71902/67).

LOTS OF *IDEAS*

His request for her opinion of a performance was a development of a process that had started almost a year before. Throughout their relationship they regularly sent each other books, cuttings and copies of poems that they liked. They had a programme for reading the same book at the same time, as it were bringing their minds closer even while their bodies were apart. Their discussion of what they read sustained that sense of closeness, as they shared opinions and analysis with each other. In this Huntington showed herself a sharply detailed reader, not only of prose but of dramatic texts. When he suggested they read Henri Becque, a naturalist playwright whose name was new to her, she bought his plays and promptly read two. Commentary, of course, followed: '"La Parisienne" is witty and amusing – and the cold-blooded, low-minded scheming of the Honnête Femme – a nice little bit of satire – but, as you say, it is all vieux jeu – [...] And this way of telling about your characters does seem a little like negro minstrels' (71915/17-18).

They also exchanged their own creative work. Here again her reading was attentive. When she read the unpublished text of *Harlequinade*, a joint work with Dion Calthrop performed in 1913 and printed in 1918, although she much enjoyed it she added: 'I think you wrote the stage directions darling – and perhaps the talk between Alice and her Uncle. The rest – which is poor – I'm sure you didn't write – and couldn't have written. So tease me if I am wrong!' (71914/206-7). It has not been definitively demonstrated that she was right, and may be impossible to do so, but she is correct about changes of register in the writing. And her willingness to identify that which is poor suggests that, for all that she was deeply in love with him, she could not compromise her aesthetic standards. In mid-August 1917 she received the newly published edition of *Rococo, Vote by Ballot* and *Farewell to the Theatre*: '"Rococo" I read when I was not in a mood to laugh, so I must read it again. But it's the one piece among the three that needs, I should think, to be acted' (71906/70-71). Although she laughed at it when read aloud, she didn't like it. And *Vote by Ballot* she thought in performance would be 'a little thin, all by itself' (71914/236).

Closeness of reading, combined with honesty of response, were clearly very useful not just after the event of publication but during the process of drafting. Exchanges of this sort probably started in spring 1916 when she saw a version of *The Morris Dance*, still with its original title *The Wrong Box*. At the same time she also saw a story of which she was highly critical, and it seems to have vanished without trace. In April that year he asked her for advice about a new play he was writing, as to the imagined response of a female character: 'I wish I could help you about the girl in your play but I fear that I can't. However I know the feeling she has – that instinct which a horse, who has never seen a wild animal shows when he scents one far off in the woods. I expect a new look in the man's eyes makes her feel as if a beast were going to spring at her - a strange thing of whose existence she had never even dreamed' (71915/33). This richly metaphoric extension of what he seems to have suggested may derive from something more specific than her capacity for imaginative reading. We hear perhaps in these words the experience of a reader herself abused. And that, in the background, gives another level of nuance to the very subtle play which finally emerged, in 1917, as *Farewell to the Theatre*.

Huntington loved it, and her reading of it can be usefully contrasted with other critical responses. Of these Eric Salmon's (1983) was misled by the title. He associated the play with Barker's supposed wholesale rejection of theatre, coming with separation from McCarthy. But Salmon's dates are askew. Barker asked McCarthy for separation in January 1916 (if the relationship breakdown were ever fictionalised it was in 'Trivialities 1', written in summer-autumn 1915 and published 1916). There was neither uncertainty nor regret in what he was doing. He began work on the play in April, finishing it just under a year later. Between starting and finishing he published 'The Promise of an American Theatre' (1916), which argues for the usefulness of theatre in building community. The other account of *Farewell* by Margery Morgan (1961) is a closer reading which, characteristically for its time, is based around analysis of theme and image. Although she concedes that the play 'can be read as the actor-manager's apologia' (1961: 197), her main argument is that the two characters, Dorothy and Edward, stand for creative imagination in dialogue with law and calculation. Through the image of the theatre the play articulates its 'hidden theme' of self in relation to other, though she doesn't make it clear to what end. The discovery of a theme so banal corresponds with an analysis of the characters that reduces them to the single positions they are said to speak for. Against this simplification Huntington's analysis was rather more complex.

She first mentions the play by title on 2 March 1917: 'First of all - the "Farewell to the Theatre" - I feel - somehow - that it is going to be particularly good - you at your best, dear - you simple - and not complex – stating the truth as it is revealed to you – and letting it go at that – not just cleverly skipping about – as Bernard Shaw does – answering or evading other people's opinions or criticism' (71904/99). She continues later: 'I've been thinking about the "Farewell to the Theatre". You say the Houssmans [*sic* : Laurence and Clemence] didn't understand it – and I'm wondering if I did. I'm going to write down the impression I had and you must tell me whether I am right or wrong. Do you remember my saying to you once that I wanted, in my writing, to lose myself in the world – not to drag bits of it into myself – ? ¶ Well, I thought your woman, the actress, had tried to do that – but people didn't want it. They just wanted <u>her</u> – a dressed-up doll, sitting for her picture – the thing she saw in the mirrors which made her smash them. Perhaps I am all wrong' (71905/97-98). (In the final version the actress merely turns the mirrors to face the wall.) Once she got it in its published form she commented: '"Farewell to the Theatre" seems to me much more brilliant and <u>poignant</u> – the woman a real creation – a personality. I like it immensely. And it's so full of protein, too – mental protein – lots of <u>ideas</u> – <u>nourishing</u>' (71906/70).

Huntington insists this is a play of ideas as much as images, and she doesn't associate it with Barker's personal life. For her the woman is not a symbol, and, perhaps above all, 'self' is not a singular entity. We know already that she was well attuned to what the stage required of women and how it represented them. In the creation of Dorothy she seems to see something to which she herself can relate, the problem of female subjectivity which is not merely objectified but compelled to be a singular entity. In her underlining in the phrase 'they just wanted <u>her</u>', Huntington points up the constraining requirement of the finite, and controllable, image rather than something more expansive that merges with the world. It's a reading that is rather finer than those of Morgan and Salmon.

OH I DO WANT THAT IT BE OUR WORK

Admire the play as she did, she agreed with him that the theatre was not ready for it. Like him, she thought much of what was produced was bad, although he of course said so publicly. She understood

247

him to have more or less 'finished' with the theatre when they met, though more specifically he had decided to give up theatre management (see pp.1–2). This is one reason why the Greek plays had such impact on her. *The Trojan Women* was an 'apotheosis' of his 'theatrical life': 'Oh, I'm glad you did "The Trojan Women" and that was a really high achievement – and <u>stopped</u>'. In her opinion for as long as theatre was culturally degraded he had no place in it. Instead, with the ending of his theatrical life, would come 'a new, <u>real</u> life – in which you will do big things for England and the world outside of England. Perhaps there will come a time when great things can be done through the theatre – it ought to be so – but now it is still much as it was when Lord Bacon wrote his essay "Of Masques and Triumphs"' (71903/132-33). He shared this opinion, barely setting foot in a theatre for much of 1916. As she said, albeit jokingly, 'you despise the theatre' (71912/184). But contempt for theatrical rubbish is, of course, very different from being against theatre itself. Barker was still making plans for directing and writing, and these she encouraged and nurtured. If she wanted him out of the theatre it was precisely so that 'when the change comes – (<u>if</u> it comes –) and the theatre is more than a toy-shop – your name will live among those who helped to make it so' (71903/133). And she wanted to assist in exactly that.

At the beginning of 1918, he told her about a new project, to do the sequel to Maeterlinck's *The Blue Bird, Les Fiançailles/The Betrothal.* This time she was invited to make suggestions in relation to the staging: 'I like best of all in what you tell me of the Maeterlinck play the figure in white which follows him but which has no voice or features or gestures because it is someone he has forgotten! And the child choosing her – and her coming to life. [...] You ask about a French composer for the music for the Maeterlinck play – and – out of nothingness – the name "Dukas" comes to me – but I give it to you as a "medium" murmurs something in a trance – nothing more!' (71910/212-13). She followed up by sending him a book of French composers pointing out that Dukas wrote the music for "Ariane [*sic*] et Barbe-Bleu"' (71910/239), but he preferred Ravel. About the script she had rather more to say: 'It seems to me "Les Fiançailles" can be made even more artistically effective on the stage than "L'Oiseau

Bleu" – don't you think so? I mean – to me – there was always something unpleasant in "L'Oiseau Bleu" – as seen acted – in a dog that was a man – and in the cat – and bread – and milk and so on. It was all right when one <u>read</u> the play, and could <u>imagine</u> it all. Now in this sequel ancestors and descendants are all in the shape of human beings –There are beautiful thoughts in it. Oh I wonder how you will put it on the stage! Won't it be very hard to get it <u>simple</u> enough? The 7th scene – "Le Séjour des Ancêtres" – sounds as complicated as a Chinese lacquer screen. And one wants to see it all – some how – far away – almost through a mist – yet clearly' (71911/50-52).

His solution to putting it on the stage, where it opened as *The Betrothal* at the Gaiety Theatre on 8 January 1921, was to work with his scenographer and composer to create a production of – as a reviewer saw it – 'surpassing beauty' (*Nottingham Journal*, 24 January 1921). The highpoint, apparently, was a ballet that owed very little directly to Maeterlinck but originated with Barker and his team, 'one of the most beautiful scenes ever put on a stage' (*Era*, 12 January 1921). Such theatrical beauty must have been rather impressive from a man who had supposedly given up on the stage. Whether any of it derived from Huntington's comments is difficult to judge, however. But one of the key production ideas bears an interesting resemblance to her description of a different play. In Barker's *The Betrothal*, Gladys Cooper 'wanders through scene after scene as a veiled, featureless figure – a graceful personality in a dream, whose identity the hero cannot remember' (*Gloucester Citizen*, 10 January 1921). The figure in a dream is rather like the seeing through mist that Huntington wanted. But more specifically it is like a figure of whom she 'got such a sense of her drifting in and out of the play – a light, heart-breaking creature – which I never got at all from the Dumas'. This figure is Marguerite, in Sacha Guitry's *Deburau*, which opened at the Théâtre du Vaudeville on 9 February 1918. Huntington saw it in March and described moments from it. Of the scene where Marguerite Gautier rejects Deburau she says 'There is something extraordinarily frail and sweet and <u>faded</u>' (71913/24, 23). That faded frailty is part of the drifting in and out which Guitry had added to the Dumas story, much as Barker added to Maeterlinck perhaps.

Judging that 'the whole play has real <u>quality</u> – what you and I like', she offered to get a copy of it for him (71913/24-25). This offer sparked a project which finally saw the light of day when *Deburau* opened for C.B. Cochran at the Belasco Theatre on 23 December 1920. It also clears up a mystery left hanging in the air by Barker's biographer Purdom: 'soon after his second marriage he translated a piece from the French by Sacha Guitry, *Deburau* (though with whom I do not know; perhaps with little help, for he had a fair knowledge of French)' (Purdom 1955: 196). In characteristic fashion, Purdom's conjecture removes from all consideration the person closest to Barker who had excellent knowledge of French, his second wife. But, in reality, as well as recommending the Guitry play in the first place, on 10 April she also offered: 'Darling – would you like to have me do the dog's work on translating "Deburau" for you? I think I could. Then you could go over it afterwards yourself – and with Sacha Guitry. I thought it might save some time for you' (71913/89). At around this time he 'settled – during a hasty lunch to do Deburau and that is cheering too. I did not say we will do Deburau but please <u>we</u> will – if my dear would like to I think it will be fun' (Texas Thursday 7-30.). He repeated the suggestion in a second letter: '<u>of course</u> beloved I meant we should do it together – talking the translation out such a good way' (Texas Friday morning 7.30 [mid-April]). Clearly he already respected her abilities as a translator, for when she offered to lend him Proust he replied: 'Yes please I will read 'Du côté de chez Swann. [...] Has it been translated and <u>would</u> it translate Cast your mind darling in the direction of doing a translation or so [...] there is much to be said as a work of "national importance" for anything that will reconcile English culture and French Closer as we have come nationally – and must stay – mentally we are still far apart – and in that lies always danger to an alliance – So anything that helps to bridge is work well done for the common cause' (Texas Wednesday morning 7.15). Note that he doesn't see this as a private hobby for his lover: it will be work of national importance. So while there is no mention of Huntington in the published translation of *Deburau* in 1921, it doesn't follow that she didn't work on it and that he didn't value that work. The fact that he encountered *Deburau* at all is almost certainly down to her.

But, as he said to Housman in June, it was only 'for bread and butter reasons' he had undertaken a translation (BM 19 June 1918). This didn't have the same status as original creation (for which there was no time). It is therefore significant that his first idea for collaboration with Huntington had proposed that she work not as translator but as fellow dramatist. The idea grew out of his – and their – ongoing thinking about post-war reconstruction and the part that they as artists might play in that. This was the project for short history plays done as panel illustrations (see pp.144–45, above). She loved the idea, likening it to 'Japanese pillar-prints' (71903/97). Her immediate understanding of the form fired him: 'it was so good that you "jumped" to my panel play scheme – for I want – oh I do want that to be <u>our</u> work – it seems like it to me – as if it suited us peculiarly' (71898/45). From here he proposed a division of the labour: 'think of the little panel pictures of bye ways of American history (your share) as I think of them – search for them in English history' (71898/52).

This offer may have been partly motivated by his belief that by focussing on her writing she could find freedom from the abuse she suffered. But the beneficial effect of her sharing the project worked two ways. In several letters he tells her how important her perceptions are to his work, how she sees things in it that he has not seen. This was the case with the history plays: 'how your mind does jump to mine How <u>always</u> you say the right thing – the thing that illuminates a problem for me' (71897/147). So the project of a writing partnership had roots deep in the emotional and intellectual needs of both of them. 'I have never yet written a thing for you or said one seriously – that you have not shown me in it a better truth – a truer meaning' (71898/188). He thought, in short, she made him a better writer. And she could do so because she had rigorously independent taste and judgement. That independence was most in evidence, as they both knew, not in the judgement of any particular text but at the very foundation of their relationship. Even though she heard her social circle regularly accuse him of being a charlatan and financially devious (see for example 71901/72), she stuck by what she had chosen. Besides love, it's intellectual courage that we hear when she says 'always I shall be proud of myself for having known you' (71908/126).

LOVE AND WRITING

The history plays project didn't eventually happen. What emerged instead was not so overtly political but continued the mood of *Deburau* and *Les Fiançailles*. This was the joint work of translating a play by the Spanish dramatist Martinez Sierra. Barker relied on Huntington for the literal translation, and it's commonly supposed that there her role came to an end. The manuscript of what they titled *The Romantic Young Lady* consists of her typed translation edited by him, together with a title page in her hand with his alterations (Sierra ?1919; THM 147/4). Beyond this there's no hard evidence either way as to how the text was finally shaped. But here it is worth noting that, quite apart from the sensibility seen in her comments on productions, her letters are shot through with a vivid sense of the dramatic. Partly it's metaphoric: 'all N.Y. seems nothing more than painted on a drop-scene – (What is a "drop-scene" really?)' (71910/163-4). But largely it's formal, as, for example, she dramatizes the real-time writing of a letter by marking the various interruptions breaking into it. And she records conversations and events as dramatic scenes (including a comic one of a dog being washed by the Seine). One such is 'Conversation at lunch'. Bear in mind that the 'story' here was by Barker.

> 'Present – Miss Maria, A. [Archer] and myself:
> Miss Maria: "I picked up the Century the other day. There was such a strange story in it. It was called – let me see! – 'Souls on Fifth'. Have you read it, Helen?"
> I – easily – "Yes, I have read it." (A. very busy with devilled crab)
> Miss Maria – "I read it aloud to your Mother and Mr. Lewis the other morning. Your Mother went to sleep (!) but Mr. Lewis became more and more interested as the story went on – "
> I – with consummate ease – (A. still busy with the crab) "The point of view is original."
> Miss Maria – hesitating – "Oh – very original!" She has been pained in her orthodoxy, it is very clear.
> A pause.
> I – desperately – "Edward Lewis is rather unusual in some ways. He has had limited opportunities in life – yet has – ". etc – etc – We are at last switched off on Edward Lewis and running smoothly'. (71913/54-55)

Note how the mode of rendering it not only articulates her social critique but puts drama to use to express and manage her anxieties about her abusive husband. The writing shows a sense of the comedic, and what comedy can do.

This, then, is the mind that collaborated on the Sierra play. The end product was acknowledged at the time, and since, as very beautiful work. When Sierra's translated plays were published in two volumes in 1923, with one volume by John Garrett Underhill and the other by Mr and Mrs Granville-Barker, the *Manchester Guardian* reviewer said: 'Sierra has been lucky in his translators ... Mr Underhill may be congratulated on having done his share of the work in a way that can bear comparison even with the exemplary versions of Mr. and Mrs. Granville-Barker, in which scholarship collaborates with a rare dramatic instinct' (2 August 1923).

In that review we see the emergence of the new entity Granville-hyphen-Barker. Some commentators suggest the new hyphen was a symptom of incipient social snobbery. But it's a somewhat unlikely suggestion given the pair's acute consciousness, and rejection, of the operation of snobbery. The explanation may be rather less seductively bitchy. For Harley, as he was known to all his close friends, Granville Barker was the professional 'stage' name. To return to that for the new work might have made sense, simply then adding his wife to the name. But the formulation 'Mrs Granville Barker', customary as it was, assumes that wives do not have first names, their identity buried in that of their husband. To link Granville to Barker with a hyphen may make a new surname but, much more importantly, puts both wife and husband in the same relation to it. Neither has a first name. Each is an equal constituent of that joint entity which is called Granville-Barker.

The first public product of that joint entity, Sierra's *The Romantic Young Lady*, opened at the Royalty Theatre on 16 September 1920. Of the translation the experienced critic St. John Ervine, a playwright himself, said: 'it has been gracefully translated. Mr. and Mrs. Granville Barker have done their work admirably, and if one wishes to discover the difference between the translation of an uninspired worker and that of an artist, it is only necessary to compare the version of another Spanish play, "Bonds of Interest," with Mr. and

Mrs. Barker's version of "The Romantic Young Lady"' (*Observer*, 19 September 1920). It was, though, billed not just as a translation but also a production 'overseen' by Helen and Harley Granville Barker (*Observer*, 1 August 1920). Conventional wisdom has it that this was a bit of marital sentimentality on his part, crediting her with work that he must have done, as the proper theatre-maker. Which, like much conventional wisdom, doesn't hold up when put alongside evidence such as the advice on the production he gave to Dennis Eadie, who was directing. The acute sense of what works on stage, and how the stage works, which she showed as an audience member persist in Huntington's views on how the Sierra text should be done. When Eadie was thinking about the scenography, Barker invoked Huntington's specialism: 'my wife testifies that Act I at least is not at all Spanish'. Again, on 22 September 1920, 'my wife suggests that she [the character Amalia] might effectively have been very "made up", pale face, <u>red, red</u> mouth – blackened eyes as all Spanish gypsies do' (in Salmon, 1986: 462, 455). Let's note here, in passing, that, twenty months later, she would be one of the financial backers of the innovatory international Theatre Exhibition.

We can never definitely know who contributed what to the Sierra and subsequent Quintero translations. Neither can we know why they chose to begin their project with *The Romantic Young Lady*. But to an external eye several features are suggestive. The play centres on the young Rosario, brought up in a household with three brothers whose freedom of movement and opportunity she envies: 'It's quite like a fairy tale', she says. 'Once on a time there were three brothers – famous, rich and happy. And they had a sister. Well, what about her?' (Sierra, 1922: 226). Then she accidentally meets, without knowing she has done so, a romantic novelist to whose works she is devoted. He falls in love with her and, after a series of misunderstandings and jealous presuppositions, he proposes marriage. In addition to these roles the play gives important parts to the grandmother and female household servant. This emphasis on the women, together with a foregrounded discourse about women's opportunities, may have appealed to Huntington and Barker, both suffragists. More locally, the situation of a woman assumed to defer to her brothers' greater knowledge and importance in the world may be seen to mirror Huntington's relationship, as a 'minor' writer, so called, to her previous husband, the celebrated Hispanic scholar Archer Milton Huntington.

Other parallels follow. Early in the relationship of the novelist, De Córdoba and Rosario the stage direction likens their behaviour to 'two children playing "tag"' (Sierra, 1922: 273). The child-like quality to their relationship was regularly articulated by both Barker and Huntington: 'I've been thinking that we are both like children in a way', she says (71903/56). 'One thing I love you for is that we make each other children again' (71910/210). More extended is the parallel offered in the closing moments of the play, when De Córdoba offers his vision of their shared future to Rosario: 'I can't promise you, or you me that love will be heaven on earth. But it will be life. No more than life. [...] We'll work a great deal and we'll always have faith in our work' (Sierra, 1922: 294-95). Their own and each other's creative work was crucial to both Barker and Huntington. He saw it as contributing to post-war reconstruction, and it was clearly bound up in their love, as she writes: 'If I lose you I shall give up writing – (for the two things – love and writing – go together)' (71899/3). But at the same time they were full of self-doubt about writing, which surfaces I think in a couple of lines of their own, a sort of private joke, that they add to Sierra's text: 'My last chapters are shockingly bad, don't you think? I'm always too anxious to finish' (Sierra, 1922: 294). Another modification of, and indeed addition to, Sierra's original seems to show the translators imbuing this final scene with their own personal experience: 'Happiness, believe me, is a very strange thing. You may find it by looking for it, or it may come by pure luck. And, looking back you may find you weren't happy when you thought you were ... or unhappy, for that matter, when you thought you were either' (Sierra, 1922: 294). Rosario and De Córdoba speak here less in Sierra's words than in Helen and Harley's.

When Rosario finally agrees to accept De Córdoba, her condition is that he alter his current novel in order that her favourite female character shall marry the man she wants him to marry. He agrees of course, and thereby the writer Sierra can bring together in Rosario's fairy-tale ending the two characters whose marriage the audience wants. The self-reference seems obvious. Almost as obvious, by this stage, is the parallelism with Sierra's translators, who in working together to translate this happy ending simultaneously united love and writing in their own partnership. Given how astute, literary, and unsentimental they were, this third level of the marital ending seems not just appropriate but arguably conscious on the part of Huntington and Barker.

By insisting on her condition Rosario may be said to do in miniature what had taken four years for Huntington and Barker. Her entry into his life became a part of his writing process, just as he became part of hers. And it was the collaboration between them that facilitated a theatrical venture which not only consolidated previous work but also, crucially, negotiated the relationship between love and writing.

VI

SOURCES

UNPUBLISHED

British Library, London

Barker, Harley Granville 1915-18. Letters to Helen Huntington. Harley Granville Barker papers Add MSS 71897, 71898, 71915

Huntington, Helen 1915-1918. Letters to Harley Granville Barker. Harley Granville Barker papers Add MSS 71901-71915

Huntington, Helen 1916. Diary. Diaries of Helen Manchester Granville-Barker: 1916-1917. Add MSS 71899-71900

Bryn Mawr College Libraries, Bryn Mawr, PA

Barker, Harley Granville 1904-1936. Letters to Laurence Housman. Laurence Housman papers Box 2, folders 3.1-2 [BM]

— and Laurence Housman c. 1909. *The Pied Piper: A Municipal Drama*. Letters to Laurence Housman. Laurence Housman papers Box 9, folders 2-3

Harry Ransom Center, University of Texas at Austin, Austin, TX

Barker, Harley Granville 1918. Letters to Helen Huntington. Harley Granville Barker Collection MS-1699, container 1.8-2.1 [Texas]

People's History Museum, Manchester

Labour Party Archive 1917-1918 [LPA]

Scott Polar Research Institute, Cambridge

Barker, Harley Granville 1917-1918. Letters to Apsley Cherry-Garrard. Granville Barker Collection MS 559/73/1-8 [SPRI]

Theatre Museum, London

Asquith, H. H. 1916. Note to Lillah McCarthy. London, Theatre Museum. THM/182.

Barker, Harley Granville c. 1919. *The Three Musketeers: scenario and notes.* THM 147/3

— 1921. *The Three Musketeers: script for opening scenes.* THM 147/4/11

— 1922. 'D[rama]. L[eague]. Dinner speech'. THM 147/2

McCarthy, Lillah 1915ff. Cuttings and writings. THM 31/3/5/113/1-8; THM/182

Sierra, G. Martinez ?1919. *The Romantic Young Lady*, translated by Harley and Helen Granville-Barker. THM 147/4

Webbs on the Web https://digital.library.lse.ac.uk/collections/webb

Webb, Beatrice 1901-1911/1911-1916. Typescript diary, accessed 20.09.20

Yale University Library, New Haven, CT

Baker, Ray Stannard 1918. Letters to Frank Lyon Polk. Frank Lyon Polk Papers MS 656/1/1/29

Barker, Harley Granville 1917. Letters to William Wiseman. Sir William Wiseman Papers MS 666/1/6/161–65 [WW]

PUBLISHED

Barker, Harley Granville. 1916. 'Acids in Solution', *Harper's Weekly*, 29 January: 107-8

— 1916. 'Trivialities: No. 1 Acids in Solution', *The English Review*, 22 (February): 129-34

— 1916. 'Souls on Fifth', *The Century*, 91: 6 (April): 817-32, simultaneously published: New York: Little, Brown and Company

— 1916. 'Backward Children Developed by Rhythm', *The Evening Post* [New York], 15 April

— 1916. 'The Promise of an American Theatre', American Number, *Manchester Guardian*, 3 October

— 1916. *The Red Cross in France.* London, New York, Toronto: Hodder and Stoughton

—— 1917. 'The Eden Theatre', *Manchester Guardian*, 11 July

—— 1917. 'Farewell to the Theatre', *The English Review*, 25 (November issue): 390-410

—— 1917. *Rococo: Vote by Ballot: Farewell to the Theatre*. London: Sidgwick and Jackson

—— 1918. 'Address' in *Eurhythmics Paper No. 3. Addresses delivered at the Annual Meeting, January 1918.* Published by the Dalcroze Society of Great Britain and Ireland: 5-7

—— 1919. 'Picket: July, 1916', *The Sun* [New York], 23 February

—— and Calthrop, Dion Clayton. 1918. *Harlequinade: an excursion.* London: Sidgwick & Jackson

—— 2004. 'Georgiana' in *'Richard Goes to Prison' and Other Stories*. Ed. Eric Salmon. Madison, NJ: Fairleigh Dickinson University Press

—— 2017. *Granville Barker on Theatre: Selected Essays.* Ed. Colin Chambers and Richard Nelson. London: Bloomsbury

Brundage, Anthony. 1994. *The People's Historian: John Richard Green and the Writing of History in Victorian England.* London: Greenwood Press

Fowler, Wilton B. 1969. *British-American Relations, 1917-1918: The Role of Sir William Wiseman.* Princeton, NJ: Princeton University Press

Froude, James Anthony. 1903. *Short Studies on Great Subjects.* Four vols. New York: C. Scribner

Gale, Maggie B. 2020. *A Social History of British Performance Cultures 1900-1939: Citizenship, Surveillance and the Body.* London: Routledge

Goffman, Erving. 1956 repr. 1990. *The Presentation of Self in Everyday Life.* London: Penguin

Green, John Richard. 1926. *A Short History of the English People.* Revised by Alice Stopford Green. London: Macmillan

Hay, Ian. 1915 repr. 1985. *The First Hundred Thousand.* Glasgow: Richard Drew Publishing

Hobson, J. A. 1916. 'The War and British Liberties 3: The Claims of the State upon the Individual', *The Nation*, 19 (10 June): 307-08

Holroyd, Michael. 1989. *Bernard Shaw: Volume 2 1898-1918. The Pursuit of Power.* London: Chatto & Windus

Howlett, John. 2017. 'The Formation, Development and Contribution of the New Ideals in Education Conferences, 1914-1937', *History of Education*, 48(4): 459-79

Judd, Alan. 2000. *The Quest for C: Sir Mansfield Cumming and the Founding of the British Secret Service*. London: Harper Collins

Kennedy, Dennis. 1985 repr. 2008. *Granville Barker and the Dream of Theatre*. Cambridge: Cambridge University Press

Kirby, David. 1983. *War, Peace and Revolution: International Socialism at the Crossroads 1914-1918*. Aldershot: Gower

Knoblock, Edward. 1915. *A War Committee*. London: Samuel French
— 1939. *Round the Room*. London: Chapman and Hall

Labour Party. 1917. The Labour Party and the Trades Union Congress. *Memorandum of War Aims*. To be presented to the Special Conference etc. Friday 28 December 1917
— 1918. *Labour and the New Social Order: A Report on Reconstruction*. (Revised in accordance with the resolutions of the Labour Party Conference, June, 1918)

Lethaby, W.R. c.1917. *Art and Labour*. London: Design & Industries Association

Marrott, H.V. 1935. *The Life and Letters of John Galsworthy*. London: William Heinemann

Martin, Laurence W. 1973. *Peace without Victory: Woodrow Wilson and the British Liberals*. Port Washington: Kennikat Press

Masefield, John. 1985. *Letters from the Front 1915-1917*. Ed. Peter Vansittart. New York: Franklin Watts

McCarthy, Lillah. 1933. *Myself and My Friends*. London: Thornton Butterworth

Messenger, Charles. 2006. *Call-to-Arms: The British Army 1914-18*. London: Cassell

Morgan, Margery M. 1961. *A Drama of Political Man: A Study in the Plays of Harley Granville Barker*. London: Sidgwick & Jackson

Newton, Douglas. 2002. 'The Landsowne "Peace Letter" of 1917 and the Prospect of Peace by Negotiation with Germany', *Australian Journal of Politics and History*, 48(1): 16–39

Onou, Alexander. 1918. 'The Russian Revolution and German Socialism', *The New Europe*, 6 (69) (7 February): 109-116

Pearson, Hesketh. 1950. *The Last Actor-Managers*. London: White Lion

—— 1951. *G.B.S. A Postscript.* London: Collins

Priestley, J.B. 1962. *Margin Released: A Writer's Reminiscences and Reflections.* London: Heinemann

Proske, Beatrice Gilman. 1963. *Archer Milton Huntington.* New York: Trustees of the Hispanic Society of America

Purdom, C.B. 1955. *Harley Granville Barker: Man of the Theatre, Dramatist and Scholar.* London: Rockliff

Roberts, Priscilla. 2005. 'Paul D. Cravath, the First World War, and the Anglophile Internationalist Tradition', *Australian Journal of Politics and History,* 51(2): 194-215

Salmon, Eric. 1983. *Granville Barker: A Secret Life.* London: Heinemann Educational Books

—— (ed.) 1986. *Granville Barker and his Correspondents: A Selection of Letters by Him and to Him.* Detroit: Wayne State University Press

Scott, Dixon. 1916. *Men of Letters.* London: Hodder and Stoughton

Shaw, Bernard. 1988. *Collected Letters, Volume 4: 1926-50.* Ed. Dan H. Laurence. London: Max Reinhardt

Sierra, G. Martinez. 1922. 'The Romantic Young Lady' in *Plays* Vol. 2. Trans. Helen and Harley Granville-Barker. New York: E.P. Dutton

Simkins, Peter. 1998 repr. 2007. *Kitchener's Army: The Raising of the New Armies 1914-1916.* Barnsley: Pen & Sword Books

Smith, Constance Babington. 1978 repr. 1985. *John Masefield: A Life.* London: Hamish Hamilton

Smith, Michael. 2011. *Six: The Real James Bonds 1909-1939.* London: Biteback Publishing

Spence, Richard. 2004. 'Englishmen in New York: The SIS American Station, 1915-21', *Intelligence & National Security,* 19(3): 511-37

Stray, Christopher (ed.). 2007. *Gilbert Murray Re-Assessed: Hellenism, Theatre, and International Politics.* Oxford: Oxford University Press

Tawney, R.H. 1916. 'Reflections of a Soldier', *The Nation,* 20 (21 October): 104-6

Wallas, Graham. 1914. *The Great Society: A Psychological Analysis.* London: Macmillan

Wright, D.G. 1978. 'The Great War, Government Propaganda and English "Men of Letters" 1914-16', *Literature and History,* 7(Spring): 70-100

NEWSPAPERS AND PERIODICALS

Era
Gloucester Citizen
Ladies' Field
Manchester Guardian
Morning Telegraph [New York]
Nottingham Journal
Observer
Vogue

VI

INDEX